India & China

Strategic Energy Management and Security

Attention Authors

Manas Publications is fighting a war to tell the world that India can win the battle not only by bullet but also by pen. We are converting fighters into writers as there is no dearth of intellectuals in our country but their knowledge is confined to them only. No sincere effort has been made by any other publisher to give right direction to their knowledge and the talent of every intellectual is lying hidden. An author always gives the raw material in the shape of a manuscript and it depends upon the publisher how to make it a finished product. We are motivating the intellectuals' mind and publishing their manuscripts for more than two decades and would like to publish your manuscript, too. If you or your colleagues have any manuscript or are working on it, please don't hesitate to contact us with detailed synopsis and contents, for its publication. We take utmost care in production and give wide publicity to the book and its author. We can also suggest you the title related to your subject for writing, as we are the publishers who believe more in quality than in quantity.

India & China
Strategic Energy Management and Security

Bimal Kumar Sikdar, IDSE
Amitabh Sikdar, IA&AS

Manas Publications
New Delhi-110002 (INDIA)

MANAS PUBLICATIONS

(We Convert Fighters into Writers)

(Publishers, Library Suppliers, Importers & Exporters)

4402/5-A, Ansari Road (Opp. HDFC Bank)

Darya Ganj, New Delhi-110 002 (India)

Off. (23260783, 23265523, Fax: 011-23272766

E-mail: **manaspublications@gmail.com**
manaspublications@vsnl.com
manaspublications@yahoo.com

© Bimal Kumar Sikdar

2012 (FP 2009)

ISBN 978-81-7049-347-1

₹ 995/-

Designed at

Manas Publications

Printed in India at
HS Offsets, Delhi and published by Mrs Suman Lata for
Manas Publications, 4402/5-A,
Ansari Road, (Opp. HDFC Bank),
Darya Ganj, New Delhi-110 002 (INDIA)

Dedicated

To the Mother India
&
To our Mother
Smt. Sadhana Sikdar
and the memory
of our Father
late Amaresh Chandra Sikdar

Contents

SECTION-IV
Development-Management of Energy Resources in China

SECTION-V
China's Strategic Energy Management

SECTION-VI
Development-Management of Energy-Resources in India

SECTION-VII
India's Strategic Energy Management

SECTION-VIII
Securitization of 'ENERGY': Its Need and Implications

SECTION-IX
Long-Run Implications of China's Energy Security Policies and Strategies on India

SECTION-X
Conclusion and Recommendations

APPENDICES

Preface

This book deals with the energy problem and kindred issues in a holistic way. It addresses a wide range of readers, planners, policy-makers, administrators, investors, and more importantly the most promising section of Indian society, the young graduates whether of applied science and technology or of political science and human resource development. The welter of information on the energy problem, to put it mildly, is mind-boggling—part science, part economics and part development. The fast depleting non-renewal energy sources and the devastating danger of environmental degradation threatening not merely modern civilization but also the very survival of life on the planet have provoked right-thinking men and women to sit up and warn the world of the threat of extinction of life on the planet looming large on the not–so–distant horizon, if urgent preventive steps are not taken. The search for newer, alternative sources of energy is being pursued on a war-footing; so also the scramble for the existing sources of non-renewal energy pushing the world into a nuclear flash-point.

Hence the need for educating all sections of society about the manifold complexity called 'energy question'. The rise of India and China as fast-growing industrial nations racing towards superpower status has added many new dimensions to the problem. Energy sources have become nodal points of conflict, economic and political.

Our effort has been to present to the reading public the essential material by viewing the energy crisis, by juxtaposing

India and China for the study to explore the varied economic, industrial, political and developmental implications of the question. The recent economic boom in both the countries necessitates a close and increased cooperation between the two not only on exploration of alternative energy sources but also on energy management.

This book provides the reader the feel of situation behind the current real world problem around energy through a critical analysis of the possible impact of China's securitized energy-management on India's energy security and economic development. It is often said that China outweighs and supersedes India in the field of energy-management. It is a self-evident truth that India too supersedes China in many other fields like IT, BPO, KPO, Banking etc. In a demographic survey of world-statistics India is projected to be stronger and in a shade advantageous position over many other countries due to her young demographic profile, abundant availability of skilled human resources, adequate natural resources and raw materials, large and growing domestic market, and established rule of law and a vibrant three-tier democracy. There is still more material in this book to feel proud of the achievements of India.

Bimal Kumar Sikdar
Amitabh Sikdar

Background Information

In course of our attempting to collect materials on various topics relating to energy-crisis we tried to have a Hand Book or something short of an Encyclopaedia and wished the most of online-information be readily available on selected-sites to make a "holistic" understanding (as much that interlinks energy-factories and energy-stricken countries) of the subject of Energy-Management, inter-woven with the present context of India then in the world context but that appeared awfully difficult. Saint Hugo confessedly waited twenty-five years before he published his new gospel. But, in our case we belatedly realized the need to be more impersonal and to shed-off our bias and ambition as the subject 'energy-management', has to be necessarily a grand public-issue needing mass-scale involvement to create apposite literature in this direction. Though the attempt to acquire a 'holistic' understanding and then cross-link and decipher all energy-related issues in a single ram appeared intellectually overwhelming and boggling yet we gathered inspiration from the contributions made by many scholars, laureates and institutions who are spreading their knowledge through internet.

The modern world realized the charisma of 'ENERGY' with the invention of electricity in 17th century. This was followed by the demands of industrial revolution and ever expanding commercial production to be indispensably met with 'ENERGY' resulting in many countries transiting from under-developed to semi-developed and to developed state across the globe at the cost of ever-increasing exploitation of the natural resources at their disposal for more and more of electricity generation. With the philosophy of industry-based, ambitious and competitive economic development adopted by the developing nations with various farsighted and strategic measures to ensure continued availability of energy to sustain their development and to achieve further new heights in the process of development among the nations, all sources of 'ENERGY', their availability, generation, import and consumption increasingly became the sole guiding-principle and the driving-force of development.

A degree of semblance reached between countries which possess the natural resources and those that have the potential and expertise to exploit and utilize the resources for furthering its development while maintaining the need based satisfaction of societies on either side inherently and independently as per the diverging preferences of the nations. The balance continued till nations developed as per their own inherent choice based on their internal, local, social fabric and regional or occasionally some international or global priorities but without much dependency on the final objective of each other.

The present trend of development, however, particularly among the developing nations, is found more intrinsically factored on dependence, common and converging economic developing-parameters of other countries, located regionally or globally, is something unique, which might not have envisaged during early period of industrial revolution where the few states which developed, did more or less in subjective isolation.

This new pattern of development has given way to increasing inter-dependence among various countries primarily linked by the energy and its resources. This dependency, on the common driving force of energy, has led to development of new matrix with elements of uncertainty, fear of discontinuity among the nations who wish to sustain their development and who wish to enter into the new bracket of developed nations. A different kind of matrix is being formed among the nations driven by the fact that energy resources across the globe are limited in the present context. The elements of matrix depends on the availability of energy resources, transport infrastructure, technical ability to exploit the resources economically and also in an eco-friendly manner, degree of dependence guided by location and availability, transporting means including geopolitical location of the state, quality of manpower etc. As a result, ENERGY, in the current trend of developmental politics, has become one of the centre-point of national strategic management and securitization.

China and India, which are the focus of this study, both are resources-rich and high-consumption countries at the macro-level taking into account the different types of energy elements viz., Oil, Gas, Coal, Nuclear, Hydro, Solar, Wind and other Non-Conventional and Renewable energy sources. However, these two countries are exclusively dependent on single domestic resource of coal for production of electricity and their potentials to exploit other available resources proportionally, based on their nations' varied requirements in different regions/provinces, are limited. The inefficiencies in the electricity utilization process in terms of huge energy losses (28-35%) in the transmission and distribution-network of such large nations with almost 10% of world area and around 40% of world population and with highest densities of population have further complicated the energy issue.

Added to above is the recent economic boom in both the countries with the prediction of China becoming the largest economy with India rising to third or fourth place in the global-economy in the near future necessitates a close and increased cooperation between both the countries to ensure easy availability of energy not only in these two countries but also in other neighbouring countries, with more joint participation in different areas of energy-management.

The energy related issues and its security for Asia, a uniquely conflict-prone region, is an especially pressing and complicated one because of the region's distinctive geopolitical structure and natural resource endowments which consists of both energy-deficient and energy-rich countries, therefore, in Asia the looming long-term problems of the energy-security dilemmas that inevitably follow are likely to be expensive, more complex, subtle, and potentially dangerous, likely to involve India from many aspects. In selecting an approach to write this book we found it more meaningful to maintain the focus of our analysis internationally, in particular, mainly on the two Energy Giants of Asia, the 'Dragon' and the 'Elephant' than making the book merely academic. Having learnt a number of lessons through the context of China's strategies on energy, we, after a two-year search on the subject decided to conclude and publish the work to share the saga, supposed to be sung in chorus in India, appearing ready but without an orchestra, foreclosing our undertaking leaving many questions and aspects for much wanted future explorations by the fellow Indians.

Certainly, it is the high time to think: Is energy-crisis the true crisis of India or is it something else? Can energy-scripts be traded in the National Stock Exchanges unless someone else somewhere produces it first? Why many of us have been wasting energy, while many more others haven't had a feel or the means to taste energy. Can India go on consuming 30% more energy than it produces while import of energy also implies import of inflation and unemployment and when India's dependence on oil import as projected by IEA is to shoot up from 1 MBD (2000) to 5 Million-Barrels/Day (2030) and that of China from 2 MBD (2000) to 10 MBD (2030).

Now, we cannot afford to be a Thinker without 'Energy'

At times you are inspired or compelled to think on 'energy' though you may not be a Thinker. At times you pose questions about 'energy' to yourself to justify your thinking capacity or to justify other's perception about you or when your own kids or youngsters give you an intelligent-tease or a brain-storm on 'energy' or when you are assigned to think on 'energy' by your boss or when you are forced to shift your target searching for an 'alternative-energy' for your home or business or when you are unduly charged for the 'energy' that you think you did not consume or when you feel getting doomed in dark in the absence of 'energy' though you are ready to pay for it or when a program inspires you to take a decision on a mutually-benefiting scheme on 'energy-cooperation' to share 'energy' with your neighbouring person (or business-entity) or when you unwillingly consent to SEB or to your neighbour pulling energy-cables over or near to your roof or lastly when you unwillingly bypass your commitment due to predisposition or lack of 'energy'.

Can we afford to be a non-thinker of 'energy' or choose to be blank to a question posed to you? Certainly not, as we have to do it ceaselessly though in many small fragments and pieces.

How to Handle the Energy-Teasers

There are certain pertinent questions, out of very many (Frequently-Asked-Questions, Appendix-E), that we may like to consider right now after reading the Preface and the Book. They may include:

Why and what Priority-Rating should be given to broad spread Energy-Awareness in India? Shouldn't we estimate the impact of the widely disseminated 'Energy-Awareness' in India firstly in the area of 'saving/conservation' of 'energy'? Why should we compare the heating-fuels in terms of their efficiency and economics and the lighting devices in terms of their illumination and unit cost?

How much will you save annually if you replace all the incandescent and fluorescent-lightings of your house with CFL or T-5/T-8 or LED lightings? Which energy resources the Nature has given to India in abundance and which ones in scarcity? How much fossil-fuel reserves (coal, petroleum, natural gas, and oil-shale) India has and how long they will last at current rate of consumption? Which institutions in

India preserve energy statistics and which institutions undertake research projects?

Does India have the required soft-database on all energy resources needed to do planning and research in a comprehensive manner? Is energy audit compulsory and sufficient in India? Whether the best practices and canons under existing corporate-governance will be sufficiently capable to administer all issues related to energy management in the country? Whether 'energy-management' needs to be a subject of strategic-governance at the national level? Does India need a Central-Coordinating-Agency or a Unified-Regulatory-Authority or a single Ministry and a separate Budget to regulate, plan for and govern all energy sources integratedly? Which class of 'industry' consume the highest share of energy? Which class of 'industry' has the highest need for energy-saving? What are the potentials of future employment opportunities in energy sector? How the criteria for investment decisions at national level best optimized, cross-optimized and sub-optimized among all energy resources?

But if we ask, how much proven and economically mineable reserves of fossil-fuel (coal, petroleum, natural gas, and oil-shale) India has and how long they will last at current and future rates of consumption against the fast-growing population, or which is the cheapest option in the comparative energy-economics of power generation out of many alternatives should you not look at the growth-trend of India's share in world population, and her resource-constraints.

Energy-Propensity of the Skilled Young-Demographic Profile of India

Per capita energy consumption of China and India, presently stands on much lower side and lags behind by some hundred odd nations. Management of Energy for India and China with almost half the world population is a critical issue, and it is likely to become supercritical keeping in view its increasing share in the near future. Destiny of the billions is going to be decided around the critical issues of energy as we are destined to progress in the scenario of high economic growth closely linked with energy growth. Currently world-population is growing by about 80 million people per year. According to the United Nations Population Division projections (according to medium-variant, TFR being 2.1) the global population is estimated at 8.04 billion for the year 2025 and at 9.37 billion for 2050. There could be a much higher increase in world-population (as per high-variant, TFR being 2.6) of 8.6 billion by 2025 and 11.2 billion by 2050. Thus, the possibility of another doubling of the world-population between 1995 and the middle (2050) of the next century is not ruled out.

The International Institute for Applied Systems Analysis (IIASA: http://www.iiasa.ac.at/ Research/LUC/Papers/ gkh1/chap1.htm), Austria while analyzing the projections estimated that between 1995 and 2050 world-population growth will be generated exclusively in developing countries. The population of the developed countries as a group increased by less than 350 million between 1950 and 2050. The developing countries, on the other hand, will have an estimated 6.8 billion people more. Among the third world countries the world population increase will be concentrated in Asia. The ten countries which will contribute most to world population-growth over the next 30 years are India, China, Pakistan, Nigeria, Ethiopia, Indonesia, United States of America, Bangladesh, Zaire, and Iran — in that order!

According to the most recent (medium-variant) UN population projection, India's population will increase by an additional 401 million between 1995 and 2025 while China will grow by only 260 million, followed by Pakistan by 133 million. India's population would increase to about 1.9 billion (with TFR being 2.6) by 2050, much higher than that of China. India will out-grow China but her population structure will be much "younger" than that of China. Just imagine the employment-seeking population in India.

IIASA further analyzed that over the next decades the world-population will inevitably age as an unavoidable consequence of large birth-cohorts during 1950s and 1960s and the rapid fertility decline since the 1970s. In 2025 the "baby-boomers" of the 1950s and 60s will be between 65 and 75 years of age. These large aging cohorts are followed by the relatively small "baby-bust" generations of the worldwide fertility decline. In 1950 there were only 131 million people of age 65 and older; in 1995 their number had almost tripled and was estimated at 371 million. Between now and 2025 the number will more than double again; and by 2050 we will probably have more than 1.4 billion elderly people worldwide. The %age of elders increased from 5.2 in 1950 to 6.2 in 1995. By 2050 every 10th person worldwide will be 65 years of age or more. While currently population aging is most serious in Europe and Japan, China will experience a dramatic increase in the proportion of elderly people by the middle of the next century. This is largely due to China's success in family planning, which rapidly reduced the relative size of her birth-cohorts since the 1970s.

Should we not necessitate ourselves to interrogate on the demographics of China and India over at least a few deep Demography-Matters invoking the well-known question of whether China will grow old before it grows rich or how young India would remain when it becomes rich. Yes, because Experts say that it is an advantage for India now since the country is entering the demographic-dividend-phase (refers to a period usually 20 to 30 years of age when population put in hard-working aiding economic-growth) while China is exiting it.

Further, research reveals that India's population will be 1.4 billion by 2026. The median-age in India in 2000 was 24, compared to 30 in China, 38 in Europe and 41 in Japan. However, India's population is still quite young; perhaps 35% of the total population is aged less than 15 years. India's younger mobile population will have propensity to spend more and more on life-style and energy.

In a demographic survey of the world statistics India is projected to be stronger and in advantage over many other countries due to her young-demographic-profile, abundant availability of skilled Human-Resources, adequate natural resources and raw materials, large and growing domestic-market, an established rule of law and a vibrant three-tier democracy.

India, in her Young-Demographic-Profile (with her mobile young population) has 24-54% of it with a median-age below 25 years, with a 61% working-population expected to rise till 2025 but marginally declining thereafter till 2050 but still remain above 60%. The younger generation of India which turns out more than 4 lakh engineering and science graduates, over 3 lakh non-engineering post-graduates, 21 lakh other graduates and 9 thousand Ph.Ds annually and whose Knowledge-Workers in software and service industry increasing 25 times from 6,800 (1985-86) to 6,50,000 (2003-04) and the strength of IT workers expected to go up to 20 lakh by 2008, will have propensity to demand and spend more on living-standard, life-style goods and energy, obviously more on clean energy.

Further, India's very large and fast growing domestic-market consisting of the increasing higher income groups with burgeoning purchasing-capacity showing an all-round predisposition for clean-energy-driven life style and the middle-class population in the size of 21 crore with sizably voluminous purchasing capacity, further increasing annually by 1.5 to 2.0 crore due to India's faster economic growth rate will show a waiting predilection to drive more on energy.

Future India's Energy-Requirement and Energy-Satisfaction levels — a battle of marathon

It will indeed be a marathon exercise to plan for and achieve the expected Energy-Requirement and Energy-Satisfaction levels for future India. While in case of India the per capita total Primary-Energy Consumption (Million Btu) increased from 6.1 (1980) to 14.5 (2004) the same for China increased from 17.8 (1980) to 45.9 (2004). China's consumption share in all energy resources in 2004 ranged between 9.62% and 64.65% in Asia-Oceania and between 1.36% and 33.82% in world while India's share remained between 3.02% and 14.99% in Asia-Oceania and between 0.57% and 7.84% in the world, consumption of coal and hydro-electricity having the highest shares in both the countries. However, the EIA projections for energy-consumption (Million Btu) is estimated at 32.5 (India) and at 139.1 (China).

Does 20% of the world's population consume 80% of the world's resources while India with 16% of the global-population uses only 3% of world's resources? But who is responsible for this imbalance and who are we going to complain to? Unfortunately, we have no one to thank but ourselves for the situation that we find ourselves in. However, it is evident that India's future consumption-requirement of energy will have to be planned and satisfied at a high-level by all means for reasons mentioned above.

Bimal Kumar Sikdar

Amitabh Sikdar

Acknowledgement

We would like to express our deep gratitude to:

Guruji Sri Achut Maharaj (Sadhan Sangh Ashram, Rishikesh) for guiding us with the way 'how to look at' and 'understand' the real-life issue in world perspective; Malay K. Biswas, Lt. Gen. (Retd.) Utpal Bhattacharya, Mrs. Preeti Sudan IAS and Sh. Rakesh Jain IA & AS for providing their constant affection, inspiration and strength; Gp. Capts. M.B. Ranade and P.R. Nawalkar and M. Bhattacharjee, of DSSC, Wellington (India) for their vision and creative guidance; Wg. Cdrs. G.S. Kochhar and S. Bhatele; Vijay Singhal (IAS), Sameer Sharma (IRS), Jai Shankar (IA & AS) and K.K. Singh (IDAS) for their persistent inspiration; and for the thoughts and friendship contributions made by Dimple Jhanwar, Neeraj Sahu, Smita, V.S. Ghantala, and Megha living in distant parts of the world; and the scholars and the institutions who spread knowledge through internet selflessly for the good of the world society; and also the web-masters and the IT force who take pains to maintain the web-sites used for this book. We give special thanks to Dr. B.K. Sthapak, Vice Chancellor of SVT University (CG, India) for his expert advice.

We also worked in the loving and inspiring memories of our father Amaresh Chandra Sikdar, brother-in-law L.D. Gupta, sister Meeta Rani Guha and nephew Samarpan.

We remain beholden to our life partners, Maj. Nagaveni and Prabha Rani for their wordless and enduring service; our nephews, Anirban and Rhitayan for their creative-peering, our little children, Meerambika, Neel, Amritanshu,

Ashwasan, and Abhipsa who kept on wishing only time from us; our revered elder sister, Supriti and our brothers, Ashok K. Guha and Sanjay and his life-partner, Ruby for their non-stop creative instincts and support; our living mother, Smt. Sadhana for showering all the strength of her love and sustenance as without them we would not be able to complete this work.

Lastly, we salute gratefully Sri Aurobindo and The Mother (Sri Aurobindo Ashram, Pondicherry) for the direction of thought that we feel inspired with from their gospel works.

Bimal Kumar Sikdar
Amitabh Sikdar

Section – I

Introduction

CHAPTER 1

Background of the Energy Problem in Asia and the World

The modern world realized the charisma of 'ENERGY' with the invention of electricity in 17th century. This was followed by the demands of industrial revolution and ever expanding commercial production to be indispensably met with 'ENERGY' resulting in many countries transiting from under-developed to semi-developed and to developed state, across the globe at the cost of ever-increasing exploitation of the natural resources at their disposal for more and more of electricity generation. With the philosophy of industry-based, ambitious and competitive economic development adopted by the developing nations with various farsighted and strategic measures to ensure continued availability of energy to sustain their development and to achieve further new heights in the process of development among the nations, all sources of 'ENERGY', their availability, generation, import and consumption increasingly became the sole guiding-principle and the driving-force of development.

A degree of semblance reached between countries that possess the natural resources and those which have the potential and expertise to exploit and utilize the resources for furthering their development while maintaining the need based satisfaction of societies on either side inherently and independently as per the diverging preferences of the nations. The balance continued till nations developed as per their own inherent choice based on their internal, local, social fabric and regional or occasionally some international or global priorities but without much dependency on the final objective of each other.

The present trend of development, however, particularly among the developing nations, is found more intrinsically factored on dependence, common and converging economic developing-parameters of other countries, located regionally or globally, is something unique, which might not have envisaged during early period of industrial revolution where the few states which developed, did more or less in subjective isolation.

This new pattern of development has given way to increasing inter-dependence among various countries primarily linked by the energy and its resources. This dependency, on the common driving force of energy, has led to development of new matrix with elements of uncertainty, fear of discontinuity among the nations who wish to sustain their development and who wish to enter into the new bracket of developed nations. A different kind of matrix is being formed among the nations driven by the fact that energy resources across the globe are limited in the present context. The elements of matrix depends on the availability of energy resources, transport infrastructure, technical ability to exploit the resources economically and also in an eco-friendly manner, degree of dependence guided by location and availability, transporting means including geopolitical location of the state, quality of manpower etc. As a result, ENERGY, in the current trend of developmental politics, has become one of the centre point of national strategic management and securitization.

This typical formulation of matrix may lead to unavoidable conflicts until and unless new methodologies and advanced technologies in the field of energy are explored and implemented on massive scale and till such time nations need to maintain a high level of cooperation in utilizing the available resources more efficiently. Otherwise the means to achieve energy security in a state will not only make energy expensive but also hamper the plan-based overall economic growth of a state, directly or indirectly affecting all the participating nations involved in the conflict/crisis encountered or anticipated based on some real or imaginary unforeseen situations. Unexpected conflict/crisis may also take place between groups of countries located in different regions, with possibility of various new combinations between nations as per their typical geo-locations.

Some nations on one hand are resource-deficient and on the other hand the richly-resourced countries are not able to utilize their potential due to remote locations of resources with respect to distant consuming centers. The options of either delivering the raw energy-material near the consumer-centres or transmitting the energy in the form of electrical-power, needs huge infrastructure in the forms of transmission-lines and transport systems duly backed by advance technical capabilities with essential cost-effectiveness. The four fundamental zones concerning energy management and security with their compelling impacts on environment, international relations and security are: (i) availability of energy from natural resources; (ii) potentials to exploit natural resources with new/advanced R&D for producing energy; (iii) efficient, economic and environment friendly utilization of energy; and (iv) import-export of more clean and efficient energy.

China and India, which are the focus of this study, both are resources-rich and high-consumption countries at the macro-level taking into account different types of energy elements viz. Oil , Gas, Coal, Nuclear, Hydro, Solar, Wind and other Non-Conventional and Renewable energy sources.

However, these two countries are exclusively dependent on single domestic resource of coal for production of electricity and their potentials to exploit other available resources proportionally, based on their nations' varied requirements in different regions / provinces, are limited. The inefficiencies in the electricity utilization process in terms of huge energy losses (28-35%) in the transmission and distribution network of such large nations with almost 10% of world area and around 40% of world population and with highest densities of population have further complicated the energy issue.

Added to above is the recent economic boom in both the countries with the prediction of China becoming the largest economy with India rising to third or fourth place in the global economy in the near future necessitates a close and increased cooperation between both the countries to ensure easy availability of energy not only in these two countries but also in other neighbouring countries, with more joint participation in all the four areas of energy management as stated above.

Focus of the Energy Problem

ENERGY, becoming the main directive principle and the driving force in the current scenario, China's emergence as a major economic power and energy consumer constitutes a very significant strategic event in Asia. Many policy-makers, strategists and scholars express significant concern over the implications of China's growing energy requirements with increased economic capability for the future security environment in Asia and beyond.

Such concern gains seriousness partly from an anticipation of the revival of the historically accompanied border security problems and foreign direct influence on the bordering states and regions warranting India's increased attention to counterbalance the effects of the emergence of a new economic power in Asia, neighbouring India, and partly from the newly emerging international ambitious trends of fast developmental economics, foreign direct investments, international joint ventures, paradigm shift of markets toward globalization with high degree of interdependency among nations and emergence of new matrices around 'energy'. For India, however, these anxieties with their impacts may get compounded by the rapidity of sustainable growth that India plans to achieve through economic expansion and capability, a large scale increase in energy requirements essential to fuel and sustain India's growth plan, a general lack of knowledge and unpredictability about China's strategies and ambitions, unipolar large population under the centralized command-structure, existence of many unresolved Chinese territorial claims and her internal political and social susceptibilities.

Each of the above factors will certainly influence India's (as also China's) future energy requirement planning, strategy, management and administration and her short term as well as long term external policy and behaviour. The present and the future capability of China in shaping the pace and content of her economic reformation, defence modernization, strategic postures, territorial claims, relation with neighbouring countries and overall leadership attempts in Asia is a critical developmental issue, therefore, the related problems have become issues of high concern not only for India but also to many leaders, planners and critics in the field of international energy-politics and energy-management around the world. As a result, the emerging as well as the possible future internal and international dynamics of the domineering China would definitely be of great concern to India, especially in view of India's large requirement of energy in proportion to her growing population, economic dimensions, accelerated pace of development, increased dependence on energy import with foreign exchange outgo, increased competition as bulk consumers of energy, and particularly when 'energy' is being treated as the greatest potential commodity tending toward securitization.

With a view to discover the implications and taking lessons therefrom, this book examines the energy-management development processes, consumption patterns of energy, future trend of energy requirements of major energy types of China which will implicate or govern the future course and pace of development of India. The information and analysis presented here are developed on an inadequate but growing literature on the Chinese economic might, energy strategies and international energy management. Since 'ENERGY' is the prime driving force for economic development of both the countries, China's energy policy and the dynamics of her strategic energy management in future, deserves a closer scrutiny considering the growing demand of energy for India's economic development so that the energy structure of India is based on a better option between (a) increasing resource-import-dependence and (b) increasing renewable energy production with proper energy-mixing and energy efficiency.

Justification for studying the related issues on 'Energy'

The issue of energy and energy security for Asia, a uniquely conflict-prone region, is an especially pressing and complicated one because of the region's distinctive geopolitical structure and natural resource endowments which consists of both energy-deficient and energy-rich countries. Therefore, in Asia the looming long term problems of the energy security dilemmas that inevitably follow are likely to be expensive, more complex, subtle, and potentially dangerous which will involve India from all aspects. Energy security was a buzz word in the late 1970s and early 1980s. But since 1990s the international politics on 'energy' with possible new multilateral, international cooperation matrices between the Western powers, the Middle East, and the Asian countries has already become a policy research agenda. While studies to date have focused more on the technical prospects for energy exploration and development to meet rising energy demand, the role of various countries in Asian energy-scenario and fueling security, global energy politics, global conflict and cooperation may now need a deeper examination.

The first thing to remember about China's relationship with the Asian and global energy market, is how little energy each Chinese has been actually consuming so far. A Chinese consumes far less per capita of virtually all types of energy than do Americans, Japanese, or South Koreans, and only 40% of the world average. They use relatively large amounts of coal, which meets 75% of primary energy demands in China, but little of anything else. The dramatic booming growth of Chinese economy in recent decades has stimulated consumer revolution, massive increases in their demand for energy, is predicted to continue to grow. Stable supply and stable prices of energy are critical to the well-being of the countries economy in the Asian region, but is unconvinced that their long term, cost-effective and efficient provision and maintenance can be assured. Thus, China's energy policy decisions may well determine the prospects for, and the timing of, a major global energy shock.

Thus, Fueling-Security and the changing international energy politics pose many fundamental questions : How China's booming economy will continue to fuel itself ? Does rising energy demand yield more security dilemmas or will efficient energy markets mitigate potential security risks arising from increased competition for energy resources? Will environmental consequences of energy exploration and development technology, new equations of international prices, increased import-dependence, energy vulnerability, energy rivalry, insufficient transportation infrastructure could deepen great power tensions in Asia. These factors also raise a host of serious security concerns, especially when considering the increasing Asian dependence on Middle Eastern oil. Strengthening Middle East Asian relations leads to potential arms for energy deals with countries that apparently sponsor international terrorism, with subsequent global geopolitical effects. In addition, the increasing importance of the transportation of oil through the strategic sea-lanes of Southeast Asia has led to tension between the status quo of guaranteeing freedom of navigation (the United States Navy) and the growing power of naval forces of

China and South East Asian countries that neighbour these sea-lanes.

The Chinese growing energy competition may provide an opportunity for a constructive cooperation matrix, may result in emergence of unforeseen international strategies, more deregulation and privatization of energy market, enhanced market competition, erratic price fluctuations in short term, politically induced price shocks, or may deepen tensions and disputes between Asian rivals, or may cause emergence of new conflicts over off-shore energy resources or new energy resources or other defence and security related fields.

There are also scary national projections which threaten to take the slide beyond the power of political goodwill and technical efficiency. As per China's 10th Five-Year Plan (2001-2005), by the year 2020, China is estimated to import about 500 million tons of oil and 100 billion cubic meter of gas to cater to its growing domestic demand. Thus, the share of China's imports in its domestic consumption of oil and gas will rise to 72% and 50% respectively of its total consumption at that time. More conservative western estimates project the rise of China's energy imports for 2020 at 30% for gas and 60% for oil.

China had also begun energy export from mid-1970s but it was too modest to impact its ideology driven politics. China's energy policies therefore had no serious linkages to energy related regional and global developments of that time. Even the price fluctuations and supply disruptions of the early 1970s made little difference to Beijing's energy-policies. It was only following the rapid economic development during the 1980s and 1990s that China developed stakes in the global energy market with a major reorganization of China's energy sector during 1988.

This reorientation of the energy sector was further hastened following China becoming a net importer of oil from 1993. This was further exacerbated when China's domestic production failed to keep pace with the qualitative change in its rising domestic consumption. As a result, in addition to its domestic sector, China's energy security strategy focused on its offshore energy assets, even promising joint development of energy in its disputed maritime areas like the South-China Sea.

China's energy strategy focus, from the early 1990s, has shifted towards 'mercantilism' and 'engagement', including joint-venture, foreign direct investment, technology transfers and other innovative approaches, towards alternative and renewable energy sources. China also experimented with privatization of its best performing firms in the energy sector. Since then, China has been on an overdrive for leasing foreign gas and oil-fields and acquiring stakes in foreign-energy establishments and joint ventures for ensuring energy supplies. It has also reoriented its procurement to more reliable pipelines from Russia and Central Asia instead of depending on volatile and US-controlled Middle East supplies through precarious Indian Ocean sea-lanes and Malacca-Straits choke points. Presently China's energy sector has emerged as an integral part of its overall maritime planning where its naval assets now form a part of China's holistic vision on energy security.

In this evolving context of China's growing energy demand and expanding stakes in global energy markets, this thesis examines the nature and profile of China's energy security related policy and strategies and highlights its implications for Sino-Indian ties. Prima facie, given the rising energy deficit and physical proximity of these two expanding economies, recent years have witnessed heightened competition as well as growing activism in Sino-Indian energy parleys. The results though as yet remain mixed. With its energy needs expanding on similar lines, India has already begun to feel the pinch of China's aggressive energy security strategies. These have not only contributed to the rise in global oil prices in recent years but also impinge on India's perceptions and policies.

Notwithstanding that real data and information about China is scarce, its future energy policy and strategies scarcer still, Indian policy makers now need to contemplate on the findings of a series of closer examinations as to when, how and to what extent India's future energy policy and energy security will get affected.

Similar problems were also experienced to get relevant information real data, comprehensive manuals and detailed guidelines at one place on the energy demand, their availability, production, distribution, pricing and end-consumption of all the energy resources relating to all the energy forms in India. For a country like India with a very vast population whom the nation is determined to provide increasing economic wellbeing, we must have an integrated knowledge-base/data-base. This book is an attempt to justify the above need.

Extended Objective of the Energy Study

The rationale and the motivation behind this publication, accepting factually that the scarce 'ENERGY' will always remain an issue of **Concern**, a point of continuing compelling **Anxiety**, an alarm of **Insecurity**, a costly **Crisis** and a potential **Conflict**, is to understand better the future dynamics of energy-policies of various countries, the energy related international politics, the network of inter-connected strategies, and the resulting security issues and that while a universally acceptable Global-Energy-Model can hardly be developed for successful implementation, "**Objective-Energy-Business-Models**", not impelled by more and more of **Securitization** of energy but enthused and guided by the principles of per capita and objective rationing; regional economic, industrial, commercial and environmental interest; agreed cooperation and mechanism for continuous dialogue and consultation; quick and effective response-mechanism in case of crisis and conflict; exerting on consistency maintenance in dealing with common regional problems; declaring the inevitability principle in the Agenda for the need to maintain national peace and well-being, providing measures to prevent aggravation of a situation threatening international peace, however, should be thoughtfully developed and effectively implemented.

But, much before the acquisition of ability to achieve the above objectives in long run by India, it will be necessary; firstly to spread the 'energy-consciousness' as widely as possible; secondly to get developed a set of Standard/Best-Operating-Practices under Corporate-Governance principles with a restructured reporting requirement/performance-measurement/accountability consideration by the existing energy-consuming industries in India; thirdly to educate the younger academics through a specialised/applied and multi-disciplinary formal programme of training and certification, and fourthly to provide free access to the documented/soft-knowledge base, current on-line information and other infrastructure to the qualified people who want to undertake research or collaborate with energy entrepreneurs willing to enter this field. In this sequel let us first recapitulate the concept of 'energy' and briefly discuss the various forms of energies and their resources available in the world together with the current trend of developments, as discussed in Chapter-2 and Chapter-3.

CHAPTER 2

A Snap-Shot of World Energy— Forms & Resources

What does 'ENERGY' mean?

'ENERGY' is the capacity of matter to perform work as the result of its motion or its position in relation to forces acting on it. Moving-energy or energy associated with motion is known as kinetic energy. Stored-energy or energy related to position is called potential energy. Thus, a swinging pendulum has maximum potential energy at the terminal points; at all intermediate positions it has both kinetic energy and potential energy in varying proportions. A falling ball has kinetic energy and hits the ground with a force. The kinetic energy of the ball is mainly converted to elastic potential energy. This elastic potential energy is then changed back to kinetic energy, and the ball bounces up again. Energy exists in various forms, namely; mechanical energy, thermal (heat) energy, chemical energy, electrical energy, radiant energy (light), and nuclear (atomic) energy. All forms of energy are inter-convertible by appropriate processes. In the process of transformation either kinetic or potential energy may be lost or gained, but the sum total of the two remains always the same.

A weight suspended from a cord has potential energy due to its position, in as much as it can perform work in the process of falling. An electric battery has potential energy in chemical form. A piece of magnesium has potential energy stored in chemical form that is expended in the form of heat and light if the magnesium is ignited. If a gun is fired, the potential energy of the gun-powder is transformed into the kinetic energy of the moving projectile. The kinetic mechanical energy of the moving rotor of a dynamo is changed into kinetic electrical energy by electro-magnetic induction. All forms of energy tend to be transformed into heat, which is the most transient form of energy. In mechanical devices energy not expended in useful work is dissipated in frictional heat, and losses in electrical circuits are largely heat losses.

How Do We Measure Energy ?

Energy is measured in many ways. One of the basic measuring unit is called a 'Btu' (British thermal unit). Btu is the amount of heat-energy required to raise the temperature of one pound of water by one degree Fahrenheit, at sea level. 1000 Btus roughly equals one average candy bar or 4/5 of a peanut butter and jelly sandwich. It takes about 2,000 Btus to make a pot of coffee.

Energy also can be measured in **joules**. 1000 joules equals one **British thermal unit** or say 1 kilojoule = 1 Btu. So, it would take 2 million joules to make a pot of coffee. The term "joule" is named after an English scientist **James Prescott Joule** who lived from 1818 to 1889. He discovered that heat is a type of energy. One joule is the amount of energy needed to lift something weighing one pound to a height of nine inches. So, if you lift a five-pound sack of sugar from the floor to the top of a counter (27 inches), you would use about 15 joules of energy. For scientific calculations around the world, energy is measured in 'joules' rather than in 'Btus'. It's much like using the metric system of meters and kilograms, instead of the English system of feet and pounds, but for measuring the heat-content in 'British thermal units' (Btu) for industrial/commercial purposes, the thermal-conversion-factor for each energy form is required. To do a meaningful comparison between different energy forms and to develop an energy-mix, acquittance with various conversion factors related to various energy forms will be essential (refer: Appendix-D).

A piece of buttered toast contains about 315 kilojoules (315,000 joules) of energy. With that energy you can jog for 6 minutes, or bicycle for 10 minutes, or walk briskly for 15 minutes, or sleep for 1.5 hours, run a car for 7 seconds at 80 kilometers per hour (about 50 miles per hour) or light a 60-watt light bulb for 1½ hours, or lift a sack of sugar from the floor to the counter 21,000 times!

Working out the Specific Energy-Efficiency/Energy-Intensity

"Energy-Efficiency" can indicate the efficiency of a process in terms of output per unit of energy consumed. "Energy-Intensity" of a process (energy consumed per unit of output) is the inverse of the "Energy-Efficiency" of the process (output per unit of energy consumed).

The 'Aggregate-Energy-Intensity or the 'Economy-wide Energy-Intensity' (Ratio of total energy consumed to GDP) can be expressed in 'Megajoules (mJ) per $, or in terajoules (TJ, 10^{12}J) per $, petajoules (PJ, 10^{15}J) per $, or exajoules (EJ, 10^{18}J) per $.

Similarly, 'Energy-Intensity' can be measured and expressed for each 'Sub-sector' separately in terms of Megajoules (mJ) per tonne of goods produced, or Megajoules (mJ) per thousand/lakh of goods produced, or Megajoules (mJ) per passenger/vehicle-kilometers, etc.

Creation or Destruction of Energy is not possible

Empirical observations in the 19th century led to the conclusion that although energy can be transformed, it cannot be created or destroyed. This concept, known as the conservation of energy, constitutes one of the basic principles of classical mechanics. The principle, along with the parallel principle of conservation of matter, holds true only for phenomena involving velocities that are small compared with the velocity of light. At higher velocities close to that of light, as in nuclear reactions, energy and matter are interconvertible. In modern physics the two concepts, the conservation of energy and that of mass, are thus unified.

Energy can be transformed into another form of energy but it can neither be created nor be destroyed because 'Energy' always exists in one form or another. For example, stored-energy in a flashlight's battery becomes light-energy when the flashlight is turned on. Food is stored-energy which is stored as a chemical with potential energy. When our body uses that stored-energy to do work, it becomes kinetic energy. If we overeat, the energy in food is not "burned" but is stored as potential energy in fat cells. When we talk (sound-energy) on the phone, our voice is transformed into electrical-energy when passed over wires. The phone on the other end changes the electrical-energy into sound-energy through the speaker. A car uses stored chemical-energy in gasoline to move. The engine changes the chemical-energy into heat and kinetic energy to power the car. A toaster changes electrical-energy into heat and light-energy (if looking into the toaster, you see the glowing wires). A television transforms electrical-energy into light-energy and sound-energy.

How Energy travels through the Food-Chain

Energy changes form at each step in the food-chain. For example, take an ear of corn. Sunlight is taken in by the leaves on the corn-stalk and transformed through photosynthesis. Plants take in sunlight and combines it with carbon-dioxide from the air and water and minerals from the ground. Plants grow tall and create the ears of corn - their seeds. The energy of the sunlight is stored in the leaves and inside the corn kernels. The corn kernels are full of energy stored as sugars and starch. The corn is harvested and is fed to chickens and other animals. Chickens use the stored energy in the corn on the cob to grow and to move. Some energy is stored in the animal in its muscle tissue (protein) and also in the fat-cells. Persons who eat chicken's meat and fat and convert that stored energy into energy in their body. As your body uses the energy from the chicken, you breathe in oxygen and exhale carbon-dioxide which is again used by other plants to grow.

To conclude, 'Energy' has mainly ten different sources: coal, propane, nuclear, natural gas, petroleum, wind, geothermal, hydropower, solar, and biomass. Renewable sources of energy include: wind, geothermal, hydropower, solar, and biomass. Non-renewable sources of energy include: coal, propane, nuclear, natural gas, and petroleum. There are six basic forms of energy: nuclear (splitting or combining of atoms), radiant (energy from light), chemical (energy from food/photosynthesis), mechanical (energy from motion), electrical (energy from moving electrons) and thermal (energy from heat). All of these forms can be transformed into another form of energy. Energy is everywhere and always conserved.

Non-renewable energy sources are sources that exhaust with use and include fossil-fuels (petroleum, coal, and natural gas) and other hydrocarbons, including gas hydrates (methane and water), tar sands, and oil shale. Renewable energy source is a natural resource that replaces itself unless overused, for example, bio-mass, wind, sunlight, moving-water, tidal-power, geothermal, hydrogen and biomass. Alternative energy sources include nuclear energy, hydroelectric energy, solar energy, wind energy, and geothermal energy.

A brief note on each type of energy source and form is shown below :

1. Bio-Energy—The term 'Bio-Energy' means energy obtained from 'bio-mass' which includes plant and animal derived organic-matter available on renewable basis, including dedicated energy-crops and trees, agricultural-food and feed-crops, agricultural crop-wastes/residues, wood-wastes/residues, aquatic-plants, animal-wastes, municipal-wastes, and other waste-materials. Biomass offers tremendous opportunity to use domestic and sustainable resources to provide its fuel, power, and chemical needs from plants and plant derived materials. Bio-Energy technologies use renewable biomass resources to produce an array of energy related products including electricity, liquid, solid and bio-fuels such as ethanol, gaseous-fuels, renewable diesel, heat, chemicals, and other materials. Bio-fuels such as bio-diesel, ethanol, and straight vegetable oil are hydrocarbon-fuels. There are non-hydrocarbon bio-fuels as well such as anaerobic hydrogen producers.

2. Coal—Coal is a basic but an economically vital energy foundation and is also the workhorse of most of the world's electric power industry but causes pollution and green-house effect on earth. Innovative technologies are on the way to develop next generation pollution-free coal-based power plants virtually eliminating the sulphur, nitrogen, and mercury pollutants released when coal is burnt. For the foreseeable future, coal will continue to be the dominant fuel for electric power production and main source of energy.

3. Electric-Power—Electrical energy is one of the most important and the commonest forms of energy used very extensively in industrialised countries. The energy sources that can be used to generate electricity include: fossil-fuels, geothermal-energy, nuclear-energy, solar energy, wind energy and moving-water.

When fossil-fuel (coal, oil or gas) is burnt, the stored chemical-energy is changed into heat. The heat is used to produce steam, which turns a turbine to produce electricity. Geothermal energy is another name for the earth's internal heat. Steam from water heated deep in the earth is used to turn turbines attached to electric generators. Nuclear energy is produced when the nucleus of an atom splits into lighter elements. The energy is released in the form of heat, which is used to produce steam, which turns turbines to produce electricity. Photovoltaic cells in solar panels convert sunlight directly into electricity, which is then stored in batteries. Moving air (wind) is used to turn turbines directly and thus generate electricity. Moving water in the form of rivers, waves and tides is used to turn turbines and thus generate electricity. The flow of water in rivers is controlled by dams, as is the ebb of tides in some areas where there is a high tidal range. In both these situations, the water can be released in a controlled way and thus turn turbines. In some coastal areas, waves are consistently large, and their energy can be harnessed to generate electricity.

The world is becoming increasingly electrified with electricity generated mostly from coal. Research is also underway to increase the fuel efficiency of coal-fuelled Power Plants. Today's plants convert only one third of coal's energy potential to electricity. New technologies after Fossil-Energy researches could nearly double the efficiency levels in the next 10-15 years. Higher-Efficiency means more affordable electricity and limited carbon/greenhouse-gases (GHG) emissions.

While coal will remain the major fuel for electric power, natural gas is the fastest growing fuel. Energy experts guess that more than 90% of the power plants to be built in the next 20 years will likely be fueled by natural gas. Natural gas is also likely to be a primary fuel for distributed power generators – mini-power plants that would be sited close to where the electricity is needed. Gas-powered Fuel-Cells being developed from fossil-energy will use hydrogen that can be extracted from natural gas or perhaps in the future from biomass or coal, will be used for distributed-generation-applications in future.

Researches are on the way to develop new technologies to modernize the electric-grid, enhance security and reliability of the energy infrastructure, and facilitate recovery from disruptions to the energy supply, energy storage systems, and energy transmission system that will contribute to energy efficiency of the future electric industry. For instance, the copper-wires used in typical transmission lines lose a significant percentage of the electricity passing through them because of resistance, which causes wires to heat up. "**Super-conductivity**" materials have no resistance, if used to transmit electricity in the future, electricity transmission losses will be minimal.

4. Fossil-Fuels—Fossil-fuels like coal, oil and natural gas, currently provide more than 85% of all the energy consumed in the world, nearly two-thirds of electricity, and virtually all of the transportation fuels. Moreover, it is likely that the reliance on fossil-fuels world over to power an expanding economy will actually increase over at least the next two decades even with aggressive development and deployment of new renewable and nuclear technologies. Innovative technologies can make the future production and use of fossil-fuels more efficient and environmentally cleaner and can locate and produce oil and gas beyond the reach of today's technologies, overcome the environmental challenges of using coal, and extract clean-burning hydrogen from fossil fuels.

5. Nuclear Energy (Fission)—Fission means to split apart. An atom's nucleus can be split apart. When this is done, a tremendous amount of energy is released. The energy is both heat and light energy. Einstein said that a very small amount of matter contains a very LARGE amount of energy. This energy, when let out slowly, can be harnessed to generate electricity. A nuclear power plant uses 'uranium' as a "fuel." Uranium is an element that is processed into tiny pellets that are loaded into very long rods that are put into the power plant's reactor. Inside the reactor of an atomic power plant, uranium atoms are split apart in a controlled chain reaction. In a chain reaction, particles released by the splitting of the atom go off and strike other uranium atoms splitting those. Those particles when given-off split still other atoms in a chain reaction. In nuclear power plants, control rods are used to keep the splitting regulated so it doesn't go too fast. This chain reaction gives off heat-energy. This heat-energy is used to boil water in the core of the reactor. So, instead of burning a fuel, nuclear power plants use the chain reaction of atoms splitting to change the energy of atoms into heat-energy. This water from around the nuclear core is sent to another section of the power plant. Here, in the heat exchanger, it heats another set of pipes filled with water to make steam. The steam in this second set of pipes turns a turbine to generate electricity.

Nuclear-Energy Research Programme on the generation of Nuclear-Energy has promoted a secure, competitive and environmentally responsible Nuclear-Technology to serve the present and future energy needs of the world. With the significant energy and environmental challenges being faced by the nations in the new century, the benefits of clean and safe nuclear-energy   are becoming increasingly apparent. As a result the world production of Nuclear Electric-Power increased by 30 times between 1970 and 2004. Advanced civilian technology researches are being conducted today to chart the way further toward introduction of the next-generation of Nuclear Power Plants, for isotope production and distribution, nuclear facilities management, and nuclear fuel security.

6. Nuclear Energy (Fusion)—Another form of nuclear-energy is called 'fusion'. Fusion means joining smaller nuclei (the plural of nucleus) to make a larger nucleus. The sun uses nuclear fusion of hydrogen atoms into helium atoms. This gives off heat and light and other radiation. The two types of hydrogen atoms, deuterium and tritium, combine to make a helium atom and an extra particle called a neutron. Scientists have been working on controlling nuclear fusion for a long time, trying to make a fusion reactor to produce electricity. But they have been having trouble learning how to control the reaction in a contained space. What's better about nuclear fusion is that it creates less radioactive material than fission, and its supply of fuel can last longer than the sun. Researches for innovative technologies are seeking to advance plasma-science and fusion-science and the related technology with the goal of harnessing fusion as a viable energy source. The research programmes are trying to identify and explore innovative and cost-effective development paths to fusion energy and to advance the science and technology of energy-producing plasmas.

7. Geothermal-Energy—Geothermal-energy has been around for as long as the Earth has existed. "Geo" means earth, and "thermal" means heat. So, geothermal means earth-heat. Geothermal-energy is clean and sustainable. Resources of geothermal-energy range from the shallow ground to hot water and hot rock found a few miles beneath the earth's surface and down even deeper to the extremely high temperatures of molten rock called 'magma'. The crust of the earth floats on this liquid magma mantle. When magma breaks through the surface of the earth in a volcano, it is called lava. For every 100 meters below ground, the temperature of the rock increases about 3^0 Celsius. Or for every 328 feet below ground, the temperature increases 5.4 degrees Fahrenheit. At about 10,000 feet below ground, the temperature of the rock would be hot enough to boil water (100^0 Celsius). Deep under the surface, the hot water can reach temperatures of more than 148^0 Celsius which doesn't turn into steam because it is not in contact with the air. The hot water from below the ground can warm or cool the buildings and swimming pools. Hot water or steam from below ground can also be used to make electricity in a geothermal power plant. California's geothermal power plants produce about one-half of the world's geothermally generated electricity. The geothermal power plants produce enough electricity for about two million homes. Innovative researches are on the way to harness the related science and technology.

8. Hydro-Power—Hydro-Power is one of the largest producers of electricity in the world. Hydro means water. Hydro-electric means making electricity from water power. When it rains in hills and mountains, the water becomes streams and rivers that run down to the ocean. The moving or falling water can be used to do work. Moving water, which has kinetic energy, can be used to make electricity. Hydroelectric power uses the kinetic energy of moving water to make electricity. Dams can be built to stop the flow of a river. The river is simply sent through a hydroelectric power plant. The water behind the dam flows through the intake and into a pipe called a penstock. The water pushes against blades in a turbine, causing them to turn. The turbine while turning spins a generator to produce electricity. Hydropower (or hydro-electric power) facilities can generate enough power to supply the world with electricity and can save trillion tons of coal and oil. Researchers are working on advanced turbine technologies that will not only help maximize the use of hydropower, but also minimize adverse environmental effects.

9. Natural Gas—Natural gas is a clean burning fuel and produces significantly fewer harmful emissions than reformulated Gasoline. Natural gas can either be stored on board a vehicle in tanks as Compressed Natural Gas (CNG) or cryogenically cooled to a liquid state, Liquefied Natural Gas (LNG). Natural Gas will become increasingly popular as an alternative transportation fuel serving the alternative fuel vehicles (AFVs). Researches are on way to develop future power plants running with natural gas.

10. Oil—Oil is truly the lifeblood of world's economy. Currently, it supplies more than 40% of our total energy demands and more than 99% of the fuel we use in our cars and trucks. Economically advanced countries maintain their **Strategic-Petroleum-Reserve** for commercial, emergency and military supplies. Oil fields are becoming increasingly costlier to produce because much of the easy-to-find oil has already been recovered. New and improvised exploration/ drilling and better technology production processes are needed to find and produce much of this "left-behind" oil for the future.

11. Renewables—Renewable energy sources like wind, solar, geothermal, hydrogen and biomass play an important role in the future of the world. Researches are in progress for the development of renewable sources of energy. Energy technology R&D programmes are on the way to help shift from production of ultra-clean forms of petroleum based fuels to low-cost production of hydrogen from coal and natural gas.

12. Solar Energy—The amount of energy we receive from the sun in 15 minutes equals the annual fossil and nuclear-fuel consumption globally. The sunlight falling on India in one day contains more than twice the energy we consume in an entire year. Plants use the sun's light to make food. Animals eat plants for food. The plants that decayed hundreds of millions of years ago produce coal, oil and natural gas that we use today. So, fossil-fuels is actually the sunlight stored millions and millions of years ago. Directly or indirectly, the sun or other stars are responsible for all our energy. Even nuclear-energy comes from a star because the uranium-atoms used in nuclear-energy were created in the fury of a nova, a star exploding. The sun's light and heat reaches earth not by conduction or convection (because space is almost completely empty) but by radiation. Radiation is the final form of movement of heat-energy. When sunlight hits the earth, its radiation is either absorbed or reflected. Darker surfaces absorb more of the radiation and lighter surfaces reflect the radiation.

Solar Energy is an unlimited and a secure, reliable, and clean energy source. Worldwide Solar Energy Technology Programmes are managed to accelerate the development of solar technologies as energy sources for the future world. Examples of solar technologies being developed are Photovoltaic-Cells (a semi-conductor device, closely related to a computer-chip that relies on the photoelectric-effect.), concentrating Solar Power technologies and low-temperature Solar Collectors.

Photovoltaic-Cells, made of semi-conductors such as crystalline-silicon or various thin-film materials, convert sunlight directly into electricity. Photovoltaic-Cells can provide tiny amounts of power for watches, large amounts for the electric-grid, and everything in-between. Concentrating Solar Power technologies use reflective materials to concentrate the sun's heat-energy, which ultimately drives a generator to produce electricity. These technologies include dish/engine-systems, parabolic-troughs, and central power-towers. Low-temperature Solar-Collectors also absorb sun's heat-energy, but the heat is used directly for hot-water or space-heating for residential, commercial, and industrial facilities.

It is advantageous to place solar-panels in the regions of highest solar-radiation. The average solar-radiation in the United States is 4.8 kwh/m2/day, but reaches 8-9 kWh/m2/day in parts of Southwest. In the Phoenix, Arizona area the average annual solar-radiation is 5.7 kWh/m2/day (or 2080.5 kWh/m2/year). Electricity demand in the continental U.S. is $3.7*10^{12}$ kW·h per year. Thus, at 100% efficiency, an area of 1.8x10^9 sq. m (around 700 sq. miles) would need to be covered with solar-panels to replace all current electricity production in the US with solar-power, and at 20% efficiency, an area of approximately 3500 sq. miles.

13. Wind Energy—We can save fossil fuels by conserving and finding ways to harness energy from seemingly "endless sources," like the sun and the wind. The kinetic energy of the wind can be changed into other forms of energy, either mechanical-energy or electrical-energy. Wind energy is used for generating electricity, charging batteries, pumping water, or grinding grain. The Wind-Turbines convert the kinetic energy of the wind into other forms of energy. Large and modern Wind-Turbines can produce electricity. Small Wind-Turbines are used by homeowners and remote villagers to help meet energy needs. Wind energy diversifies the nation's energy supply, takes advantage of a domestic resource, and helps the nation meet its commitments to curb emissions of greenhouse gases, which threaten the stability of global-climates.

The wind energy has been in use for many years for sailing, pumping water from wells/low-lying areas using windmills, for turning large grinding stones to grind wheat or corn and also as currently doss to make electricity. Blowing wind spins the blades on a wind turbine, just like a large toy-pinwheel. This device is called a wind turbine and not a windmill. A windmill grinds or mills grain, or is used to pump water. The blades of the turbine are attached to a hub that is mounted on a turning shaft. The shaft goes through a gear-transmission-box where the turning speed is increased. The transmission is attached to a high-speed shaft which turns a generator that makes electricity. Single smaller wind-turbines are used to power homes and schools.

In order for a wind-turbine to work efficiently, wind speeds usually must be above 12 to 14 miles per hour to generate electricity. The turbines usually produce about 50 to 300 kilowatts of electricity each. A kilowatt is 1,000 watts (kilo means 1,000). We can light ten 100 watt light-bulbs with 1,000 watts. So, a 300 kilowatt (300,000 watts) wind turbine could light up 3,000 light bulbs that use 100 watts! These turbines can be grouped together to be called "Wind-Farms". Once electricity is generated by the turbine, the electricity from the entire "Wind-Farms" can be collected together and sent through a transformer where the voltage can also be increased to send it through long distances over high power lines. The wind energy related technology should be propagated and made competitive in global market to strengthen the domestic economy.

14. Tidal Sea-Level Energy—Tidal-power utilizes the twice-daily variations in sea-level caused due to the gravitational effect of the moon, to a lesser extent of the sun on the world's oceans and also by the effect of centrifugal forces due to earth's rotation. Tidal energy involves use of traditional hydropower technologies to generate electricity from the elevated water in the tidal-basin. Tidal range may vary over a wide range (4.5-12.4 m) from site-to-site. A tidal range of at least 7 m is required for economical operation of the turbines. The energy potential of tidal-basins can be large. One 240 MWe facility has been in operation in France since 1966, another 20 MWe facility in Canada since 1984, and the third 100 MWe unit in China since 1987. A proposal for installing new facilities on the Severn estuary (UK) to produce 8.2 GWe is underway.

15. Tidal Stream-Power—Researchers are also trying to extract energy directly from tidal-flow-streams, a relatively new technology development. Tidal-Stream-Generators draw energy from underwater currents in much the same way that the Wind-Generators are powered by the wind. The much higher density of water means that there is the potential for a single generator to provide significant levels of power. Tidal stream technology is at its early stages of development and will require significantly more research before it becomes a significant contributor to electrical generation needs. Several prototypes of tidal stream power have shown some promise.

For example, in the UK in 2003, a 300 KW Seaflow marine current propeller type turbine was tested off the north-coast of Devon, and a 150 KW oscillating hydroplane device, the Stingray, was tested off the Scottish coast. Another British device, the Hydro-Venturi, is to be tested in San Francisco Bay. Canada has plans for installing very large arrays of tidal current devices mounted along a 'tidal-fence' in various locations around the world, based on a vertical axis turbine design.

16. Ocean Thermal Energy Conversion (OTEC)—Using the temperature of water to make energy actually dates back to 1881 when a French Engineer by the name of Jacques D'Arsonval first thought of OTEC. The final ocean energy idea uses temperature differences in the ocean. If you ever went swimming in the ocean and dived deep below the surface, you would have noticed that the water gets colder the deeper you go. It's warmer on the surface because sunlight warms the water. But below the surface, the ocean gets very cold. Power plants can be built that use this difference in temperature to make energy. A difference of at least 38 degrees Fahrenheit is needed between the warmer surface water and the colder deep ocean water. Using this type of energy source is called Ocean Thermal Energy Conversion or OTEC. It is being demonstrated in Hawaii.

17. Synthetic Fuels—Synthetic fuels do not occur in nature but are made from natural materials. 'Gasohol', for example, is a mixture of gasoline and alcohol made from sugars produced by living plants. Although making various types of fuel from coal is possible, the large scale production of fuel from coal will likely be limited by high costs and pollution problems, some of which are not yet known. The manufacture of alcohol-fuels in large quantities will likely be restricted to regions, such as parts of Brazil, where a combination of low cost labour and land, plus a long growing season, make it economical. Thus, synthetic fuels are unlikely to make an important contribution to the world's energy supply anytime soon until a significant breakthrough in research is made.

18. Solar Power Satellites—One suggestion for energy in the future is to put huge solar-power satellites into orbit around the earth. They would collect solar energy from the sun, convert it to electricity and beam energy to the electrical power-grids on earth as microwaves or in some other form of transmission. The space solar-power satellite-system would have no greenhouse gas emissions, but the microwave beams might affect the human health adversely.

19. 'Alternative-Fuels' for transportation—More than one-half of all the current energy sources we use goes into transportation – for our cars, planes, trucks, motor-cycles, trains, buses and of all the oil we use about three-quarters of it goes into making gasoline and petro-fuel for vehicles. Excessive dependence on the limitedly available current petroleum based transportation-fuels (petrol, aviation-fuel, gasoline, diesel-fuel and reformulated gasoline) brings severe environmental problems, need for avoidable securitization of energy, international unrest, and economic imbalance. Because of these concerns new clean-burning fuels made from fuels other than petroleum are being introduced. These fuels include : methanol, ethanol, natural gas, propane, batteries and even electricity which are called 'alternative fuels' because they are an alternative to gasoline and diesel. Automobiles that use 'alternative-fuels' are called 'Alternative-Fuel-Vehicles' or AFVs. (Just as the automobiles out-threw the horse-carts, so the future energy technologies may make today's smoke-stacking and gasoline-powered automobiles uneconomical and redundant by the new energy-devices using new definition of Horse-Power, not of the automobile engines but relating to energy and energetics.)

20. Batteries (Energy-Storage Devices)—According to a 2005 estimate, the worldwide battery industry generates US$48 billion in sales annually.

A **battery** (electricity) is of one or more electro-chemical cells, which store chemical-energy and make it available as electrical-energy. There are many types of electro-chemical cells, including galvanic-cells, electrolytic-cells, fuel-cells, flow-cells, and voltaic-cells. Formally, an electrical "battery" is an array of similar *voltaic-cells* connected in series. However, in many contexts it is common to call a single cell a *battery*. A battery's characteristics may vary due to many factors including internal chemistry, current drain, and temperature. Generally, battery-life can be prolonged by storing the battery in a cool place and using it at an appropriate current.

Widespread use of batteries not only served the economy forward but also created many environmental concerns, such as toxic metal pollution. Many reclamation companies recycle batteries to reduce the number of batteries going into landfills. Rechargeable batteries can be charged hundreds of times before wearing out; and even after wearing out they can be recycled.

There are two types of batteries, Primary (chemical-reactions they use are non-reversible, so disposable) and Secondary (chemical-reactions they use are reversible, so rechargeable), both of which convert chemical-energy to electrical-energy. Primary batteries can only be used once because they use up their chemicals in an irreversible reaction.

Secondary batteries are recharged by running a charging-current through the battery, but in the opposite direction of the discharge current.

The first known artifacts that might have served as batteries were the Baghdad Batteries (between 250 BC and 640 AD). The story of the modern battery began in the 1780s with the discovery of electric-circuit which was further developed into a voltaic-cell. In 1799, Volta invented the modern-battery by piling many voltaic-cells in series. This Voltaic-Pile gave a greatly enhanced net emf for the combination, with a voltage of about 50 volts for a 32-cell pile. In many parts of Europe batteries continue to be called piles. Although early batteries were of great value for experimental purposes, their limitations made them impractical for large current drain. Later, starting with the Daniell cell in 1836, batteries provided more reliable currents and were adopted by industry. These wet cells used liquid electrolytes, which were prone to leaks and spillage. In the 19th century, the invention of dry-cell batteries replaced liquid-electrolyte with a paste made portable electrical devices practical. The battery has since become a common power source for many household and industrial applications.

Types of Disposable Battery – They are not designed to be rechargeable and called "primary-cells". "Disposable" may also imply that special disposal procedures that must take place for proper disposal according to regulation, depending on battery-type.

Examples of Disposable Battery include: Zinc-Carbon battery (mid-cost, used in light drain applications); Zinc-Chloride battery (similar to zinc-carbon but slightly longer-life); Alkaline battery (alkaline/manganese "long-life" batteries, widely used in both light-drain and heavy-drain applications); Silver-Oxide battery (commonly used in hearing-aids, watches and calculators); Lithium-Iron-Disulphide battery (commonly used in digital-cameras, sometimes used in watches and computer-clocks, very long-life (up to ten years in wristwatches) and capable of delivering high currents but expensive, operates in sub-zero temperatures); Lithium-Thionyl-Chloride battery (used in industrial applications, including computers, electric-meters and other devices which contain volatile memory circuits, act as a "carryover" voltage to maintain the memory in the event of a main power failure, also used for providing power for wireless gas and water-meters, cells are rated at 3.6 Volts and come in 1/2AA, AA, 2/3A, A, C, D & DD sizes, relatively expensive, but have a proven ten-year shelf life); Mercury battery (formerly used in digital-watches, radio communications, and portable electronic instruments, manufactured only for specialist applications due to toxicity); Zinc-Air battery (commonly used in hearing-aids); Thermal battery (high-temperature reserve, almost exclusively military applications); water-activated battery (used for radiosondes and emergency applications); and Nickel-Oxyhydroxide battery (ideal for applications that use bursts of high-current, better performance and cheaper in this application than Lithium-Iron-Disulphide battery).

Types of Rechargeable Battery - The oldest form of rechargeable battery still in modern usage is the "wet-cell" lead-acid battery. A common form of lead-acid battery is the modern wet-cell car battery. This can deliver about 10,000 watts of power for a short period, and has a peak current output that varies from 450 to 1100 amperes. An improved type of liquid electrolyte battery is the sealed valve regulated lead acid (VRLA) battery, popular in automotive industry as a replacement for the lead-acid wet cell, as well as in many lower capacity roles including smaller vehicles and stationary applications such as emergency lighting and alarm systems. Other portable rechargeable batteries include several "dry-cell" types, which are sealed units and are therefore useful in appliances like mobile phones and laptops. Cells of this type (in order of increasing power-density and cost) include Nickel-Cadmium (NiCd), Nickel-Metal-Hydride (NiMH), and Lithium-Ion (Li-Ion) cells. Recent developments include AA Batteries with embedded functionality such as 'USBCELL' with built-in charger and 'USB' connector within the AA format, enabling the battery to be charged by plugging into a USB port without a charger.

Homemade Cells for children – Almost any liquid or moist object that has enough ions to be electrically conductive can serve as the electrolyte for a cell. When two electrodes made of different metals are inserted into a lemon, potato, etc. can generate small amounts of electricity. "Two-Potato-Clocks" are available in toy-stores made from a pair of cells, each consisting of a potato (lemon, etc.) with two electrodes inserted into it, wired in series to form a battery with enough voltage to power a digital-clock. Similarly, a voltaic-pile can be made from two coins (such as a nickel and a penny) and a piece of paper-towel dipped in salt-water and when such voltaic-piles are stacked together in series, they can replace normal batteries for a short amount of time. Sony has developed a biologically friendly-battery that generates electricity from sugar in a way that's similar to what's found in living organisms. The battery generates electricity through the use of enzymes that break down carbohydrates, which are essentially sugar. Lead acid cells can easily be manufactured at home, but a tedious charge/discharge cycle is needed to 'form' the plates. This is a process whereby lead sulfate forms on the plates, and during charge is converted to lead dioxide (positive plate) and pure lead (negative plate). Repeating this process results in a microscopically rough surface, with far greater surface area being exposed. This increases the current the cell can deliver. For example, Daniel-cells or Aluminium-air batteries can also be produced at home.

[For more detailed reference on Battery one may refer: "The-Battery-Bible" (http://www. pureenergysystems.com/); "New-Technology-Batteries Guide" (http://www.nlectc.org/); and "Battery Handling and Maintenance" (http://www.nlectc.org/)].

The Human Body, Bio-engineering & Bioenergetics

Discussion of energy-value of foods, bio-engineering, bio-energetics, aura, yoga, tai-chi etc. is not the purpose of this book; yet the absence of their passing mention will leave the subject incomplete. All the branches of arts and sciences on earth discovered and function within or without human-body always exist in a balancing mode where attempt to draw the lines of demarcation becomes meaningless, on the contrary the study of correspondence gains more importance.

All living things on earth need to use energy. Plants use energy as they make new cells and grow and manufacture their food. Animals use energy to sustain their life activities. Human body also needs energy for all its body functions, complex systems and activities (breathing, digestion, blood-circulation, thinking, for developing new cells for growth or for the repair of damaged tissue, and even during sleep), not for just obvious movements such as running, walking or jumping and survival.

Human-Body 'Energy-engineering' is an application of engineering-principles and design-procedures to medical problems which includes its sub-disciplines like bio-mechanical, bio-chemical, and bio-electrical engineering. 'Bio-energetics' is the study of the processes by which living-cells use, store, and release energy. A central component of bio-energetics is energy-transformation, the conversion of energy from one form to another. All cells transform energy. Plant cells, for example, use sunlight to make carbohydrates (sugars and starches) from simple inorganic chemicals. In this process, called photosynthesis, radiant energy from the sun is converted into stored chemical energy. If these plant-carbohydrates are eaten by us, they will be broken down and their chemical-energy turned into movement (kinetic energy), body-heat (radiant-energy), or new chemical-bonds (Adenosine-Triphosphate, Citric-Acid Cycle, Metabolism).

In all such transformations, some energy is lost to the environment. This lost energy, which is no longer available for useful work, is called "entropy". The second law of thermodynamics states that every system tends to run down, that is, increases its entropy, over time. However, the energy security and the steady-influx of "Solar Energy", free and infinite, has been and will always remain to be required for the certitude in survival and growth of all the earth's plants, animals and mankind, faithfully and divinely, with a natural energy-retreat in entropy.

The self-perpetuating human body is also considered as a type of battery composed of three vital parts : (i) Structure - the cells and the organs, bones, muscle, skin layers, blood vessels, nerves and other physical structures that they form; (ii) Liquid — the intra and inter-cellular liquids that play important roles in the generation of electrical energy; and (iii) Electrical charge — the charge responsible for activating the body and its structures. It is called the "life-force", life-energy, spirit or bio-electromagnetism. The Chinese refer to this as "chi".

Of the three components, the last, 'electrical-charge' is least understood, since its presence is not immediately obvious to the naked eye. Electrical energy is detected only in a roundabout way, because it is most obvious when it is absent. If there is partial absence of energy in the body, weakness or disease invades. When there is total absence of vital energy, there is death. Cessation of heartbeat does not necessarily mean death, for many yogis have stopped their own heartbeat, yet remain alive because their bodies still hold vital energy.

Exhaustion is a symptom of low energy levels. Anytime you use your body or your mind you lose energy. According to scientific studies, if you focus your eyes on an object for one minute it will take twenty minutes of rest to regain the amount of energy lost. Furthermore, studies have been done in which dying people have been put on a scale and weighed, at the point of death, there has been recorded a weight loss of six ounces, varying from person to person. It is believed that the six ounces weight loss reflects the weight of vital energy, which is material and measurable.

The 'aura' (electro-magnetic energy-field) around a person's body has been researched for many years, but it has now been proved to exist with the advent of Kirlian photography. A simple description of the aura suggests that it is made up of coloured flames of energy that are emitted from the human body. The radiance and the colours of the aura have been determined to be reflective of health and energy levels. Brilliant light, clear colours indicate good health and high energy levels, whilst dark, heavy colours indicate disease.

Minute after minute and day after day we lose energy by body movements and mental activities. In time, if this constant loss of energy is not replenished, weakness and illness will follow. Of course we also acquire vital energy, through the food we eat, the air we breathe and the cosmic radiation we are exposed to. We also require normal, restful sleep, which relaxes the acupoints of exit and entry and allows the universal energy to travel through the meridians and reach and recharge every cell in the body. Besides the external techniques consisting of various forms of physical-exercises (gymnastics, running, swimming, dancing, cycling, walking etc.), scientific-dieting, physio-therapy, sun-bath and bio-engineering, the other ways to increase our vital energy, is by practising the internal art of psycho-therapy, Yoga, Music, Qigong, Tai-Chi and similar other techniques regularly.

Kardashev Theory (Energy Based) of Technologically Advanced Civilisation

It may not be out of place to mention here that many great theorists (social-theories and social-evolutionism) of the earth studied and attributed the advancement in the stages of human-civilisation mainly to 'Technology' and 'Energy'.

The "Kardashev-scale" (first proposed in 1964 by the Soviet-astronomer "Nikolai Kardashev") is a method of classifying how technologically advanced a civilization is. His theory scaled civilization into three categories (Type-I, II & III), based on the amount of 'Usable-Energy' a civilization has at its disposal. A Type-I civilization is able to harness all of the 'power' (approximately 10^{16} W) available on a single planet (EARTH). A Type-II civilization is able to harness all of the 'power' (approximately 10^{26} W) available from a single star (SUN). Again, this figure is variable; the sun outputs approximately 3.86 ×10^{26} W. (Kardashev's original definition was 4 ×10^{26} W). A Type III civilization is able to harness all of the 'power' (approximately 10^{36} W) available from a single galaxy (MILKY-WAY).

Usage and examples of Kardashev's theory

Human civilization is currently somewhere below Type-I, as it is able to harness only a portion of the earth's energy. The current state of human civilization has thus been named 'Type-O' by 'Carl-Sagan' who by interpolating and extrapolating (using a power-output of ~10TW and the formula: $K=(\log_{10}W-6)/10$) the values (K = a civilization's Kardashev rating and W= its power-output in watts) given by Kardashev calculated humanity's current civilization to be 0.7.

A possible method by which earth can advance to a 'Type-I' civilization is to begin the heavy use of 'ocean thermal-energy conversion' and 'wind-turbines' to obtain the energy received by earth's oceans from the sun. However, there is no known way to successfully utilize the full potential of earth's energy-production without complete coating of the surface with man-made structures. In the near and medium future, this is an impossibility given the current-lifestyle of humanity. Currently, we are already "harnessing" earth's production through our dependence upon ecosystem-services, which may prove more efficient and sustainable than our own technology well into the future. If humans choose never to fully substitute synthetics for nature's services on this planet, they may still achieve a Type-I civilization by assuring that earth's ecosystem services are maximally functional. A simpler and far less intrusive method would be to place solar collectors with sufficient surface area into orbit.

Kardashev's theory is an extension of social-theories & social-evolutionism

Kardashev's theory can be viewed as extension of some social-theories, especially from social-evolutionism. It is close to the theory of 'Leslie-White', author of *'The Evolution of Culture: The Development of Civilization to the Fall of Rome'* (1959). White considered 'Technology' as the most important factor in the entire history of humanity and emphasized that the *Social-systems are determined by technological systems* echoing the earlier theory of 'Lewis-Henry-Morgan'. He considered 'Energy-Consumption' as a measure of society-advancement of a given-society (thus his theory is known as "Energy-Theory of Cultural-Evolution").

White introduced a formula $P = E \times T$, where 'P' measures the advancement of the culture, 'E' is a measure of energy consumed, and 'T' is the measure of efficiency of technical factors utilizing the energy and differentiated between the five-stages of human-development as the 1st Stage (people use muscular-energy); 2nd Stage (people use energy of domesticated animals); 3rd Stage (people use the energy of plants); 4th Stage (people learn to use the energy of natural resources, such as coal, oil and gas); and 5th Stage (people harness nuclear-energy).

Criticism of Kardashev's Theory

It has been argued that, because people on earth cannot understand advanced civilizations, their behaviour is unpredictable; thus, Kardashev's visualization may not reflect what will actually occur for an advanced civilization. Though such civilizations are hypothetical at this point of time, Kardashev scale is of use to **SETI** (Search for Extra-Terrestrial Intelligence, an organized-effort, widely endorsed by the scientific community as hard-science, to survey the sky to detect existence of transmissions from a civilization on a distant planet) researchers, science-fiction authors, and futurists as a theoretical framework.

CONCLUSION

The technological advances of the 20th century relied to a great extent on exploitation of the earth's fossil-fuels. In the 21st century research and application development of energy sources as alternatives to fossil-based energy sources was done on a significant scale. The achievements made by USA, Denmark, France, Canada and China are spectacular. Many experts believe that a transition toward renewable, carbon-free energy technologies would go a long way toward addressing the problems of dwindling oil reserves and the potentially ruinous environmental impacts linked to the burning of fossil-fuels. Such a transition could make the 21st century the age of renewable energy leaving the 20th century as the age of fossil-fuels. Observers believe that in 21st century a series of revolutionary new and nano-technologies — including a wide range of traditional and renewable energy resources as well as use of advanced and nano solar-cells, wind-turbines, fuel-cells and hydrogen will be commercialized in wide scale. A host of other resources, including geothermal-heat, bio-mass, and ocean-power, may also figure prominently in the world's next energy systems.

Considering the population of India, even a single successful and sustainable step taken toward Energy-Conservation and Energy-Efficiency may bring very large annual economic impact on the whole in the country. For example, creation and free distribution of a knowledge-base on Energy-Management; more of distributed/decentralized energy-generation systems; Government sponsored policy and programme for strategic cost-reduction to incentivise increased use of renewable energy technologies to make them commercially competitive; national programmes to introduce energy-revolution and economic-revolution in energy sector; wide-scale use of solar-lighting; launching of nation-wide solar-roof programmes by the Central and all State Governments in India (like the United States and the European Union) providing tax-incentives, low-cost financing, and other assistance; time-based tariff for electricity; rationing or consumption-based tariff in case of subsidised petroleum products for corporate sector and high taxable-income; use of advanced insulation on walls and attics to reduce energy-consumption for heating or cooling buildings and store-houses; and use of recycled wastes. Use of recycled-wastes (newspapers, tires, aluminium cans, tin cans, plastic bottles and many other goods) can prove to be an important source of energy-conservation because recycling these waste-items, grinding them up and reusing the material, uses less energy, reduced manufacturing process time and cost than it would take to make them from the stage of brand new raw materials.

To make sure we have plenty of energy in the future, it is upto all of us to use energy wisely. We must all conserve energy and use it efficiently. It is also upto those who will create the new energy technologies of the future. All energy sources have an impact on the environment. Concerns about the greenhouse effect and global warming, air pollution, and energy security have led to increasing interest and more development in renewable energy sources. But we will need to continue to use fossil-fuels and nuclear-energy until new, cleaner technologies can replace them. One of you who is reading this book might become another Albert Einstein or Marie Curie and find a new source or form of energy Until then, it is upto all of us. The future is ours, but in any case we will need 'energy' to get there.

CHAPTER 3

Trend and Current Researches & Developments for Future Energy Sources

For the sake of going beyond petroleum-based economy (with its high and volatile energy prices) and keeping the economic development (being re-defined from the angle of National Security) moving, growing, secured and sustainable, countries, in the growing world-trend for having more and more of clean, affordable, reliable and secured energy sources, have also been internally committing on undertaking research and development projects on energy[1] related technologies continuously, improvement of energy-efficiency, development of alternative and renewable energy sources, cost-competitive production of cellulosic-ethanol in place of corn-based ethanol, zero-emission coal-fired technology, solar

---

1. There are still other forms or industrial-sources of energy which are industry-specific and not discussed here. Examples: Blast-Furnace-gas, Coke-Oven-gas, LD Converters-gas, Steam from Boilers, Pitch-Creosote-Mixture from coal etc. generated and used in Steel Plants.

and wind technologies, safe and clean nuclear technology, advanced battery technologies, hybrid electric automobiles, hydrogen fuel-cells, and more. This chapter contains only some examples to show the current trend of development in respect of less known or less popular energy sources in the world.

(1) Non-Conventional Oil

Production or extraction of 'Non-Conventional Oil' is done using techniques other than the traditional oil-well method. Currently, the non-conventional oil production is less efficient and some types have a larger environmental impact relative to conventional oil production.

Production of 'Non-Conventional Oil' types, detailed below, include: tar-sands, heavy-oil, oil-shale, bio-fuels, thermal-depolymerization (TDP) of organic matter, and the conversion of coal or natural gas to liquid hydrocarbons through processes such as 'Fischer-Tropsch' synthesis. These non-conventional sources of oil may be increasingly relied upon as petro motor-fuel for transportation when conventional oil becomes "economically non-viable" due to depletion. Currently conventional oil-sources are preferred because they provide a much higher ratio of extracted energy over energy used in extraction and refining processes. Technology, such as using steam-injection in tar-sands deposits, is being developed to increase the efficiency of non-conventional oil production.

(i) Extra Heavy-Oil and Tar-Sands – Extra heavy-oils are extremely viscous, with a consistency ranging from that of heavy-molasses to a solid at room temperature. Tar-sands is a common name of what are more properly called bituminous-sands, also commonly referred to as oil-sands or extra-heavy oil, were used by the ancient Mesopotamians and Canadian First Nations, among others. They are' a mixture of sand or clay, water, and extremely heavy crude-oil. The hydrocarbon content of these deposits is called 'bitumen', on which the fuel 'Orimulsion' is based. Heavy crude-oils have a density (specific-gravity) approaching or even exceeding that of water. As a result, they cannot be produced, transported, and refined by conventional methods. Heavy crude-oils usually contain high concentrations of sulphur and several metals, particularly nickel and vanadium. These properties make them difficult to pump out of the ground or through a pipeline and interfere with refining. The oil extraction process requires either strip-mining or in-situ processing, steam and caustic-soda (NaOH). Oil production from these fossil-fuels will be difficult since the extraction process takes a great deal of capital, manpower and land. The process is more energy-intensive than conventional oil and thus more expensive. Despite the difficulty and cost, oil-sands are now being mined on a vast scale to extract the oil, which is then converted into synthetic-oil by oil-upgraders, or refined directly into petroleum products by specialized refineries.

In course of time many extraction/production processes/ technologies have been used for separating 'Raw-Bitumen' from the oil-sands in giant separation cells which include: Surface Mining, Open-Pit Mining, In-Situ Mining, Cold Flow through progressive cavity-pumps, Cold Heavy-Oil Production with Sand, Cyclic Steam Stimulation, Steam Assisted Gravity Drainage, Vapour Extraction Process, and Toe to Heel Air Injection.

Oil-sand deposits are found in over 70 countries worldwide. Countries having large deposits of oil-sands, include the United States, Russia, and various countries in the Middle East. However, the world's largest deposits occur in two countries: Canada and Venezuela, both of which have oil-sands reserves approximately equal to the world's total reserves of conventional crude-oil. The Venezuelan extra heavy oil deposits differ from tar-sands in that they flow more readily at ambient-temperature and could be produced by cold-flow techniques, but the recovery rates would be less than the Canadian techniques (about 8% versus upto 90% for surface mining and 60% for steam assisted gravity drainage).

However, as a result of the development of these reserves, most Canadian oil production in the 21st century is from oil-sands or heavy-oil deposits, and Canada is now the largest single supplier of oil and refined products to the United States. Venezuelan production is also very large, but due to political problems its oil production has been declining since the start of the 21st century.

(ii) Oil–Shale – Oil-Shale (a fine-grained sedimentary-rock) is a general-term applied to a group of fine black to dark brown shales rich enough in organic-material (called kerogen) to yield petroleum and combustible gas upon distillation. The 'kerogen' in oil-shale can be converted to synthetic crude-oil through the chemical process of pyrolysis. During pyrolysis the oil-shale is heated to 450–500°C in the absence of air where the kerogen is converted to oil and separated out, a process called "retorting". Oil-shale has also been burnt directly as a low-grade fuel for power generation and heating purposes, and can be used as a raw material in the chemical and construction material industries. Oil-Shale requires extensive processing, consumes large amounts of water and energy. An operation producing 100,000 barrels per day requires approximately 1.2 GW of dedicated electric-power to heat the oil-shale.

However, a critical measure of the viability of oil-shale as an energy-source is the ratio of the energy produced by the shale to the energy used in its mining and processing, a ratio known as "Energy-Returned on Energy-Invested" (EROEI). A 1984 study estimated the EROEI of the various known oil-shale deposits as varying between 0.7 and 13.3.

Deposits of oil-shale are located around the world, including major deposits in the United States. Global deposits are estimated around 2.8–3.3 trillion (2.8–3.3×10^{12}) barrels of recoverable oil. The United States (Office of Naval Petroleum and Oil Shale Reserves) estimated the world-supply of oil-shale at 1662 billion barrels (264 billion m³) of which 1200 billion barrels (191 billion m³) is in the United States. Estonia, Russia, Brazil, Australia and China too currently mine oil-shale, however production is declining due to economic and environmental factors. If oil-shale could be used to meet a quarter of the current 20 million-barrels per day demand, 800 billion barrels of recoverable resources would last for more than 400 years. However, attempts to develop these reserves have been going on for over 100 years with limited success. Oil-shale has gained attention as an energy-resource as the price of conventional sources of petroleum has increased and as an alternative to secure independence from external suppliers of energy.

Main industrial uses of Oil-Shale – Currently, oil-shale is used industrially in Brazil, China, Estonia and to some extent in Germany, Israel, and Russia. At the beginning of the 21st century, several other countries were assessing their reserves or had built experimental production-plants, while others had phased out their oil-shale industry. Oil-shales are used for oil production (in Estonia, Brazil, and China), for power-generation (in Estonia, China, Israel, and Germany), for cement-production (in Estonia, Germany, and China), and by chemical industries (in Estonia and Russia). At present, Estonia alone accounts for about 70% of the world's oil-shale production.

Use of Oil-Shale for power-generation – Oil-shale can be used as a fuel for thermal power plants, where, like coal, it is burnt to drive steam-turbines; some of these plants employ the resulting heat for heating of homes and businesses. Sizable oil-shale-fired power plants are located in Estonia, which has an installed capacity of 2,967 (MW), Israel (12.5 MW), China (12 MW), and Germany (9.9 MW). While some countries, such as Romania, have shut down their oil-shale-fired power plants, others, including Russia, have switched over to other fuel-sources. Jordan and Egypt are planning to construct new oil-shale-fired power plants, while Canada and Turkey plan to burn oil-shale along with coal for power generation. Oil-shale is used as the main fuel for power generation only in Estonia, where its oil-shale-fired Narva Power Plants accounted for 95% of electrical generation in 2005.

Other Application of Oil-Shale – In addition to its use as a fuel, oil-shale is also being used for production of speciality carbon-fibers, adsorbent-carbons, carbon-black, phenols, resins, glues, tanning agents, mastic, road bitumen, cement, bricks, construction and decorative blocks, soil additives, fertilizers, rock-wool insulation, glass, and pharmaceutical products. However, oil-shale use for production of these items is still small or only in its experimental stages. Some oil-shales also yield sulphur, ammonia, alumina, soda-ash, uranium, and nahcolite as by-products. Between 1946 and 1952, a marine type of Dictyonema-shale was used for 'uranium' production in Sillamäe and Estonia. Between 1950 and 1989 alum-shale was used in Sweden for the same purposes. Another of its proposed use is as a substitute for natural gas.

(iii) Thermal Depolymerization – Thermal-depolymerization is also considered a future energy-crisis solution. If all the 6 billion people (including 1.2 billion Chinese and 1.1 billion Indians) in the world demand the same standard of energy-living enjoyed by the 1 billion people in the West the petroleum production would need to be increased by 4 or 5 times than what it is now. Thermal-Depolymerization (TDP) has been noticed as a powerful alternative solution to the present energy crisis. TDP is a process which seems to be able to convert any organic-material into any product now produced from oil (natural gas, propane, kerosene, gasoline, diesel-fuel, petroleum-coke, jet-fuel, home heating-oil, and lubricating-oil). Organic materials include wood, leaves, grass, food, paper, all agricultural waste, plastic, paint, cotton, synthetic fabrics, sludge from sewage, animal parts, bacteria, any carbo-hydrates, or hydro-carbons (with the exception of metal, ceramics, and glass).

TDP is a form of solar energy. Sunlight converts H_2O and CO_2 into carbo-hydrates in living-plants giving off Oxygen in the well-known process of photo-synthesis. In a completely TDP based economy the amount of CO_2 produced (when fuels are burnt) is exactly balanced by the plants grown to be used for TDP feedstock. In other words, it is a closed system, there is no net gain in CO_2 levels, regardless of how much fuel is produced and burnt. The amount of solar energy hitting the earth is about 5000 times more than the entire amount of energy used in all human activities. Even by a 1% increase in solar energy efficiency-rate there is the potential by many times to increase our current energy use. With optimum use and a mature TDP technology, the earth might comfortably support 10 times its current population at a high standard of energy-living. There is enough bio-mass existing now accessible on the surface of the earth to provide 100 years of human energy-use.

Further, TDP occurs under conditions of temperature and pressure absolutely guaranteed to kill all living things including any microbe/virus and the related diseases. TDP energy-farms can be used as a habitat for other species and as recreational space for people. TDP plants can be located near agricultural waste, landfills, and markets reducing transportation cost and risk. TDP based energy can be produced anywhere the sun shines.

TDP was invented by USA, and the first-patent was acquired in the mid 90's when a bench-scale proof of the principle was done by 'Changing-World-Technologies' (CWT). In 2000 a small-scale plant was built in Philadelphia and used to test the whole range of feedstock. In 2003 a full-scale plant was started-up in Missouri and is now (April 2004) running at full capacity. Five more TDP larger-plants are under construction (2007). Thermal-Depolymerization is different from other similar processes known as *Thermo-Chemical-Conversion* (limited to the changing of manure to crude-oil) and *Thermal–Conversion-Process* (limited to the changing of manure and vegetable waste to crude-oil). Thermal-Depolymerization can change many carbon-based materials into crude-oil and methane, and is not limited to the use of manure or vegetable waste.

What is 'TDP' technically - It mimics the natural geological processes thought to be involved in the production of fossil-fuels. Under pressure and heat, long-chain polymers of hydrogen, oxygen, and carbon decompose into short-chain petroleum hydrocarbons with a maximum length of around 18 carbons. TDP uses steam under pressure to cook and crack organic chemicals in the absence of oxygen then by manipulating temperature and pressure, assemble useful selectable hydrocarbon chains. TDP is a closed-process which produces no harmful waste. About 15% of the btu content of feed-stock is required to power the process. That is, a TDP plant where feedstock containing 100 btus went in one end and oil will come out the other. No other inputs. TDP will convert energy in a useless form to very useful oil. Many previous methods which create hydrocarbons through depolymerization used dry materials (anhydrous-pyrolysis), which requires expending a lot of energy to remove water.

However, the work has been done on hydrous-pyrolysis methods, in which the depolymerization takes place with the materials in water. The fixed-carbon solids produced by the TDP process have multiple uses as a filter, a fuel source and a fertilizer. It can be used as activated carbon in wastewater treatment, as a fertilizer, or as a fuel similar to coal. TDP process is considered more efficient and economic for reasons shown in braces when compared with other thermal based biomass processes that have been tried : Rendering (not hot enough, no chemical reaction, open to atmosphere, smells bad); Pyrolysis (too high temperature/not uniform temperature); Ethanol (requires too specialized feedstock-sugar, energy required to produce ethanol is more than it releases when burnt); Bio–diesel (specialized feed stock– just takes oil produced by plants); and Biomass (not done in techno-commercially way to contribute much to world energy supplies). CWT expanded the technology with further improvements into what is now referred to as TCP where the water improves the heating process and contributes hydrogen to the reactions. TCP even efficiently breaks down many types of hazardous materials, such as poisons and difficult-to-destroy biological agents such as prions.

A biofuel tax-credit of roughly $1 per US gallon (26 ¢/L) on production costs as allowed in USA was not available because the oil produced did not meet the definition of "biodiesel" according to the relevant American tax legislation. The US Energy Policy Act of 2005 specifically added thermal depolymerization to a $1 renewable diesel-credit.

Alternative process of 'Thermal-Depolymerization' using Microwaves

In 2007, "Popular-Science" reported that Frank-Pringle used 'microwaves' to extract oil from various types of waste. The machine used was a microwave-emitter that extracted the petroleum and gas hidden inside everyday objects, or at least anything made with hydro-carbons, which, it turned out, is most of what's around us. Every hour, the first commercial version will turn 10 tons of auto waste—tires, plastic, vinyl—into enough natural gas to produce 17 million BTUs of energy (it will use 956,000 of those BTUs to keep itself running).

Feedstocks and outputs with thermal depolymerization

Feed-Stock	- OUTPUT -			
	Oil	Gas	Carbon-Solids	Water
Plastic bottles	70 %	16 %	6 %	8 %
Sewage sludge	26 %	9 %	8 %	57 %
Turkey offal	39 %	6 %	5 %	50 %
Medical waste	65 %	10 %	5 %	20 %
Paper (cellulose)	8 %	48 %	24 %	20 %
Tires	44 %	10 %	42 %	4 %

(iv) Coal and Gas conversion – The conversion of coal and natural gas has the potential to yield great quantities of non-conventional oil albeit at much lower net-energy-output. Because of the high cost of transporting natural gas, many known but remote fields are not being developed.

Conversion can make this energy available even under present market conditions. The 'Karrick' process is a Low-Temperature-Carbonization (LTC) of coal, shale, lignite or any carbonaceous materials. These are heated at 360 °C to 750 °C (680 °F to 1380 °F) in the absence of air to distill out oil and gas. Production works out at about $35 per barrel. The 'Fischer-Tropsch' process operates on similar principle to the 'Karrick' process, but is less efficient for coal gasification because more of the energy content of the coal is lost. For producing liquid-fuel from natural gas, the Fischer-Tropsch process is currently an area of significant process research by most major oil companies.

(v) **Vegetable-Oil used as Fuel** – Many **vegetable oils** have **fuel**-properties similar to diesel-fuel, except for higher viscosity and lower oxidative stability. If these differences can be overcome, vegetable-oil may substitute for #2 Diesel-fuels, most significantly as engine-fuel or home-heating-oil. For engines designed to burn #2 diesel-fuels, the viscosity of vegetable-oil must be lowered to allow for proper atomization of fuel, otherwise incomplete combustion and carbon built-up will ultimately damage the engine. Many enthusiasts refer to vegetable-oil used as fuel as **Waste-Vegetable-Oil** (WVO) if it is the oil that was discarded from a restaurant or **Straight-Vegetable-Oil** (SVO) or **Pure-Plant-Oil** (PPO) to distinguish it from bio-diesel.

The first known use of vegetable-oil as fuel in a diesel-engine was demonstrated by the 'Otto' company at the 1900 World Fair. While engineers and enthusiasts have been experimenting with using vegetable-oils as fuel for a diesel-engine since at least 1900, it is only recently that the necessary fuel-properties and engine-parameters for reliable operation have become apparent. A number of peer reviewed studies exist that show reliable long term use of vegetable-oil. Most diesel car engines are suitable for the use of SVO, also commonly called Pure-Plant-Oil (PPO), with suitable modifications. In principle, the viscosity and surface-tension of the SVO/PPO must be reduced by preheating it, typically by using waste heat from the engine or electricity, otherwise it results into poor-atomization, incomplete-combustion and carbonization which are, however, commonly solved by adding a heat-exchanger, and an additional fuel-tank for "normal" diesel-fuel (petro-diesel or bio-diesel) and a three-way valve to switch between this additional-tank and the main-tank of SVO/PPO. Single-tank conversions (to provide reliable-operation with rape-seed-oil that meets the German rapeseed oil-fuel Standard:DIN-51605) have also been developed in Germany, and used throughout Europe followed by modified Indirect-Injection (IDI) engines (proven to be operable with 100% PPO down to temperatures of 10°C); Direct-Injection (DI) engines; and Turbocharged Direct-Injection engines. Many cars powered by Indirect-Injection engines supplied by in-line injection pumps, or mechanical Bosch injection pumps are claimed to be capable of running on pure SVO/PPO in all temperatures except in acute winter.

While the main form of SVO/PPO used in UK is rape-seed-oil (known as Canola-oil, used in the United States and Canada) has a freezing-point of -10°C, use of Sunflower-oil, which freezes at -17°C, is currently being investigated as a means of improving cold-weather starting. Unfortunately oils with lower gelling-points tend to be less saturated (leading to a higher iodine-number) and polymerize more easily in the presence of atmospheric oxygen.

Coconut oil is also being used as fuel by some Pacific Island-nations due to high/volatile prices of imported fuels. Coconut oil is usable where temperature do not drop below 17°C unless two-tank SVO/PPO kits or other tank-heating accessories, etc. are used. Fortunately, the same techniques developed to use, for example, Canola and other oils in cold climates can be implemented to make coconut oil usable in temperatures lower than 17°C.

As of 2000, the United States was producing in excess of 11 billion liters of Waste–Vegetable-Oil (WVO) annually, mainly from industrial deep fryers in potato processing-plants, snack-food-factories/fast-food restaurants whose energy-equivalent replacement amount of petroleum would be significant. Use of Waste-Vegetable-Oil (WVO) as a fuel is competing with some already established uses.

Pure-Plant-Oil (PPO) or Straight-Vegetable-Oil (SVO), in contrast to Waste-Vegetable-Oil (WVO), is not a by-product of other industries, and thus its prospects for use as fuel are not limited by the capacities of other industries. Production of vegetable oils for use as fuels is theoretically limited only by the agricultural capacity of a given economy.

(2) Advancements in Battery-Technology

Rechargeable-Battery - Examples of secondary-batteries (accumulators) include: A rechargeable Lithium-Polymer battery (used in Nokia mobile-phone); Nickel-Cadmium (NiCd) battery (best used for motorized-equipments and other high-discharge, short term devices, can withstand even more drain than NiMH, the mAh rating is not high enough to keep the device running for very long, the memory-effect is far more severe), Nickel-Metal-Hydride (NiMH) battery (best used for high-tech devices, can last upto four times longer than alkaline-batteries because NiMH can withstand high current for a long while); and the rechargeable alkaline-battery (use similar chemistry to non-rechargeable alkaline-batteries and best suited for similar applications, but hold their charge for years unlike NiCd and NiMH batteries).

Flow-Batteries – Flow-batteries are a special class of rechargeable-battery where additional quantities of electrolyte are stored outside the main power-cell of the battery, and circulated through it by pumps or by movement. Flow-batteries can have extremely large capacities and are used in marine-applications and are gaining popularity in grid energy-storage applications. Zinc-Bromine and Vanadium-Redox batteries are typical examples of commercially available Flow-batteries.

Traction-Batteries - Traction batteries are high-power batteries designed to provide propulsion to move a vehicle, such as an electric-car or tow motor. A major design consideration is power-to-weight-ratio since the vehicle must carry the battery. While conventional lead-acid batteries with liquid-electrolyte have been used, gelled-electrolyte and AGM-type can also be used, especially in smaller sizes. The largest installations of batteries for propulsion of vehicles are found in submarines, although the toxic-gas produced by seawater contact with acid-electrolyte is a considerable hazard. Battery types commercially used in electric vehicles include: lead-acid battery (flooded type with liquid electrolyte, gel type, Absorbed-Glass-Mat type); Zebra Na/ $NiCl_2$ battery (operating at 270 °C requiring cooling in case of temperature excursions); and NiZn battery (higher cell voltage 1.6 V and thus 25% increased specific-energy, but have very short lifespan).

Advanced Batteries for Hybrid Battery-electric vehicles

Accelerated consumer adoption of hybrid-electric vehicles offers the potential to significantly reduce oil consumption in the short term. Further gains are possible with a "plug-in-hybrid-vehicle", a hybrid-electric vehicle that can run either on electricity from its own batteries or on gasoline. Unlike current hybrid vehicles, which can use only the gasoline engine to charge the on-board battery, a plug-in hybrid can be plugged into a common household electrical outlet to recharge its batteries. This allows a consumer to drive as an electric vehicle for the majority of driving that takes place within a range of 40 miles around home. For longer trips, the gasoline engine kicks in, and the vehicle drives like a regular hybrid-electric vehicle. As a result, fuel efficiency of plug-in hybrids could exceed 80 or more miles per gallon, particularly when the hybrids are driven in urban areas. Plug-in hybrids would generally be charged at night, when electric utilities have spare generating capacity available.

The Electric-Power-Research-Institute (EPRI-USA), in an attempt to assess the state of advanced battery technology for all Electric-Vehicle (EV) applications, collected and analysed data from battery-industry. It concluded (May, 2004) that the Nicle-Metal-Hydride (**NiMH**) batteries appeared capable of exceeding recent cycle life and durability projections to meet the life-time requirements of full-function

Battery-Electric-Vehicles (BEVs), Plug-In-Hybrid-Electric-Vehicles (PHEVs) with 40–60 miles of EV range, city EVs, and possibly even PHEVs with 20 miles of EV range. Economic analysis showed that Life-Cycle-Cost-Parity is possible for power-assist HEV 0s, PHEV 20s, and BEV 40s (short-range city EVs) compared to their gasoline counterparts. The Report provided important implications for decision-makers looking for cost-effective ways to reduce criteria pollutants, greenhouse gas emissions, and petroleum consumption for car and light-trucks.

Current battery technologies used in today's hybrid-electric vehicles store only enough energy to drive the vehicle in an electric-only mode at low-speed/short-range. Simply adding additional batteries is not practical as each hybrid-electric vehicle battery adds a sizeable increase to the price of the hybrid-electric vehicle. To address these issues, advanced battery technologies such as "**lithium-ion**" batteries ('Advanced-Energy-Initiatives' issued by the White House NEC, Feb. 2006), similar to batteries used in cellular-phones and other consumer-electronics are being considered for adaptation for vehicle use. These batteries, coupled with the development of advanced electric-drive technologies, will enable the commercialization of plug-in hybrids that can deliver the desired range. In addition to the gasoline savings they make possible, plug-in hybrids represent a practical step toward hydrogen fuel-cell vehicles, which have some of the same electric-drive and power-management technologies. Through the large scale replacement of gasoline with electricity and hydrogen produced from clean-coal, nuclear and renewable technologies, future oil use, balance-of-payment deficits, and emissions of air pollutants and greenhouse gases could be dramatically reduced.

Note: [The pace of innovations and R&D in the battery sector is fast enough where the manufacturers worldwide are introducing newer products each year with varying claims on performance/efficiency and battery-life. For a more detailed reference on latest product range of battery one must refer : "Directory-of-Battery-Resources" (http://www.freeenergynews.com/Directory/Battery/]

Battery capacity and discharging

The more electrolyte and electrode material there is in the cell, the greater the capacity of the cell. Thus a small cell has less capacity than a larger cell, given the same chemistry (e.g. alkaline-cells), though they develop the same open-circuit voltage. Because of the chemical reactions within the cells, the capacity of a battery depends on the discharge conditions such as the magnitude of the current, the duration of the current, the allowable terminal voltage of the battery, temperature, and other factors. The available capacity of a battery depends upon the rate at which it is discharged. If a battery is discharged at a relatively high rate, the available capacity will be lower than expected. Therefore, a battery rated at 100 A·h will deliver 5 A over a 20-hour period, but if it is instead discharged at 50 A, it will run out of charge before the theoretically expected 2 hours. For this reason, a battery capacity rating is always related to an expected discharge duration, such as 15 minutes, 8 hours, 20 hours as the case may be.

The relationship between current discharge time, and capacity for a lead acid battery is expressed by Peukert's law. The efficiency of a battery is different at different discharge rates. When discharging at low rate, the battery's energy is delivered more efficiently than at higher discharge rates. Battery manufacturers use a standard method to rate their batteries. The battery is discharged at a constant rate of current over a fixed period of time, such as 10 hours or 20 hours, down to a predetermined terminal voltage per cell. So a 100 ampere-hour battery is rated to provide 5 A for 20 hours at room-temperature. Ampere-hours are commonly called amp-hours. In general, the higher the ampere-hour rating, the longer the battery will last for a certain load. Installing batteries with different A·h ratings will not affect the operation of a device rated for a specific voltage.

Life of Primary Batteries

Even if never taken out of the original package, disposable (or "primary") batteries can lose 8-20% of their original charge every year at a temperature of about 20°–30°C. This is known as the "self-discharge" rate and is due to non-current-producing "side" chemical reactions, which occur within the cell even if no load is applied to it. The rate of the side reactions is reduced if the batteries are stored at low temperature, although some batteries can be damaged by freezing. High or low temperatures may reduce battery performance. This will affect the initial voltage of the battery. For an AA alkaline battery this initial voltage is normally distributed around 1.6 volts.

Life of Rechargeable Batteries

Rechargeable batteries traditionally self-discharge more rapidly than disposable alkaline batteries, upto 3% a day (depending on temperature). However, modern Lithium designs have reduced the self-discharge rate to a relatively low level (but still poorer than for primary batteries). Due to their poor shelf-life, rechargeable batteries should not be stored and then relied upon to power flashlights or radios in emergency. For this reason, it is a good idea to keep alkaline batteries on hand. NiCd Batteries are almost always "dead" when purchased, and must be charged before first use.

Although rechargeable batteries may be refreshed by charging, they still suffer degradation through usage. Low-capacity Nickel-Metal-Hydride (NiMH) batteries (1700-2000 mAh) can be charged for about 1000 cycles, whereas high capacity NiMH batteries (above 2500 mAh) can be charged for about 500 cycles. Nickel-Cadmium (NiCd) batteries tend to be rated for 1,000 cycles before their internal resistance increases beyond usable values. Normally a fast charge, rather than a slow-overnight-charge, will result in a shorter battery lifespan. However, if the overnight charger is not "smart" (i.e. it cannot detect when the battery is fully charged), then overcharging is likely, which will damage the battery.

Degradation usually occurs because electrolyte migrates away from the electrodes or because active material falls off the electrodes. NiCd batteries suffer the drawback that they should be fully discharged before recharge. Without full discharge, crystals may build up on the electrodes, thus decreasing the active surface area and increasing internal resistance, decreasing battery-capacity and causing the dreaded "memory-effect". These electrode crystals can penetrate the electrolyte-separator, thereby causing shorts. NiMH, although similar in chemistry, does not suffer from 'memory-effect' to this extent.

Automotive lead-acid rechargeable batteries, because of vibration, shock, heat, cold, and sulfation of their lead plates hardly last beyond six years or less of regular use. Automotive starting batteries have many thin plates to provide as much current as possible in a reasonably small package. Typically they are only drained a small amount before recharge. Care should be taken to avoid deep discharging a starting-battery, since each charge-and-discharge cycle causes active material to be shed from the plates. Hole formation in the plates leads to less surface area for the current-producing chemical reactions, resulting in less available current when under load. Leaving a lead-acid battery in a deeply discharged state for any significant length of time allows the lead sulfate to crystallize, making it difficult or impossible to remove during the charging process. This can result in a permanent reduction in the available plate surface, and therefore reduced current output and energy capacity.

"Deep-Cycle" lead-acid batteries such as those used in electric golf-carts have much thicker plates to aid their longevity. The main benefit of the lead-acid battery is its low cost; the main drawbacks are its large size and weight for a given capacity and voltage. Lead-acid batteries should never be discharged to below 20% of their full-capacity, because internal resistance will cause heat and damage when they are recharged. Deep-cycle lead-acid systems often use a low-charge warning light or a low-charge power cut-off switch to prevent the type of damage that will shorten the battery's life.

Special "reserve" batteries intended for long-storage in emergency equipments or munitions keep the electrolyte of the battery separate from the plates until the battery is activated, allowing the cells to be filled with the electrolyte. Shelf times for such batteries can be years or decades. However, their construction is more expensive than more common forms.

Extending the Battery Life

Battery life can be extended by storing the batteries at a low-temperature (as in a refrigerator or freezer) to reduce chemical reactions in the batteries. Such storage can extend the life of alkaline batteries by ~5%; while the charge of rechargeable batteries can be extended from a few days up to several months. In order to reach their maximum voltage, batteries must be returned to room-temperature; therefore, alkaline-battery manufacturers like Duracell do not recommend refrigerating or freezing batteries.

Battery heat, explosion, hazards and Environmental considerations

A battery explosion is caused by the misuse or malfunction of a battery, such as attempting to recharge a primary (non-rechargeable) battery, or short-circuiting a battery. With car-batteries, explosions are most likely to occur when a short-circuit generates very large currents. In addition, car-batteries liberate hydrogen when they are overcharged (because of electrolysis of the water in the electrolyte). Normally the amount of overcharging is very small, as is the amount of explosive-gas developed, and the gas dissipates quickly. However, when "jumping" a car-battery, the high current can cause the rapid release of large volumes of hydrogen, which can be ignited by a nearby spark (for example, when removing the jumper-cables).

When a battery is recharged at an excessive rate, an explosive gas mixture of hydrogen and oxygen may be produced faster than it can escape from within the walls of the battery, leading to pressure build-up and the possibility of the battery case bursting. In extreme cases, the battery acid may spray violently from the casing of the battery and cause injury. Battery explosions can also occur in maintenance free lead-acid batteries if the valves fail by being blocked. The pressure rises within the cells until a short-circuit ignites the hydrogen-oxygen mixture. Such explosions can cause severe personal injury. The problem can be detected in car-batteries if the sides appear at all swollen. Additionally, disposing of a battery in fire may cause an explosion as steam builds up within the sealed case of the battery. Overcharging (attempting to charge a battery beyond its electrical capacity) can also lead to a battery-explosion, leakage, or irreversible-damage to the battery. It may also cause damage to the charger or device in which the overcharged battery is later used. A short-circuit can lead to a battery-fire or explosion. It often occurs when a battery is connected to itself, creating two points on a circuit with different potentials connected with zero or near-zero resistance.

Since their development over 250 years ago, batteries ha·e remained among the most expensive energy sources as their manufacturing consumes many costly resources besides using hazardous chemicals. Used batteries also contribute to electronic-waste, so availability of Battery-Recycling services to recover some of the more toxic (and sometimes valuable) materials from used batteries is now a necessity. Batteries are harmful or fatal if swallowed. It is also important to prevent dangerous elements, such as lead, mercury, and cadmium, that are found in some types of batteries from entering the environment.

(3) Nano-Technology based Paper-Battery

The 'Rensselaer-Polytechnic-Institute' (http://en. wikipedia.org/wiki/) developed (2007) a paper-battery which is a nano-technology based integration of super-battery and super-capacitor. The nano-engineered battery (a sheet of black-paper infused with aligned-carbon-nanotubes) is made of cellulose by more than 90%, lightweight, ultra-thin, completely-flexible, and geared toward meeting the trickiest design and energy requirements of tomorrow's gadgets, implantable medical equipment, and transportation vehicles. The creation of this unique nano-composite paper drew from a diverse pool of disciplines, requiring expertise in materials science, energy storage, and chemistry.

The nano-tubes act as electrodes and allow the storage-devices to conduct electricity. It can provide long, steady power-output comparable to a conventional battery, and a supercapacitor's quick burst of high-energy. The researchers used ionic-liquid (essentially a liquid-salt) as the battery's electrolyte. Use of ionic-liquid which contains no water enables the battery to be free from getting ozen or evaporated and also to withstand extreme temperatures. The battery is a single, integrated device where the components are molecularly attached to each other: the carbon-nanotube-print is embedded in the paper, and the electrolyte is soaked into the paper with the end result that the device looks and weighs the same as paper.

Alongwith its ability to function in temperatures upto 300^0F and down to -100^0F, the device is completely integrated and can be printed like paper. The device is also unique in that it can function both as a lithium-ion high-energy-battery and a high-power-supercapacitor, which are generally separate components in most electrical systems. Another key-feature is the capability to use human blood or sweat to help power the battery. The device can be rolled, twisted, folded, or cut into any number of shapes with no loss of mechanical integrity or efficiency. The paper-batteries can also be stacked, like a ream of printer paper, to boost the total power-output.

Alongwith its use in small handheld electronics, the paper batteries' light weight could make them ideal for use in automobiles, aircraft, and even boats. The paper also could be moulded into different shapes, such as a car door, which would enable important new engineering innovations. Because of the high paper-content and lack of toxic-chemicals, it's environmentally safe. Paper is also extremely biocompatible and these new hybrid battery/supercapacitors have potential as power suppliers for devices implanted in the body. It is demonstrated that naturally occurring electrolytes in human sweat, blood, and urine can be used to activate the battery device.

Mass scale production of this paper-battery both for the energy and the electronics markets is still underway to further boosting the efficiency of the batteries and supercapacitors, and investigating different manufacturing techniques before a commercially viable trial-produciton is held.

Scientists and Technologists claim that energy storage is an area that can be addressed by nano-manufacturing technologies through an inter-disciplinary collaborative research activity to bring together advances and expertise in nano-technology, room temperature ionic-liquids, and energy-storage-devices in a creative way to devise super-battery and super capacitor devices in future.

Protein powered Solar-Cell produces electricity from spinach and bacterial proteins

Demonstrating a new strategy for making long lasting photovoltaic-cells, a protein-powered solar-cell (prototype) from spinach and the bacterium (Rhodobacter-sphaeroides) has been developed by the Massachusetts Institute of Technology (MIT) using molecular-biology, creative-chemistry, and nano-technology causing the photosynthetic-proteins (protein-complexes isolated to get associated chlorophylls, approximately 2 billion isolated proteins accommodated inside a cell-membrane) absorb light and pump electrons (e^-) through the semiconductor layer into a silver-electrode. This opened possibilities for making not just solar-cells but also other protein-based electronic-devices. Though production of protein-powered commercial/nano photovoltaic-devices will depend on the solar-cell's efficiency, a protein based solar-cell could be self-repairing like living plants replenishing their photosynthetic-proteins against many solar-cell materials which degrade over time.

(4) Cellulosic–Ethanol

Transportation fuels derived from bio-mass can be produced either by the conversion of sugar or starch-crops to ethanol, or by conversion of soyabean or other plant-oils to produce bio-diesel. These clean-burning fuels are currently mixed with gasoline or diesel-fuel in small amounts (upto 10% for ethanol and upto 20% for bio-diesel) and used in conventional vehicles to help reduce petroleum demand. The 3.4 billion gallons of ethanol blended into gasoline in 2004 amounted to about 2% by volume of all gasoline sold in the United States. Greater quantities of ethanol are expected to be used as motor-fuel in US in the future, in part due to two federal policies: an excise tax exemption of $0.51 per gallon of ethanol used as motor fuel, and a new requirement for at least 7.5 billion gallons of renewable fuel to be used in gasoline by 2012 (included in the recently passed US Energy Policy Act).

Virtually, all domestically produced ethanol currently comes from corn. However, corn and other starches and sugars are only a small fraction of bio-mass that can be used to make ethanol. A recent DOE/USDA study suggested that, with aggressive technology-developments, bio-fuels could supply some 60 billion gallons per year – 30% of current U.S. gasoline consumption in an environmentally responsible manner without affecting future food production. To achieve greater use of "homegrown" renewable-fuels, use of advanced technologies that will allow competitively priced ethanol to be made from cellulosic-biomass, such as agricultural and forestry residues, materials in municipal solid waste, trees, and grasses are being considered. Advanced technology would be used to break those cellulosic materials down into their component sugars and then ferment them to make fuel ethanol. (The US Budget 2007, increasing its bio-mass research funding by 65%, targets to make cellulosic-ethanol cost-competitive with corn-based ethanol enabling greater use of this alternative fuel.)

(5) Hydrogen Energy

Hydrogen is a colourless, odourless gas that accounts for 75% of the universe's mass. Hydrogen is found on earth only in combination with other elements such as oxygen, carbon and nitrogen. To use hydrogen, it must be separated from these other elements. Presently, hydrogen is used primarily in ammonia manufacturing, petroleum refining and synthesis of methanol. It is also used in NASA's space programme as fuel for the space shuttles, and in fuel-cells that provide heat, electricity and drinking water for astronauts. Fuel-cells are devices that directly convert hydrogen into electricity. In the future, hydrogen could be used to fuel vehicles (such as the DaimlerChrysler **NeCar 4**) and aircraft, and to provide power for our homes and offices. Hydrogen can be made from molecules called hydrocarbons by applying heat, a process known as "reforming" hydrogen. This process makes hydrogen from natural gas. An electrical current can also be used to separate water into its components of oxygen and hydrogen in a process called electrolysis. Some algae and bacteria, using sunlight as their energy-source, give off hydrogen under certain conditions. Hydrogen as a fuel is high in energy, yet a machine that burns pure hydrogen produces almost zero pollution. NASA has used liquid-hydrogen since the 1970s to propel rockets and now the space shuttle into orbit. Hydrogen fuel cells power the shuttle's electrical systems, producing a clean by-product, pure water, which the crew drinks. We can think of a fuel-cell as a battery that is constantly replenished by adding fuel to it, it never loses its charge. A flash-video showing how a fuel-cell works is available at the Ballard-Power-Systems website (http://www.ballard.com/).

Hydrogen is a clean energy-carrier (like electricity) made from diverse domestic resources such as renewable-energy (e.g. solar, wind, geothermal), nuclear-energy, and fossil-energy (combined with carbon-capture sequestration). Hydrogen, in the long run will simultaneously reduce dependence on imported oil and emissions of greenhouse gases and criteria pollutants. Fuel-cell vehicles operating on hydrogen will be zero-emission vehicles. As transportation accounts for over two-thirds of the oil consumed daily, the current researches are focused on developing hydrogen-technology for the transportation sector. The best near-term technology solution, based on hydrogen-economy, is to reducing the oil consumption and emissions by making energy-efficient choices such as purchasing gasoline hybrid electric vehicles.

Hydrogen Fuel-Cell for Transportation – An energy-carrier of future

An energy carrier stores, moves and delivers energy in a usable form to consumers. Fuel-cells are a promising technology for use as a source of heat and electricity in buildings, and as an electrical power source for vehicles. Auto companies are working on building cars and trucks that use fuel-cells. In a fuel-cell vehicle, an electro-chemical device converts hydrogen (stored on board) and oxygen from the air into electricity, to drive an electric motor and power the vehicle. Although these applications would ideally run-off pure hydrogen, in the near future they are likely to be fuelled with natural gas, methanol or even gasoline. Reforming these fuels to create hydrogen will allow the use of much of our current energy infrastructure – gas stations, natural gas pipelines, etc. – while fuel-cells are phased in. In future, hydrogen could also join electricity as an important energy carrier. Hydrogen can store energy until it is needed and can be transported to where it is needed. Some experts think that hydrogen will form the basic energy infrastructure that will power future societies, replacing today's natural gas, oil, coal, and electricity infrastructures. Experts see a new "hydrogen-economy" to replace our current "fossil fuel-based economy".

The US 'Hydrogen-Fuel-Initiative' and related 'FreedomCAR' programme, pursued since 2003, has been striving to develop the hydrogen-technology commercially viable for making clean and cost-effective hydrogen-powered fuel-cells to power automobiles, homes, and businesses with no pollution or greenhouse gases. The US Department of Energy is also conducting research in partnership with industry to make the hybrid-electric vehicle-components more affordable as these components are expected to be needed for tomorrow's hydrogen-vehicles. Some limited but significant success in reducing the high-cost of a fuel-cell by more than half has been achieved, further research is continued to make the technology cost-competitive, to develop improved materials/methods to allow for economic and effective hydrogen-storage in vehicles and at refuelling stations and to develop technology to enable safe production and delivery of hydrogen.

The promise of hydrogen-technology is too great to ignore. According to US (Dept. of Energy) estimates if hydrogen reaches its full potential, its Hydrogen-Fuel-Initiative and FreedomCAR programme could reduce country's oil demand by over 11 million barrels per day, approximately the same amount of crude oil America imports today.

(6) Hybrid Solar-Lighting Technology

In commercial buildings, lighting (lighting accounts for more than 1/3 of the total electricity consumed for commercial purposes in the United States) consumes more electric-energy than any other use. Typically, less than 25% of that energy actually produces light; the rest generates heat, which increases the need for air-conditioning. ORNL developed a system (HSL) to reduce the energy required for lighting and the air-conditioning loads associated with it, while generating power for other uses (heating or cooling the spaces in buildings). That means, the HSL concept separates and uses different portions of sunlight for two applications — interior-lighting and distributed-power-generation. This concept takes advantage of two facts. First, the luminous-efficacy (light-output per unit of energy, expressed as lumens per watt) of the visible part of the solar-spectrum is more than double that of electric lamps.

Second, photovoltaic (solar) cells, and especially thermo-photovoltaic cells, are very efficient in converting the infrared-portion of the spectrum to electricity.

While Hybrid-Solar-Lighting (HSL) technology is still in its infancy compared to solar-photovoltaic (PV) and solar-thermal, the technology is slowly gaining recognition as a legitimate contender in the race to become a commercially viable technology. The US Oak-Ridge-National-Laboratory (ORNL) developed (2006) a multifunctional and adaptive solar energy system (HS , Hybrid Solar Lighting) that uses sunlight both directly and indirectly to more efficiently leverage the entire solar spectrum. With hybrid-cars making waves in the auto-industry, hybrid solar-lighting might be the next big splash, combining the benefits of sunlight with the consistency of traditional electric-lighting.

HSL currently transports sunlight into buildings to illuminate interior spaces. HSL technology uses rooftop, 4-ft-wide mirrored dishes that track the sun with the help of a GPS receiver. The collector (removing the infrared-light) focuses the sunlight onto 127 optical-fibers (used as flexible light-pipes), are connected to hybrid light-fixtures that have special diffusion-rods that spread out the light in all directions, that also contain electric-lamps. As the two light-sources work in tandem, control systems keep rooms at a constant lighting level by dimming the electric lights when the sunlight is bright and turning them up as clouds move in or when the sun sets. As a result, HSL is close to an order of magnitude more efficient than the most affordable solar-cells today and has many advantages over conventional day-lighting practices. One collector powers about eight hybrid light fixtures—which can illuminate about 10,000 square feet. According to ORNL, the system is estimated to save about 6,000 kilowatt-hours (kWh) per year in lighting and another 2,000 kWh in reduced cooling needs for a total savings of 8,000 kWh per year.

HSL is different from traditional solar-power, which converts sunlight into electricity. HSL does not convert sunlight to electricity but captures sunlight and channels it directly into a room, using optical-fibers. The Prototype HSL systems are made up of roof-mounted concentrators that collect and separate the visible and infrared portions of sunlight. The visible portion of the light is distributed through large-diameter optical fibers to hybrid luminaires. (Hybrid luminaires are lighting-fixtures that contain both electric-lamps and fiber-optics to distribute sunlight directly.) Unlike conventional electric-lamps, the solar-component of HSL produces little heat. The remaining "invisible" energy in the sunlight, mostly infrared-radiation, is directed to a concentrating thermo-photovoltaic (solar) cell that very efficiently converts infrared radiation into electricity. The resulting electric-power can be directed to other uses in a building. When sunlight is plentiful, the fiber-optics in the luminaires can provide all or most of the light needed in a particular area. But when there is little or no sunlight, sensor-controlled electric lamps turn on to maintain the desired illumination level.

The current R&D Solar-Technology Programme will use Hybrid System-Components (control-board, fiber-optics, etc.), Buildings-Integration, Hybrid-Solar-Lighting, Photovoltaic-Material, Photo-sensors (automatically adjusting how much electric-current is needed to keep a room uniformly bright) and an environmental-chamber with an electronic load-bank to perform cyclic voltametry on fuel-cells. During times of little or no sunlight, HSL light-fixtures use electricity to provide a constant amount of illumination. If used in a top-floor of a building, HSL can deliver 50% of collected sunlight as indoor-lighting which is far more efficient than photovoltaic-cells, which convert about 15% of sunlight into electricity and then have to change this electricity back into light. Since light-bulbs lose a lot of energy in the form of heat, the end-result is only between 2% to 8% of the sunlight being used. Besides the more direct use of sunlight, HSL light-fixtures generate less heat than conventional bulbs, which can mean less energy spent on air conditioning. HSL also provides a full spectrum of light — as compared to fluorescent bulbs that only emit at certain frequencies. Full spectrum natural-light has health benefits as well (helps set our body's internal-rhythms and check against Seasonal-Acquired-Depression).

Use of Nano-Technology with Solar-Technology

Solar-power has not taken off as a serious contributor to national energy system because of very low energy-efficiency and the cost is too high per-kwh produced though the amount of annual solar energy received by the earth is 10,000 times more than the amount of energy that all humans currently consume and 13 times more than the energy stored in all fossil-fuels currently stored in the earth. Scientists and Technologists working on this are very hopeful that in the long run solar energy will be cost-competitive to flow on the grid. The trend of development suggests it be true. Ray Kurzweil (http://www.amazon.com/) points out that the efficiency of solar-power increased from 4% in 1952 to 24% in 1992; modern multilayer- cells reaching 34%; Hybrid-Solar-Lighting (HSL) technology reaching 50%; and a recent analysis of applying nano-crystals to solar energy conversion estimated that the efficiency going above 60% is feasible. Today solar-power is estimated at $2.75/W. Once solar-power falls below $1/W it will be competitive on the grid. 'Nanosolar' (http://www.nanosolar.com/) has a design based on titanium-oxide nano-particles that, if mass-produced, is estimated to bring down the solar-power costs significantly.

(7) Compressed Air energy storage

Compressed Air Energy Storage (CAES) refers to the compression of air to be used later as energy source. It can be stored during periods of low energy demand (off-peak), for use in meeting periods of higher demand (peak-load). Off-peak (low-cost) electrical-power is used to compress air into an underground air-storage "vessel" (the Norton mine), and later the air is used to feed a gas-fired turbine generator complex to generate electricity during on-peak (high-price) times.

Compressed-air energy-storage can be done in two ways: with an electrically powered turbo-compressor or with an eolo-compressor; thereafter expansion is done with a natural gas powered 'expander' (heater) which drives a combustion turbine or air-engine (generator) to produce renewable electricity. Compressed-air can be stored in mass quantity in an underground cavern created by solution mining (salt is dissolved away) or in an abandoned mine. Compressed-air energy-storage can also be used to describe technology on a smaller scale such as exploited by air-cars or wind-farms in carbon-fiber tanks. One type of reversible air compression and expansion is described by the 'isothermal-process' where the heat of compression and expansion is removed or added to the system at the same rate as it is produced. As the 'isothermal-process' is reversible, the efficiency of compressed air storage approaches 100% where the maximum energy storable is calculable.

In the real world, gas heats when it is compressed. If this heat is lost to the surroundings, efficiency suffers. That is why commercial energy storage systems are located at natural underground caverns. Because of the large volume, energy can be stored with only a small change in pressure, hence a small heat-loss. The system can be a hybrid power-generation system, with stored compressed-air mixed with natural gas before being combusted in a conventional gas-turbine engine (for example a modified aero-engine). Two plants exist with this design at Huntorf in Germany (1978) and Mckintosh in Alabama, USA (1991) both using off-peak energy for the air compression. The Power-Output of the Mckintosh and Iowa gas/compressed air generation systems is shown at 2-300 MW. The duration of the Mckintosh plant is 24 hours, with the extended operation being achieved through the combined burning of a natural gas/compressed-air mix. Additional plants are under development in Norton, Ohio and Iowa Stored-Energy-Park (ISEP).

Use of 'Compressed-Air' for future transportation is imminent

Air has been used since the 19th century to power mine locomotives, and has been the basis of naval torpedo propulsion since 1866. Compressed air vehicles (CAVs) are vehicles that are powered by Compressed-Air-Engines and fuelled by Compressed-Air-Technology (CAT), that is, it uses 'compressed-air' as energy-storage (compressed-air is stored in a tank (likely to be made of extra-strong/light-weight carbon-fiber) under high pressure, such as 30 MPa (4500 psi or 300 bar) following ISO:11439) with or without combining with hybrid-electric-engine and regenerative braking. Instead of mixing fuel with air and burning it to drive the pistons with hot expanding gases; the *air-cars* use the expansion of compressed-air to drive pistons. 'Compressed-air' has a low energy-density. At 0.14 MJ/L, 300 litre of 'air' at 300 bar only amounts to about 12kWh (the equivalent of 1.4 litre of gasoline). While gasoline or diesel fuel-tank have the same amount of energy per-litre of fuel from the first to the last litre, compressed-air tanks rely on the pressure in the tank, which falls as 'air' is drawn off.

The first official launch (2000) of the T0P (Taxi 0 Pollution) vehicle was in Barcelona. This followed development (2003) of first prototypes of the MiniCat's and the first outlines of the MultiCat. Compressed-air is currently used in race-cars to provide the initial energy needed to start the car's main power plant, the internal combustion engine (ICE).

Compressed-air vehicles are comparable in many ways to electric-vehicles, but use compressed-air to store the energy instead of batteries. Their potential advantages over electric-vehicles include: slow cyclic-movement (10 to 60 cycles/minute); high torque for minimum volume; sequential mechanical design of the engine is simple and robust; they do not suffer from the effect of corrosion of batteries in hot, humid climates; low manufacture and maintenance costs as well as easy maintenance; compressed-air bottles can be disposed of or recycled with less pollution than batteries;

the tank may be able to be refilled more often and in less time than batteries can be recharged, re-fueling rates comparable with liquid-fuels; and the Refueling-Stations (petrol/gas/diesel) can be easily modified with low investment to support air-infrastructure. Considering many advantages, the presently known disadvantages of using 'compressed-air' (thermal effect of compression/ decompression produces excess heat when *refueling* and later cooling the engine during use; compressed-air offers no thermal-byproduct for reheating while users of 'compressed-gas-fuels', such as a propane BBQ or a LOX rocket engine, can utilize some of the heat of combustion to reheat the gas prior to its use) are likely to be handled technologically.

Tata Motors has gone for the commercial production of its least-cost 'CityCAT' in 2009 (a 'Tata-Nano' car powered by an air-engine). The compressed-air car is mentioned by 'Popular Mechanics' and 'Green News' as being the true car of tomorrow, with the same mileage and zero emissions as a fuel-cell car without the dangers currently associated with the use of 'hydrogen'. The cost of air-fueling is estimated approximately at $2.00 (1.5€) per 200 km with the tank re-filling time, using the volume-transfer-system, of 3 or 4 minutes. A full-scale launch of Tata's air-car may be followed by a growing demand for aftermarket-kits to repl..ce (in cars, buses and trucks) the Internal-Combustion-Engines (ICEs) by Compressed-Air-Engines' (CAEs) manufactured by Mitsubishi, RATP, K'Airmobiles, MDI, Quasiturbine, Tata Motors and ZAP.

(8) 'Flywheel-Energy-Storage' system

Flywheel Energy Storage (FES) works (example, NASA G2 Flywheel) by accelerating a rotor to a very high speed and maintaining the energy in the system as rotational-energy. The energy is converted back by slowing down the flywheel. Most 'FES' systems use electricity to accelerate and decelerate the flywheel, but devices that directly use mechanical energy are being developed. Advanced 'FES' systems have rotors made of high-strength carbon-composite filaments that spin at speeds from 20,000 to over 50,000 rpm in a vacuum enclosure and use magnetic-bearings. Such Flywheels can come up to speed in a matter of minutes, much quicker than some other forms of energy-storage devices.

Main Components of FES system– A typical system consists of a rotor suspended by bearings inside a vacuum-chamber to reduce friction, connected to a combination electric-motor/electric-generator. First-generation flywheel energy storage systems use a large steel flywheel rotating on mechanical bearings. Newer systems use carbon-fiber composite rotors that have a higher tensile strength than steel and are an order of magnitude lighter and magnetic-bearings (essential as in conventional mechanical-bearings, friction is directly proportional to speed resulting in high energy-loss at high speed due to friction). High cost of refrigeration led to the early dismissal of low-temperature superconductors for use in magnetic bearings. High-temperature superconductor (HTSC) bearings though economical and could extend the energy storage period economically, had problems providing the lifting forces necessary for the larger designs.

Therefore, in hybrid-bearings, permanent magnets support the load and HTSC are used to stabilize it. The reason superconductors can work well stabilizing the load is because they are good diamagnets. In hybrid-bearing systems, a conventional magnet levitates the rotor, but the high temperature superconductor keeps it stable. If the rotor tries to drift off center, a restoring force due to flux-pinning (magnetic-stiffness of the bearing) restores it. Since flux-pinning is the important factor for providing the stabilizing and lifting force, the HTSC can be made much more easily for FES than for other uses. HTSC powders can be formed into arbitrary shapes so long as flux pinning is strong.

An ongoing challenge that has to be overcome before superconductors can provide the full lifting force for a FES system, is finding a way to suppress the decrease of levitation force and the gradual fall of rotor during operation caused by the flux-creep of SC material. Parasitic-losses such as friction, hysteresis, and eddy-current loss (of both magnetic and conventional bearings) in addition to refrigerant costs have been limiting the economical energy storage period of FES system. However, further improvements in superconductors may help eliminate eddy-current losses in existing magnetic-bearing designs as well as raise overall operating temperatures. Even without such improvements, however, modern flywheels can have a zero-load rundown time measurable in years.

FES system is more economical than other systems – In spite of above limitations, FES systems, compared with other ways of storing electricity, have long lifetimes (lasting decades with little or no maintenance; full-cycle lifetimes quoted for flywheels range from in excess of 10^5, upto 10^7), high energy-densities (~ 130 W·h/kg, or ~ 500 kJ/kg), and large maximum power-outputs. The energy efficiency (*ratio of energy out per energy in*) of flywheels can be as high as 90%. Typical capacities range from 3 kWh to 133 kWh. Rapid charging of a system occurs in less than 15 minutes.

Wider applications of FES system is possible – In 1950s flywheel-powered buses were used in Switzerland. There is ongoing research to make the flywheel-systems smaller, lighter, cheaper, and with higher capacity. It is hoped that flywheel-systems can replace conventional costlier chemical-batteries for mobile-applications, such as for electric-vehicles. Proposed flywheel-systems would eliminate many of the disadvantages of existing battery power systems, such as low-capacity, long charge-times, heavy-weight, and short usable-lifetimes. In Vancouver, BC, flywheels were used in buses to retain their electric power when disconnected from overhead lines. Flywheel systems have also been used experimentally in small electric-locomotives for shunting or switching, e.g. the Sentinel-Oerlikon-Gyro-Locomotive. Larger electric locomotives, e.g. British-Rail-Class-70, have sometimes been fitted with flywheel boosters to carry them over gaps in the third-rail. Advanced flywheels, such as the

133 kWh pack of the University of Texas at Austin, can take a train from a standing start upto cruising speed. Recently, there has been a new incentive to develop 'continuously-variable-transmissions' (CVTs) for use in the new kinetic energy-recovery-systems' (KERS) proposed for Formula-One motor racing.

Flywheel power storage systems are mainly used to provide load-leveling for large battery-systems, such as an 'Uninterruptible-Power-Supply' and for maintaining power-quality in Renewable-Energy-Systems. Developers of flywheel energy storage systems include Active-Power, AFS Trinity, Beacon Power, Hitec Power Protection, Pentadyne, Piller, Powercorp and VYCON. Flywheel maintenance in general runs about one-half the cost of traditional battery UPS systems with only an annual preventive-maintenance routine and replacing the bearings every three years, which takes about four hours. Since FES can store and release energy quickly, they have found a niche providing pulsed-power. In motor-sports applications, Flywheel system is used to improve acceleration rather than reduce CO^2 emissions, although the same technology can be applied to road cars to improve fuel-efficiency. Flywheels are also advantegeous as they are not affected by temperature-variations, and by a simple measurement of the rotation speed it is possible to know the exact amount of energy stored. However, one of the primary limitations relating to flywheel-design is referred to as "flywheel-explosion". While traditional flywheel-systems require strong containment-vessels filled with red-hot sand as a safety-precaution, the modern flywheel power-storage-systems prefer to have them embedded in the ground to halt any material escaping the containment vessel.

(9) Problems of Intermittency in various power sources

Currently, 56% of India's 700 million rural residents lack adequate and reliable power-supplies. Renewable-energy and distributed-generation technologies will be critical in future, energy-mix as the renewable energy and distributed-generation (REDG) sector harnesses a wide range of resources and includes a diverse range of technologies at different stages of development. Transmission and distribution losses estimates for India are as high as 30-50% (as per Asia-Pacific-Partnership:Task-Force on REDG, 2006). Renewable energy currently accounts for 7% of China's total primary energy consumption and in India between 3–4%. As such large-scale investments are to be committed in the renewable-energy sector, the sector which has one inherent limitation (problem of 'intermittency').

Intermittent Power-Sources are sources of electric power-generation that may be variable or intermittent, primarily sources of renewable-energy such as wind and solar generated electricity. The variable nature of power-generation from intermittent sources has raised concerns about the ability of electricity-grids to absorb intermittent power and the related economic implications. However, in small amounts, integration of intermittent power-sources has little effect on grid operations. Non-renewable power-sources are also intermittent to some degree since there is no such thing as a totally reliable source of electricity.

Intermittency affects all energy sources

The intermittent energy losses from power-sources are caused by a number of events: intermittency in energy availability (primarily in renewable-energy sources); water-shortages (in conventional and nuclear); operator-error (primarily in conventional and nuclear); planned-outages; unplanned-outages (accounted for 1.6% of worldwide nuclear power plant capacity in 2006); component failures; design-flaws; grid disconnects; natural disasters and terrorism. All of these can cause an immediate loss of power production and its true intermittency, a particular type of variability that switches between full-power and no-power (however it is hard to see how this true intermittency can apply to the main contenders for mass renewable replacements of fossil-plant such as wind and solar, since the wind and sun cannot suddenly disappear simultaneously for a large numbers of necessarily small renewable-sources.) Several conventional units can fail without warning, and simultaneously if a common failure mechanism arises such as an earthquake, an airburst nuclear explosion, a grid disconnect, or a common design flaw manifests or is discovered, or a transmission-line breaks down unexpectedly as a result of over-loading, or a tree falling, or bushfires, lightning strike, icing, high-winds, providing a source of intermittency in existing grids by the disconnection of major power stations, or wind-blown debris causing widespread black-outs.

Intermittency inherently affects all Solar-energy generation

Intermittency inherently affects Solar-energy, as the production of electricity from solar sources depends on the amount of light-energy in a given location. The extent to which the intermittency of solar-generated electricity is an issue will depend to some extent on the degree to which the generation profile of solar corresponds to demand cycles. In areas with high solar production possibilities, and where air conditioning is a driver of demand and corresponds to periods of high sunlight, variability may actually be beneficial. For example, solar thermal-power plants designed for solar-only generation (such as Nevada Solar-Plant) are ideally matched to summer noon-peak-loads in prosperous areas with significant cooling demands, such as in south-western United States. Using thermal-energy storage systems, solar thermal operating periods can even be extended to meet base-load needs. Using a variety of energy sources in combination can help to overcome intermittency. For example, stormy weather, bad for direct solar collection, is generally good for wind power.

Intermittency inherently affects all Wind Energy generation

Intermittency also affects wind-generated power which is an inherently variable-resource, and the amount of wind-generated electricity produced at any given point-in-time by a Plant will depend on wind speeds and turbine-characteristics (among other factors). While the output from a single turbine can vary greatly and rapidly, as more turbines are connected over larger and larger areas, the slower and less variable the aggregate rate of change becomes, and as the number of units need to replace a single large conventional unit is very high, these cannot all fail simultaneously. As compared to many other types of electricity generation, wind is not normally *dispatchable* - it cannot be turned on at will by human or automatic dispatch to meet increased demand. Intermittency caused by the variability in wind-flow will imply an alternating presence or absence, i.e., generation that is either on or off. A study during the 2006 California heat storm revealed that output from wind power in California significantly decreased to less than 5% during peak-demand. A similar result was seen during the 2003 European heat wave, when the output of wind power in Germany fell to 10% during peak demand times, resulting in importing a peak of around 2,000 MW of electricity.

Intermittency affects Nuclear Power Plants

Nuclear power is considered a Base-Load power-source, in that its output is nearly constant and other types of plants are adjusted with changes in demand. This is done because output changes can only be made in small increments, and because of small fuel costs — there is little marginal cost between running at a low power and a high power, therefore it is cheapest for the system to run the nuclear plants at high power. Every year or two (depending on the plant), the plant must be shut down for *planned-outages* for about a month. This is typically done in the spring or fall when electricity demand is lower, as such, on a national scale power output from nuclear increases corresponding with demand during the peak summer and winter months. This change in output commonly occurs on a yearly scale, it is rare that nuclear power plants adjust their power-output to correspond with demand on a daily basis, which would be much more likely to happen in countries where over 50% of their power comes from nuclear plants (such as France). Nuclear power plants are also subject to *unplanned-outages* as noted above. For instance, unplanned outages in the United States caused a total capacity loss of 1.7% in 2000, which was drastically improved from 11.6% in 1980.

In the UK, the largest nuclear plant, Sizewell B, of total output 1.32GW regularly suffers 'unplanned-outages' which sets the required spinning reserve margin on the total UK generating system due to its being the largest single intermittent source. The plant typically has a load factor of 80 to 85%. In UK, the spring of 2006 and the fall of 2007 saw times when half the nuclear capacity in the country was offline due to a combination of 'planned' and 'unplanned-outages'. The relevance of this is that every grid-system has to allow sufficient reserves for sudden loss of large numbers of conventional plant and this reserve can equally well be made available to variable and intermittent renewable sources, at no extra cost, since it is already existing.

Large-scale Diesel Engine Generation to check Intermittency

It is not commonly appreciated even amongst industry experts that small high speed diesels of automotive or rail traction sizes (200kW-1.2 MW) as opposed to large slow speed marine diesels that are very commonly used within large power-grids throughout North America and Europe. France uses about 5GW of such diesels to cover intermittency on nuclear-stations.

In USA and UK these are largely diesels that they have usually been purchased for other reasons i.e., emergency standby, in water works, hotels, hospitals, etc. and in some cases electricity substations - e.g. Cuyahoga Falls, USA (10 x 1.6 MW Caterpillar) and Tregarron Mid Wales UK, 3 x 1.6 MW Caterpillar) but can be readily used to automatically synchronize and feed into the grid. Typically in the UK for example 500 MW of such plant is routinely started in a few minutes and this is perfectly acceptable to the engines life times in a scheme operated by National Grid called Reserve

Service. It is established that there are 20 GW of such diesel plants in the UK and it has been pointed out that there is no technical reason why this quantity could not be brought in to the Reserve Service scheme to assist handling very rapid changes in renewable output, whilst conventional plant is started or indeed stopped.

Economic impacts of Intermittency/Variability

All electricity generating plants (wind, solar, fossil-fuel) have costs ("external" or "hidden") that are separate from the standard/regular cost-of-production, including, for example, the cost of any necessary transmission-capacity or reserve-capacity in case of loss of generating-capacity. The cost estimates of wind energy may not include estimates of certain "external" costs due to wind-variability. Many types of generation, particularly fossil-fuel derived, will also have cost-externalities such as pollution, greenhouse gas emission, and habitat destruction which are generally not directly accounted for. The magnitude of the economic-impacts varies by location, but is expected to rise with higher penetration-levels. At low penetration-levels, costs such as operating-reserve and balancing-costs are believed to be insignificant. Intermittency may introduce additional costs that are distinct from or of a different magnitude than for traditional generation types. These may include:

- Transmission capacity: transmission capacity may be more expensive than for nuclear and coal generating capacity due to lower load-factors. Transmission capacity will generally be sized to projected peak-output, but average capacity for wind will be significantly lower, raising cost per unit of energy actually transmitted.

- Additional operating reserve: if additional wind does not correspond to demand-patterns, additional operating reserve may be required compared to other generating types, resulting in higher capital costs for additional plants. Contrary to statements that all wind must be backed by an equal amount of "back-up capacity", intermittent-generators contribute to base-capacity "as long as there is some probability of output during peak-periods." Back-up capacity is not attributed to individual generators, as back-up or operating reserve "only have meaning at the system level."

- Balancing costs: to maintain grid-stability, some additional costs may be incurred for balancing of load with demand. The ability of the grid to balance supply with demand will depend on the rate of change of the amount of energy produced (by wind, for example) and the ability of other sources to ramp production up or scale production down. Balancing costs have generally been found to be low.

- Storage, export and load management: at high-penetrations (more than 30%) for dealing with high-output of wind during periods of low demand may be required. These may require additional capital expenditures, or result in lower marginal income for wind producers.

- A detailed study for the UK National Grid estimated that for the case with 8000MW of wind needed to meet the 10% renewables target for 2010, the balancing-costs was expected to increase by around £2 per MWh of wind production, representing an additional £40 million per annum.

In view of above continuing problems, it will be necessary that a Task-Force at national level conducts a cross-sectoral study and recommend relief or subsidy against the technical and financial implications of perennial nature of losses due to 'intermittency' in energy sources to attract more private sector participation in this field, particularly in the renewable energy sector.

Section – II

The Economy-dance Between
The 'Dragon' And The 'Elephant'
— Some Lessons To Be Learnt

CHAPTER 4

A Quick View on the Industrial-Economic Development of China

Growth of China's Industrial Sector

In earlier decades of 20th century China's economic reform had more value-addition in the agricultural sector. In the later decades the emphasis shifted progressively to the industrial sector. The service sector which includes financial markets did not appear to have expanded to match the demand of the immensely growing industrial sector.

China's industrialization over the past 30 years has been epochal. Its industrial revolution has been marveled by the rest of the world. The share of GDP (Industry, value-added, as % of total GDP) contributed by the Industrial Sector of China was throughout higher than her other sectors (agriculture and services) between 1960 and 2002, was recorded at 44.89% (1960), 35.09% (1965), 40.49% (1970), 45.72% (1975), 48.52% (1980), 43.13% (1985), 41.61% (1990), 48.80% (1995), 50.22% (2000), and 51.09% (2002).

China's GDP has grown at an average rate of about 10%. China has earned her place as the leading newly industrialized economy of the world. Her average Annual Rate of Growth of Output was 10.3% (1980-1990) and 9.7% (1990-2002).

As of 2000, the industrial sector's share of GDP has grown to 64% of the total from 44.6% (1970) as shown below. China has emerged as a leading industrial economy. The share of the agricultural sector of GDP has expectedly declined from 42.2% in 1970 to 11.9% in 2000. China's economic development profile has been mainly industrial and its total GDP is due to the expansion of its industrial sector which has immensely increased.

Sectoral Shares (in %age) of GDP in China
(1970 to 2005)

Sector/Year	1970	1980	1990	2000	2002	2005
Agriculture	42.2	25.6	11.8	11.9	15.38	11.7
Industry	44.6	51.7	75.9	64.0	51.09	48.0
Service	13.2	22.7	12.3	24.1	33.53	40.3
Total	100.0	100.0	100.0	100.0	100.0	100.0

As China cannot sustain a growth-rate of her GDP at an annual rate of 10% for an indefinite period which resulted in overheating of its economy and rising inflation, taking lessons from the Asian financial crisis of 1997-98, a process of softening is found to be in effect through administrative-measures and tightened monetary policy as a macro-economic control tool. By 2002 the industrial sector's share of GDP is appearing to be shifting more to service sector followed by the agriculture sector. Issue of softening is in recognition by the economists.

Progressive augmentation of high-tech oriented productivity of the Chinese manpower to minimize cyclical-fluctuations in the process of progression of China's fabulous industrial revolution merits serious attention. As other competing economies of other developing countries, particularly in non-OECD Asia and in this context India, will successfully make high-tech productivity gains, the Chinese economy will continue to strive to remain still more competitive in the global-market in future.

The issues discussed are inter-related and are expected to be managed by an appropriately designed, well-specified macro-economic agenda of China. China's Monetary and Fiscal policies are likely to become more dynamic, as such, will be the core-agenda of its economy's and macro-economic policy in future, be it a capitalist-market-economy or a socialist-market-economy. In China's socialist-market-economy, its monetary and fiscal policies are expected to be more premeditatedly strategic and competitive, well defined and operationally more transparent in future to sustain the present growth rate of industrialization.

Highlights of the overall Economic Development of China

The World Bank's major Development-Parameters (Appendix-F) showing the economic-overview of China for the past six years (2001 to 2006) is given below –

Parameters/Year	2001	2002	2003	2004	2005	2006
Agricultural land (% of land area)	59.52515	59.43916	59.49245	..	..	..
CO_2 emissions (metric tons per capita)	2.363746	2.720112	3.216	..	..	..
Electric power consumption (kWh per capita)	1069.308	1184.223	1378.527	1585.122	..	..
Energy imports, net (% of energy use)	-0.12576	0.867065	2.071314	4.509031	-	-
Energy-Use (kg of oil equivalent per capita)	880.9372	947.2251	1072.103	1241.63	..	-
Exports of goods and services (% of GDP)	22.60025	25.13327	29.55604	33.95057	37.29692	36.77002
Fixed line and mobile phone subscribers (per 1,000 people)	255.6811	328.1998	413.4586	498.8437	570.2269	..
Foreign direct investment, net inflows (BoP, current US$)	4.42E+10	4.93E+10	4.71E+10	5.49E+10	7.91E+10	..
GDP growth (annual%)	8.3	9.1	10	10.1	10.2	10.7
GNI per capita, Atlas method (current US$)	1000	1100	1270	1500	1740	2010

Gross capital formation (% of GDP)	36.26775	37.86576	41.20289	43.26324	43.27007	40.69522
High-technology exports (% of manufactured exports)	20.56835	23.30854	27.09555	29.80557	30.60326	..
Imports of goods and services (% of GDP)	20.48037	22.56195	27.35739	31.39927	31.73516	**32.90485**
Industry, value added (% of GDP)	45.15252	44.78988	45.96865	46.22525	47.34212	**47.00047**
Inflation, GDP deflator (annual%)	2.052264	0.584614	2.611465	6.912397	4.360426	2.881533
Long-term debt (DOD, current US$)	1.29E+11	1.2E+11	1.2E+11	1.32E+11	1.33E+11	..
Market capitalization of listed companies (% of GDP)	39.54933	31.85239	41.51247	33.11907	34.79563	90.93932
Merchandise trade (% of GDP)	38.46989	42.69863	51.8591	59.76854	63.36896	**65.991**
Military expenditure (% of GDP)	1.969814	2.102499	2.083594	2.026545	1.974242	..
Net barter terms of trade (2000 = 100)	102.5022	102.7052	98.6925	93.10394	86.82748	..
Official development assistance and official aid (current US$)	1.47E+09	1.47E+09	1.33E+09	1.69E+09	1.76E+09	..
Population growth (annual%)	0.726381	0.67	0.622861	0.600296	0.641573	0.557865
Population, total	1.27E+09	1.28E+09	1.29E+09	1.3E+09	1.3E+09	1.31E+09
Revenue, excluding grants (% of GDP)	7.86193	8.671139	8.759562	9.468469	..	..
Services, etc., value added (% of GDP)	40.69764	**41.71507**	**41.465**	40.66726	40.11084	**41.09037**
Time required to start a business (days)	..	..	48	48	48	35
Total debt service (% of exports of goods, services and income)	7.922806	8.280203	7.332966	3.415015	3.104496	..
Workers' remittances and compensation of employees, received (US$)	8.39E+09	1.3E+10	1.78E+10	1.9E+10	2.25E+10	2.25E+10

China has a rapidly growing mixed-economy. Economic development has proceeded unevenly, with urban coastal areas, particularly in the south-east, experiencing more rapid economic development than in other areas of the country.

It has a combination of state-owned and private firms. A number of state-owned firms have undergone partial or full privatization in recent years. The Chinese government has encouraged mass-scale foreign investment in some sectors of the economy and subject to constraints, since the 1980s, offering several "special economic zones" in which foreign investors receive tax relief, tariff, and preferable investment treatment. Breaking with previous policy, China in July, 2005 delinked its currency from the U.S. dollar, resulting in a devaluation of 2.1%. The Chinese 'Yuan' now will float within a very narrow-band against a basket of currencies from the country's major trading partners.

In March, 2003, a long-expected transition in China's political leadership took place. Hu Jintao assumed the country's presidency, as well as chairmanship of the ruling Communist Party. Wen Jiabao became the new premier. In March, 2005, Hu Jintao replaced former president Jiang Zemin as chairman of the Central Military Commission, completing the leadership transition.

With China's entry into the World Trade Organization (WTO) in Nov. 2001, the Chinese government made a number of specific commitments to trade and investment liberalization which, if fully implemented, will substantially open the Chinese economy to foreign firms. In the energy sector, this will mean the lifting or sharp reduction of tariffs associated with imports of some classes of capital-goods, more imports of clean and efficient energy and the eventual opening to foreign competition of some areas such as retail sales of petroleum products.

Despite moves toward privatization, much of China's economy remains controlled by the large State-Owned-Enterprises (SOEs), many of which are inefficient and unprofitable. Restructuring of the SOE sector, including the privatization of some enterprises, is a major priority of the government, as is the restructuring of its banking sector. Many Chinese banks have had to write-off large amounts of delinquent debts from state-owned enterprises. Layoffs have been part of the restructuring of the SOEs, as many were severely overstaffed. This has created unemployment, and also has been a burden on the government budget, as the government begins to provide social-benefits which were previously the responsibility of the SOEs. The geographic concentration of privately-owned industry in the urban centers along the coast has also created social strains.

China's real Gross-Domestic-Product (GDP) grew at a rate of 9.5% in 2004, held steady from 2003's growth rate. Real GDP for the first quarter of 2005 was up 9.5% year-on-year, a pace most observed expecting to slow down in coming years. Real GDP growth is forecast to drop to 9.0% for 2005 as a whole, and 7.8% in 2006. Much of the increase in the GDP growth rate has come from excessive spending on capital goods and construction, particularly in the state sector.

In an effort to cool its economy seen as overheating, the Chinese government took a number of steps in 2004 designed to counter this trend, including tightening bank lending policies. China's banking sector remains a key concern for the country's economic stability, as the ratio of problem-loans has been rising.

Inflows of Foreign Direct Investment (FDI) into China in 2004 totalled $57.0 billion, a high record and modestly up from the 2003 figure of $53.5 billion increasing to $86.1 billion in 2005, a new record and roughly double the level of 2001. Japan, South Korea, Taiwan, and the United States are China's most important sources of FDI.

China's major Trading-Partners were Japan, United States, European Union, South Korea, and Taiwan. Its major Export-Products included: Light industrial and textile products, mineral fuels, heavy manufactures, and agricultural goods. Its major Import-Products included : oil, machinery, steel, chemicals, miscellaneous manufactures, industrial materials, and grain.

China's imports increased by 35.8% in 2004, largely capital goods being acquired to refurbish outdated industrial facilities. Exports increased by 35.4% in 2004. China's merchandise trade-surplus rose in 2004 to $32.6 billion, from $25.3 billion in 2003; forecasted to rise to $83.0 billion in 2005 which actually soared to $102 billion.

In the late 1970s the fact became pronounced that China's communist economy failed to deliver what it promised to China's over one billion–plus population. An agenda for economic reform was formulated. The new Communist Party leadership took full responsibility for the committed implementation of China's economic reform agenda. The immediate priorities were agricultural reform and food-supply for a billion-plus people. The commune-system of the earlier regime was replaced by the Family-Responsibility-System where land now bélonged to the family of a farmer, not to the Commune, as was the case in earlier communist regime. This brought Green Revolution to China.

No sovereign state's economy can maximize its economic-gain in splendid isolation. China has a leadership position in the United Nations Organization with a permanent member-status in the Security Council, a membership in International Monetary Fund and World Bank, a recent member of World Trade Organization, a 147 member-nation group with an agenda of global-free-trade, and also a member of World Economic Community. The European Union paradigm based on the emerging concept of continental-economic-regionalization will be a learning model for China and her fellow Asian economies.

As China's pre-industrial economy was agriculture-dominant, 68.7% (1980) of employment was in its agricultural sector, declined to 53.5% (1990) and to 46.9% in 2000. Employment in the industrial sector over the same time period has been around a fifth of the total employment; 18.2%, 19.0% and 17.5% in 1980, 1990, and 2000, respectively. Employment percentage in the service sector has been 11.7% in 1980, 9.5% in 1990 and 12.3% in 2000. Compared with the employment profile of the mature industrialized economies of the world, China continues to be too much dependent on its agricultural sector. China's industrial progress has yet to cover her one billion-plus people across the vast territory.

Successful reforms in the agricultural sector made substantive contributions to the reform in the industrial sector by way of higher value-addition in the agricultural sector due to increased labour-productivity; surplus farmers able to migrate to the manufacturing sector and easing the labour-cost and demand; and augmented farmers' incomes/ purchasing capacity to spend more money on consumption of goods and services produced by the manufacturing-sector. Thus the new supply and demand levers became features of China's emerging socialist market economy.

China finding her reform in the industrial sector not profitable through Contractual-Joint-Ventures (CJV), with Equity-Joint-Ventures (EJV) between China's State-Owned-Enterprises (SOE) and the Foreign Investors and also not being able to direct the reform with her domestic savings, shifted to Foreign Direct Investment (FDI), units fully owned/ managed by Foreign Investors. This resolved the situation as the Foreign Investors were attracted, as detailed below, by relatively abundant low-cost labour-supply and natural-resources waiting to be exploited and the potential market of one billion-plus consumers in China.

China's GDP and Foreign Direct Investment Inflows

Year	GDP (constant 1995 US$, in billions)	Foreign Direct Investment, net (BOP, constant 1995 US $, in millions)	Foreign Direct Investment, net inflows (% of GDP)
1980	172	236	0.14
1985	272	1,482	0.54
1990	398	3,910	0.98
1995	700	35,849	5.12
2000	1,041	36,995	3.55
2002	1,209	47,080	3.89

Thus, China needed and successfully managed a massive inflow of FDI, thereby increased employment and income to broaden her economy which could not have been done without substantive reform of her industrial sector and FDI. Inflow of FDI into China over the past 23 years (1980-2002) stood at US$ 434 billion. Thus, a marriage between China's socialist market economy and the savings-rich, high-income capitalist market economies of the world happily worked out her industrial reform. Now China is perceived to be one of the most FDI-friendly economies of the world. Foreign investors were able to repatriate profit from their investments in China by way of exporting a part of their Chinese products to the world market and earning export revenues in convertible currencies. Repatriation of profit encouraged further investments into China by the FDIs, a win-win game plan.

As China's exports grew, her foreign exchange reserve also grew and contributed to her international credit-rating. China's ability to offer Credit-instruments in the international market warrants recognition. By 2003, China's foreign exchange reserves reached US$ 434 billion. The net result is China's emergence as an empowered member of the world economy. With its huge foreign-exchange-reserve China made investments abroad by buying US bonds. This matches the fact that much of China's foreign exchange-reserve is earned on exports of manufactured products of China, much attributable to FDI in China.

China's successfully inviting large scale FDIs, imported-technology and know-how, specialized-equipments and capital goods from a number of mature industrialized economies and their adaptation to the indigenous resources, low cost domestic labour, required exploitation of natural resources, became the key to China's industrial success.

China also focused on innovation/R&D so that adaptation of imported-technology could profitably contribute to her faster industrial progress, enabling the pre-industrial, agriculture-dominant economies of Asia to manufacture cost and quality competitive products, planned with a large-scale exports to the world market, earning export revenues in convertible currencies, creating a resource pool to enable repatriation of profits by the FDIs and to encourage FDI continuation in China. This way, China adopted a growth model which was truly an "import-export led" rather than only an "export-led" growth model.

China's economic development proceeded unevenly with urban-coastal areas experiencing more rapid growth than in other areas of the country. As strong growth continues unabated, the Chinese government took measures to cool the economy by raising the reserve requirement for commercial banks by 0.5% (June 2006) to 8.5% required and raising the interest rates by 0.27% (August 2006) to bring lending rates to 6.12%, the second rate increase in 2006. These moves served to take money out of the money supply to help ward-off possible economic-overheating. Breaking with previous policy, China also delinked its currency, the renminbi, from the U.S. dollar in July 2005, resulting in an initial devaluation of 2.1%. Since the devaluation, the renminbi appreciated about 1.4% against the U.S. dollar in July 2006.

With China's entry (2001) into World Trade Organization (WTO), it made a number of specific commitments to trade and investment liberalization which, if fully implemented, will substantially open the Chinese economy to foreign firms. In the energy sector, this will mean the lifting or sharp tariff-reduction associated with imports of some classes of capital goods, and the eventual opening to foreign competition of some areas such as retail sales of petroleum products and possibly many more other products.

The World-Development-Indicators (2001) reported that nearly 17% of people in China were living on less than $1 a day and nearly 47% of the population was living on less than $2 a day. Reportedly at the opposite-end, 10% of the people in China have become progressively high income-groups. The %age of high income group must have gone high by 2005 which also shows augmentation of human-capital with more competitive ability and skill, higher living standards and resultant increasing energy consumption. As at a given time there is a limited supply of highly skilled human-capital in the global market, now China must be planning on augmentation of the supply of its more skilled human-capital into the economy to accept the global challenge triumphantly.

It may be observed from above that China's economic accomplishment is an eloquent testimony to the fact that the socialist market-economy anchored itself into the core-principle of market-economy by way of offering incentives to production agents in all the sectors of the economy for maximization of economic gains. China's economic reform agenda adopted the open-economic policy, because without internationalization, China's industrialization would not have been operationally successful. China seems to be in the process of progressively completing the marketization of her state-owned as well as managed-enterprises in order to become a member of the world economic community, to share some of the global responsibility and prove her leadership in the world economy.

In can be concluded that China must be preparing for her second phase of industrial revolution by controlling the recent-past industrial growth rate; by improvised policy and plans to resolve income-distribution problem both at inter-regional and intra-regional levels; by progressive augmentation of her human capital and productivity; by proper and improvised restructuring of the macro-economic framework of China's socialist market economy; by further reform of her monetary and fiscal policies in order that China can sustain her ability to compete in the world market and successfully establish a continental economic regionalization of Asia to play a leadership role therein.

China's economy during the last quarter century has changed from a centrally planned system that was largely closed to international trade to a more market-oriented economy that has a rapidly growing private sector and is a major player in the global economy. Reforms started in the late 1970s with the phasing out of collectivized agriculture, and expanded to include the gradual liberalization of prices, fiscal decentralization, increased autonomy for state enterprises, the foundation of a diversified banking system, the development of stock markets, the rapid growth of the non-state sector, and the opening to foreign trade and investment.

China has generally implemented reforms in a gradualist or piecemeal fashion. The process continues with key moves in 2005 including the sale of equity in China's largest state banks to foreign investors and refinements in foreign exchange and bond markets. The restructuring of the economy and resulting efficiency gains have contributed to a more than tenfold increase in GDP since 1978. Measured on a purchasing power parity (PPP) basis, China in 2005 stood as the second largest economy in the world after the US, although in per capita terms the country is still lower middle-income and 150 million Chinese fall below international poverty lines.

China's **11th Five-Year Plan** (2006-2010) calls for a 20% reduction in energy-consumption per unit of GDP by 2010 and an estimated 45% increase in GDP by 2010. The plan states that conserving resources and protecting the environment are basic goals, but it lacks details on the policies/reforms necessary to achieve these goals. For China, the goal of sustainable-development is already under emphasis as reflected in its White-Paper on Agenda-21 which states, 'Because China is a developing country, the goals of increasing social productivity, enhancing overall national strength and improving people's quality of life cannot be realized without giving primacy to the development of the national economy and having all work focused on building the economy.' (http://www.acca21.edu.cn/chnwp2.html).

Further, China's 11th Five-Year Plan stresses on scientific-concept of development, the goal of building a harmonious society, on attaining a GDP of US$4 trillion-yuan, a per-capita GDP share of 2,400 US$ in 2010 and 3,000 US$ by 2020. It includes ambitious objectives such as environmental protection; curtailing pollution/energy-waste, propagating more energy-saving, higher value-added industries as well as expansion of the services sector, in particular, ensuring that GDP growth to go hand-in-hand with marked improvement in education, employment, social-security and poverty-reduction. The World Bank pointed out that 150 million Chinese, mostly farmers in the western-provinces, still live in acute poverty. The 11th Plan estimates that China's average urban per capita disposable income in 2010 would increase from the existing 10,493 yuan to 13,390 yuan, while rural per capita net income will rise from 3,255 yuan to 4,110 yuan.

The 11th FYP stipulated that the industrial sector must cut energy use by 20%. The emission-levels of major pollutants will be cut by 10% and the forest coverage rate will be increased to 20%. On the 11th FYP, the official New China News Agencies (NCNA) deplored the fact that institutional and systematic problems hindering the healthy development of the economy and society are still very outstanding and one of the reasons behind the fuel-wastage is that the prices of oil, gas, and other types of energy have been kept artificially low by the government. China's 11th FYP has drawn strategic lines, on the industrial sector, stressing not on expansion in scale, but structural upgrading to turn China's big industry into a powerhouse, mainly stressing on saving resources and on building an innovation-oriented country and implementing the strategy of developing the country with talents.

Morgan-Stanley-Asia (economist-institution), noticing the main slogan of 11th Plan as China's shifting from its economic dependence on exports and foreign direct investments to more of domestic-demand and consumption through boosting of internal market due to growing protectionist threats from US and Europe against its fast increasing exports, pointed to the dangers: rising internal tension over inequality and external friction over China's noticeable trade success suggests that China's government-led and export/investment-driven development model may be reaching its limits. As Chinese bureaucracy has little control over the market forces it has unleashed, it is in China's interests to change its economic model before the tension reaches the point of triggering an economic crisis.

However, though most of the economic targets were advisory and difficult, if not completely speculative, yet China's 11th Plan shows the Chinese leadership's ambitious blueprint for socio-economic take-off and more concerns for energy and environment.

CHAPTER 5

A Quick View on the Industrial-Economic Development of India

Growth of India's Industrial Sector

Since independence, India has achieved a good measure of self-sufficiency in the manufacture of a variety of basic and capital goods. The output of the major industries includes aircraft, ships, cars, locomotives, heavy electrical machinery, construction equipment, power generation and transmission equipment, chemicals, precision instruments, communication equipment and computers. The economic reform process set in motion since mid-1991 has further put the Indian economy on a fast-track. India has achieved spectacular developments through its key industries which includes: iron and steel industry; engineering and machine-tools industry; telecommunication, aviation, broadcasting and strategic electronics industry; chemicals, computer-software; nuclear, textiles; transportation; service; and cottage industries.

Highlights of the overall Economic Development of India

The World Bank's major Development-Parameters (Appendix-G) showing the economic overview of India for the past six years (2001 to 2006) is given below –

INDIA: Parameters/Year	2001	2002	2003	2004	2005	2006
Agricultural land (% of land area)	60.65539	60.64866	60.54104	60.61503	60.60158	..
CO2 emissions (metric tons per capita)	1.128304	1.172499	1.196145	..	..	..
Electric power consumption (kWh per capita)	403.0312	416.5955	434.8098	457.3245	-	-
Energy imports, net (% of energy use)	17.9901	18.22428	17.87898	18.5001	-	-
Energy-Use (kg of oil equivalent per capita)	503.4377	508.9551	515.4657	530.5546	-	-
Exports of goods and services (% of GDP)	12.74658	14.46476	14.74613	18.20034	20.32767	..
Fixed line and mobile phone subscribers (per 1,000 people)	43.55338	51.59788	64.0309	84.52182	127.6742	..
Foreign direct investment, net inflows (BoP, current US$)	5.47E+09	5.63E+09	4.58E+09	5.47E+09	6.6E+09	..
GDP (current US$)	4.78E+11	5.08E+11	6.02E+11	6.96E+11	8.06E+11	9.06E+11
GDP growth (annual %)	5.208022	3.726654	8.391931	8.325039	9.23218	9.19511
GNI per capita, Atlas method (current US$)	460	470	530	630	730	820
Gross capital formation (% of GDP)	24.45137	25.57427	27.45111	30.98203	33.35161	..
High-technology exports (% of manufactured exports)	5.393494	4.759841	4.753784	4.884294	..	..
Import of goods and services (% of GDP)	13.63622	15.45842	16.03325	20.02002	23.28671	-
Industry, value added (% of GDP)	25.30879	26.41915	26.19551	27.46584	27.32813	27.71214
Inflation, GDP deflator (annual %)	3.128165	3.889109	3.795513	4.368794	4.448521	5.274544
Long-term debt (DOD, current US$)	9.57E+10	1.01E+11	1.08E+11	1.17E+11	1.14E+11	..
Market capitalization of listed companies (% of GDP)	23.08131	25.79372	46.37427	55.73708	68.64243	90.35723
Merchandise trade (% of GDP)	19.60169	20.82364	21.85356	25.22406	29.64273	32.50078

Military expenditure (% of GDP)	3.020318	2.916849	2.751378	2.935603	2.872983	..
Population growth (annual %)	**1.615975**	**1.553746**	**1.491518**	**1.42929**	**1.367061**	**1.381639**
Population, total	1.03E+09	1.05E+09	1.06E+09	1.08E+09	1.09E+09	1.11E+09
Revenue, excluding grants (% of GDP)	11.2055	11.757	11.91474	12.49106	..	..
Services, etc., value added (% of GDP)	**51.49979**	**52.71478**	**52.87258**	**53.74419**	**54.36764**	**54.73819**
Surface area (sq. km)	3287260	3287260	3287260	3287260	3287260	3287260
Time required to start a business (days)	..	..	89	89	71	35
Total debt service (% of exports of goods, services and income)	14.68581	17.32037	19.10136	..	..	..
Workers' remittances and compensation of employees, received (US$)	1.43E+10	1.57E+10	2.1E+10	1.88E+10	2.13E+10	2.57E+10

India's real GDP, over the past 24 years, grew at an average pace of 5.9% a year. Never in human history has a democracy containing more than 1020 million people achieved such growth rates over a two-decade period which was no less than an "economic miracle". India's huge and growing population is the fundamental social, economic, and environmental problem yet India's economic growth was faster than all the Asian economies except China since 1992. In fact, India's growth-rate has been slightly above the average growth-rates of all the eight Asian countries since 1980 during that decade. Though India's GDP growth-rate has been impressive, the HDI rank has deteriorated between 1990 and 2003 despite scoring a better HDI value. The Human-Development-Index/World-Rank were 0.297 (121) in 1990, 0.595 (127) in 2002, and 0.602 (127) in 2003.

However, after economic reform in early 1990s, the economy has grown at faster rate of approximately 6%. Currently the growth rate stands at just over 7%. Increased economic performance has reduced the incidence of poverty by raising over 10% of the population above the poverty line. (The %age of population below poverty line declined from 44.48% in 1983 to 35.97% in 1993-94 and to 26.10% in 1999-2000.)

However, nearly 25% of the population, which in absolute terms exceeds 250 million people, are still below the poverty-line. The public distribution system, which is now managed through the open-market-mechanism, awaits optimisation in the distribution of foodgrains. Though food has increased substantially over the last four decades, starvation, in tribal areas, is still reported. Inequality in India exists in many forms, mainly the economic and the rural-urban divide. For example, in 1999 the share of income enjoyed by 20% of the poorest and the 20% of the richest Indians were 8.9% and 43.3% respectively. India's GDP in 2002 was: Agriculture (23.6%), Industry (28.4%), Services (48%). India's per capita GDP were Rs. 8258.29 (1990-91) and Rs. 12,496.32 (2002-03).

India's share (2005) in the global trade was less than 1% (0.8%). Though India now enjoys a positive balance-of-payments, its trade-balance is still negative. Among the principal imports, petroleum-crude accounts for the largest share. With regards to exports, manufactured goods enjoy the maximum share. In a global production system dominated by transnational corporations, much of these manufactured exports are intra-subsidiary transfers. However, software-exports showed remarkable growth; between 1993-04 and 2003-04, the average growth rate of software export was 40%. The exchange rate over the past few years was by and large stable. The average exchange rates of Indian rupees per US dollar in 2000 were Rs. 44.942 and had an average rate of Rs 45.317 in 2004.

Comparison between Chinese and Indian Economy seems inappropriate on several counts

Comparison between **China** and **India** seems inappropriate on several counts, apart from the fact that India is a multi-polar democracy with all the attendant strengths and weaknesses of democracies while China inheriting many opportunities has a unipolar dictatorship:

(a) In 1984 China inherited Hong Kong, a world-class financial centre that China had done nothing to create.

Although Hong Kong was formally handed over to China in 1997, the 1984 Sino-British agreement obliged Hong Kong's businessmen to orient themselves toward China, which they vigorously did. China's growth/performance cannot properly be compared with other economies that has not similarly inherited a world-class financial centre.

(b) Today's dynamic, coastal parts of China's economy were all part of Japan's pre-1945 empire, for example, Manchuria. The legacy of Japanese rule was superior than the physical infrastructure and the rudiments of industrial revolution.

(c) Taiwan, one of the world's main high-technology-industry centres, made mainland China the primary focus of its investments with high-tech machinery and technology, which are the key-driver of China's on-going industrial revolution. Today, Taiwan accounts for more than half of all Foreign Direct Investment (FDI) into China, and runs a bilateral-trade-surplus of about US\$ 55 billion annually with mainland China.

(d) China inherited many ports with associated infrastructure from the period of "unequal treaties". China, not colonized by a single-power, had only "leased" its ports to different powers who competed to build the best possible urban infrastructure in the port that they controlled.

(e) Japan's post-WW-II industrial revolution, preceded by the build-up of its human-capital, achieved both universal-literacy and a broad-based/developed vocational-educational-system. Taiwan and Korea similarly built significantly on the legacy of human-capital inherited from Japanese rule. While Japan, Korea and Taiwan had painstakingly developed their "human-capital", China was able to "import" largely the human-capital it did not have - specifically entrepreneurs, experienced engineers, accountants, lawyers, investment bankers, etc. - from Hong Kong, Taiwan and elsewhere.

(f) Being a communist-economy, China did very well in achieving basic levels of literacy, health, nutrition, life-expectancy – and most other social indicators – and considerably exceeded India's achievements in these areas.

The above unique features of China's economic "inheritance" placed it in an extraordinary position in relation to India. It is, therefore, inappropriate to compare China's growth experience with India, not having these unique advantages conferred by history and circumstances.

India also supersedes China on many fronts

In spite of above specially favourable inheritances of China, India also supersedes on many fronts on China as discussed below:

(i) India's Green Revolution occurred earlier than China's but without an adequate focus on nation-wide equality: (focus concentrated primarily on Punjab, Haryana, western Uttar Pradesh and West Bengal) which constrained growth of productive areas in other parts of the country.

(ii) India Scores on High-Quality Tertiary-Education over China: Just as China's achievements in basic literacy and primary education considerably exceeded, India's achievements in secondary, tertiary-education, internationally-traded services and knowledge-based industry exceeded China's attainments. India had a literacy rate of less than 14% in 1947 which increased to 65.6% by 2001. Though the high-quality tertiary-institutions (ISI, IITS, IIMs, IISC etc.) of India are unique in the developing world, the Indian private-sector was slow to benefit fully from this enormous pool of highly skilled personnel.

(iii) India Scores More on Financial System and Stability over China: India has a better-regulated and more well-functioning financial system and capital-market opening it (especially equity-market, bond-market) to foreign investment. China, by contrast, has given foreigners very limited access to its own-equity and bond-markets but opened a window for more foreign-portfolio-investments.

This introduced the system of qualified Foreign Institutional Investors to acquire controlling access to China's equity-markets. Thus China allowed unfettered foreign access to and foreign-ownership of her domestic financial instruments.

India's stock-markets have been well functioning, regulated by SEBI and with equity-prices properly reflecting companies earnings-growth and future prospects. In Indian financial system, companies that fail to live up to earnings-expectations are punished by the stock-market. In China, on the other hand, the sheltered "A" shares of Chinese companies remain massively over-valued using poorly audited accounts. As a result, Chinese domestic investors face severe financial uncertainty in their capital-market. However) India, by opening its capital-market early, suffered consequences of the 1994 crisis and learnt an early salutary lesson, one that China will have to painfully learn in the future, with even more severe financial crisis because its stock-market will by then be much larger relative to the overall economy than India's was in 1994.

(iv) India's Banking System is in substantially better shape than that of China: India's banking system is also in substantially better shape. S&P estimated (Aug. 2003) that Non-Performing-Loans (NPLs) in China's banks amounted to 50% of all loans. Such high NPL rate when China's economy growing at a spectacular 9% rate suggests that things may get substantially worse when a genuine economic slowdown comes. This is due to Chinese banks facing a basic problem of "adverse-selection": the best potential borrowers (export-oriented firms, predominantly foreign-owned or foreign-invested) have negligible need for bank-credit, while banks' primary customers (State-owned Enterprises) share the maximum borrowings to help keep the SOEs afloat by continuing to lend to them regardless of their ability to service debt, without penalty, and also permitting SOEs to shift their NPLs from their own-books to that of Asset-Management-Companies (AMCs). The AMCs, in turn, sell NPLs in secondary market for less than

10 cents per dollar, implying that banks should have taken a loss of over 90% of the face value of these loans when transferring them to AMCs.

If China persists with these lending-practices it will end-up bearing an even larger burden in future. At 173% of GDP, China's domestic-credit/GDP ratio is already exceedingly high for a developing economy, and if its NPLs are 45% of total credit, they will amount to 77% of annual GDP. To make up, even if China's public-debt is conservatively raised to about 90% of GDP from the current 45% and the additional issuance of government-debt will likely raise the whole structure of interest-rates in China, slowing her economic growth in the medium-term as bank-rehabilitation takes precedence over the "growth-at-any-cost" doctrine during communist-stewardship of the Chinese economy.

In early 1990s, Indian banks when lending to public enterprises, agriculture sector and exporters had many similar problems raising their gross NPLs estimated at 30% that Chinese banks face today. But once the loss-recognition norms were tightened, BIS capital-adequacy ratios stringently applied and Banks' prudential norms made more consistent with international practices. But India's state-owned banks gradually reformed over the past decade, restraining their lending-growth. The Securitization Act (2002) further strengthened Indian Banks' ability to seize the assets of delinquent borrowers. Consequently, by the end of Mar. 2004, India's Nationalised Banks had gross NPL of only 7.8% of total loans.

Comparing India and China it can be concluded that it is unlikely that India can emulate China's growth-rate of past two decades because China's geo-political circumstances and her historic "inheritances" were unique. However, India, apart from the long term strengths of its democracy, has two significant sources of strength that will provide India's economy greater stability and robustness in the medium and long-terms: India's financial-systems (capital-markets and banking-system) are significantly more sound than those of China; and India's attainments in post-secondary and tertiary-education ensures that India will comfortably sustain her lead over China in internationalized services and knowledge-based industry. In order to better understand and appreciate the economic development of India, a period-based detailed analysis seems necessary.

India's Economic Growth Experience from 1950 to 1990

The facts about India's economic performance over the past half-century (1950 to 1990) can be best summarised as below:

Between 1900 and 1950 (under the British Rule), India's real GDP grew 0.7% a year (implying a decline in per capita income). Between 1950 and 1980 real GDP grew at an average pace of 3.7% per year (per capita income just 1.5%), marginally above the global-average for that period. Between 1980-90 period the real GDP accelerated to 5.9% growth (per capita income to 3.8%). Between 1999-2000 period real GDP accelerated to 6.2% (per capita income to 4.4%) annually. At the average pace of 1980-2000, India will achieve the per capita income levels of the present-day United States by 2061.

The noteworthy features of India's economic growth were: that there were greater fluctuations before 1980. After 1980 there was period of faster-growth (averaging over 5% annually for about 5 years). The 1950-80 period was followed by a year of severe recession. These recessions were caused either by a foreign-exchange crisis (FY1957-58), a food crisis in the aftermath of war (FY1965-66), the first oil crisis (FY1973-74) and drought coupled with an oil-related inflationary surge (FY1979-80), when the Iran-related oil price surge was exacerbated by food price inflation which raised prices of agricultural products, and aggravated by the worst drought since the mid-1960s.

Since 1980, India has had no genuine recession (i.e., in no year since 1980 has real GDP declined). China too has had no year of decline in real GDP over that period, but all other Asian economies have had at least one recession, and most have had two (around 1984-86 and 1997-98).

The FY1990-91 oil-crisis which resulted in huge oil related inflation and collapse in overseas worker-remittances from Kuwait and Iraq led to yet another Balance-of-Payments crisis in India, but this time a full-blown recession was avoided, despite severe import-compression, as major structural reforms rebuilt confidence in the currency and induced significant new foreign capital inflows for the first time.

In the 1950s, India focused on Import-Substituting-Industrialization (ISI). The ISI strategy was founded on the belief (among developed economies) that the developing countries would primarily substitute imports of consumer goods with domestic production but would still need to import capital goods from the developed world. It was argued that the successful growth of the developing countries would boost their demand for capital goods, so the ISI strategy was seen as a win-win situation for both sides.

India's economy had its best performance in FY1975-76 (during the period of Emergency) since independence, real GDP grew 9% and the current-account gained a comfortable surplus. The "controlled experiment" with autocracy showed that India could indeed generate substantially stronger growth under authoritarianism even with the "socialist" perversions and policy excesses introduced in the period 1969-75.

Since 1980 a modest liberalization of the economy began after taking a massive US$5 billion loan from the IMF (then the largest loan ever given by the IMF), a modest liberalization of the industrial-licensing-regime, industrial de-licensing made a little more progress, with piecemeal liberalization of imports continued accompanied by fiscal-reforms viz., substantial reduction in direct taxes, introduction of a modified value added tax to ease collection of indirect taxes.

As a result, India's real GDP growth accelerated to 5.8% in the 1980s (above the average achieved by the eight East Asian miracle economies), India's external-debt rose from US$ 20.6 billion in 1980 to US$ 70.2 billion in 1990. In FY1990, commercial-loans accounted for 26.3% of external-debt; loans from international institutions (World Bank) made up 45.2%; borrowing from foreign governments (Japan, Germany, United States) accounted for 28.5%. Aided by a 26% depreciation of the rupee in REER terms between 1984 and 1990, however, India's exports doubled from US$ 8.9 billion in FY1985-86 to US$ 18.1 billion in FY1990-91.

The 1990s and Beyond: India capitalises on Globalisation

In FY1990-91, India's current-account deficit widened to 3.2% of GDP, external-debt-service payments rose to 35% of current-receipts. Since 1991-92 reforms included mainly: stabilization measures to compress imports and reduce the current-account deficit; a two-step devaluation of the rupee; fiscal and monetary contraction; a slew of micro-economic reforms aimed at wholesale structural adjustment; a sweeping de-licensing of virtually all of industry; a substantial phased reduction in import tariffs; and the removal of almost all non-tariff barriers to imports of capital and intermediate goods; and linearization of capital-market. India's Banking sector got benefited from a gradual de-regulation of interest-rates. By mid-1990s, the rupee was fully convertible on current-account, and virtually all lending-rates/deposit-rates were deregulated except Small Savings and various Provident Fund schemes.

The external-sector responded powerfully to these reforms with a large voluntary inflow of foreign-capital (mainly portfolio investment and substantial inflows from NRIs, but also the first significant inflows of FDI). By 1993, the annual increases in external-debt was just US$ 1 billion (down from US$ 8 billion annually in the last couple of years). Three years after the introduction of 1991-92 reforms a rebound in the current-account balance and strong capital-inflows allowed foreign reserves to rise to US$ 21.6 billion

(July 1994) to US$ 127 billion (Nov. 2004). There was a moderation in export-growth in the late 1990s. Exports of "invisibles" (services, transfers and investment income) rose nearly seven-fold, from US$ 7.49 billion (June 1991) to US$ 59.1 billion (June 2004). Merchandise exports also rose by about 260% from US$ 18.48 billion to US$ 66.48 billion. India's exports of goods and services have nearly quintupled over the past 13 years to US$ 125.6 billion.

India's exports are predominantly generated by its own companies (as is true in Japan, Korea and Taiwan) rather than by foreign companies that generate the vast majority of the exports of China. "Services" were traditionally considered to be 'non-tradable' across borders, thereby limiting developing countries' ability to take advantage of their much lower costs for producing services. Foreign tourists arrival rose 26% in 2003 and 35% in 2004 which contributed to the improvement in the services balance-of-payment. While all "invisible" exports were about 13% of India's GDP, exports of software services accounted for about 2.5% of GDP. Over the past eight years, the real growth of the services-sector has usually exceeded 8% annually. The strong growth of the services sector underpinned the overall-growth of the economy. Although agriculture remained volatile, the services sector's steady growth ensured that even in a bad-year (such as 2002-03), the floor for real GDP growth is now set at 4%, and average real GDP growth is in excess of 6%.

After growing at an average pace of 11% in real terms in the four years period (93-94 to 96-97), the real manufacturing growth slumped to just 2.8% in the subsequent three years as industrial investments declined while industrial companies restructured in the face of the heightened international competition. This period marked a slump in Asia in 1997-99, during which there was an average real effective depreciation of over 20% in Asian currencies. The Indian rupee consequently appreciated in real-terms during the period, thereby both weakening the export performance and hurting import-competing industries that faced deflationary pressures from the declining price of imports from the east.

By 2003, recovery in industrial sector was visible by knowledge-based manufacturing sectors (automobiles, auto components, electronics and pharmaceuticals), extending to commodity manufactures (aluminium, steel, cement and petrochemicals), capital goods and also the consumer goods. Additionally, in recent years, the textile and garment industry has begun to gear up to take advantage of the dismantling of the Multi-Fiber-Arrangement (MFA) at the beginning of 2005. Studies by the World Bank and WTO suggest that India's share of the global market for textiles and garments should rise to about 15% from 2.5% as a result of the dismantling of MFAs.

The fiscal improvements have continued into the current fiscal year, aided by the continued strengthening of the industrial sector (which remains the main contributor to government revenues; agricultural income is untaxed, and services sector incomes have just started being taxed in recent years, and are still small by comparison). In the first half of 2004-05, the fiscal deficit was just 3.7% of GDP. Net corporate-tax revenues (which rose 37% in 2003-04) are greater than customs revenue, thereby completing the transition of the Indian fiscal system from its unhealthy dependence on customs duties to a more sustainable reliance on direct taxes and on personal and corporate income taxes.

Though India's economy grew at 4% per annum from 1990 to 2003 (compared to 3.3% from 1975 to 2003), a large section of population suffered. A key-feature of India's economic growth in the 1990s was the decline of "employment-elasticity" (employment generated per unit growth of output). The employment-elasticity dropped from 0.5 (1980s) to 0.16 (1990s). The higher capital-intensity of economic growth due to globalization and competitive-pressure were responsible for this. The net effect was increased layoffs and closure of uncompetitive production units. Pressure on the government to privatize public utilities was increased.

On the whole, India's economic achievement over the past quarter-century was unprecedented among large democracies, outstanding by comparison with the fastest-growing economy of Asia, yet India's economic achievements remain subject to endless unflattering comparisons with China. In fact, India suffers by comparison with China on most standard-measures of economic-achievement viz., growth rate, per capita income, and consumption of key consumer and food items, social-indicators such as life expectancy, literacy and infant mortality.

CONCLUSION: Indian Economy is likely to grow faster in the future

India's physical infrastructure remains noticeably worse than virtually anywhere in East Asia but India's real GDP grew at an average pace of 6.2% a year over the past ten years (faster than all the East Asian economies except China and Vietnam). The reason is primarily that while the absolute level of physical infrastructure remains poor, it is slowly but steadily improving at the margins. For examples: tele-density improved from 7 phones per 1000 people in 1993 to 86/1000 in 2004; construction of national-highways / Golden-Quadrilateral-highway; increase in domestic airports with privatization of international airports; and electricity reforms are likely to make progress in the years ahead.

India, in her Young-Demographic-Profile (with her mobile young population) has 24-54% of it with a medium-age below 25 years, with a 61% working population expected to rise till 2025 but marginally declining thereafter till 2050 but still remain above 60%. The younger generation of India which turns out more than 4 lakh engineering and science graduates, over 3 lakh non-engineering post-graduates, 21 lakh other graduates and 9 thousand Ph.Ds annually and whose Knowledge-Workers in software and service industry increasing 25 times from 6,800 (1985-86) to 6,50,000 (2003-04) and the strength of IT workers expected to go up to 20 lakh by 2008 will have propensity to demand and spend more on living standard, life style goods and energy, obviously more on clean-energy. India produces more than 28 lakhs of college-graduates/post-graduates each year which is about 50% more than the number passed out from the next biggest producer (USA). Tertiary enrolments in India, especially in engineering, technical and management schools, are also rising rapidly, and are expected to rise by 50% from the levels of last year by 2008.

India also retains its lead in software exports, BPO and other internationalized services over the next 10-15 years. While software-export revenues are just 2.5% of GDP now, they should rise to 6 to 7% of GDP by 2008. Thus the total "invisible" exports may rise from the current 13% to about 25% of GDP by 2010. As that happens, the multiplier-effects on the economy (generated by the domestic-spending of the Dollars and Euros earned through services exports) will be progressively larger than they are now. Additionally, knowledge-based manufacturing may gather momentum with the consumer-electronics joining the already buoyant pharmaceutical, automobile, auto-component and fine-chemical export sectors. The abolition of MFA quotas may also generate a multi-year boom in textile and garment manufacturing and exports.

India's demographic-dividend unfolded late than in all of East Asia. Most East Asian countries had dependency-ratios begin declining around 1970, India began to see the dependency-ratio decline only after 1980. As dependency-ratios decline, national saving rates typically rise, which will boost a higher investment-GDP ratio, a higher labour-productivity which, in the long-run, is the main determinant of national prosperity.

With everything else remaining broadly unchanged, India should grow at about 7% a year over the next 10 years, benefitting from the demographic-dividend, the growing share of services-exports, a more sustainably buoyant manufacturing-sector, and the knowledge-based industry. The impact of bio-technology on the agriculture sector could also deliver gains. If the already enacted power-sector reforms are truly implemented, and infrastructure bottlenecks are rapidly eliminated, as the fiscal situation improves, India's real GDP growth may accelerate to 8 to 8.5% annual growth over the decade.

India's economic growth in future decades may accelerate to China-like figures of over 9% a year, only possibly when the labour-sector/human-capital/brain-drain repatriation reforms and re-deployment also occur in India. However, in the likeliest scenario, India may grow at a little over 7% a year which is the fastest pace of growth ever witnessed in a large democratic economy.

To conclude, Indian economy posted an average growth rate of more than 7% in the decade since 1994, reducing poverty by about 10% points. India achieved 7.6% GDP growth in 2005, significantly expanding manufacturing. India is capitalizing on its large numbers of well-educated people skilled in the English language to become a major exporter of software services and software workers. Despite strong growth, the World Bank and others worry about the combined state and federal budget deficit, running at approximately 9% of GDP; government-borrowings has kept interest rates high. Economic deregulation would help attract additional foreign capital and lower interest rates.

India's relations with all major nations traditionally have been based on principles of 'non-alignment' which was seriously tested as a viable basis for its foreign policy and its capacity in playing influentially in regional and world politics with increased need of energy-securitization and also the international terrorism are leading India to create stronger bilateral relations with US, China, Israel, and other nations. Thus, India's overlapping domestic and external dimensions will continue to compel it to rapidly shift its emphasis from domestic-self-sufficiency to the major-promoters of free-trade, economic-liberalization, increased bi-lateral trade and energy-cooperation/dependence with Nepal, Sri Lanka, and particularly Pakistan whose necessity has evidently increased to provide both security and sustainable development to the Future-India.

India's 11ᵗʰ Five-Year Plan (2007-12) will need to give priority to increase infrastructure in manufacturing sector and curtail the present (38%) 'aggregate technical and commercial losses' in Energy Sector

India's Planning Commission (IPC) through its approach-document (14 June 2006) to the 11ᵗʰ FYP (2007-12) held a series of consultations with the States for political consensus being a vital important component of reform proposed to achieve an average growth-rate of **8-9%** in the 11ᵗʰ Plan, against only 7% in 10ᵗʰ Plan, through strong fiscal efforts that is difficult but not impossible combined with other correctives on sector policies, contending that high economic growth is an essential part of the strategy for India's development. IPC stressed that India's economic-fundamentals have improved to the point where they have the capacity to make a decisive impact on common people's economic welfare if only accompanied with completion of the reform-agenda after evolving a political consensus.

The 11ᵗʰ Plan approach document proposes growth in agricultural sector from 2 to 4%; in manufacturing sector from single-digit to double-digit; to control inflationary pressures by additional imports (also by stimulation of domestic supply); increase foreign exchange earnings; controlling the current-account-deficit due to higher payment on oil import by passing on the increased cost to the consumer in a gradual manner; to increase the shares of comparative advantages in areas like tourism, services and labour-intensive manufactures; to modernize the 35 non-metro airports.

For attaining higher growth rate in **manufacturing sector** IPC made a detailed focus on bottlenecks viz., inadequate infrastructure, need to extend improvement in the investment-climate of all Indian States; remove the skill-constraints of graduates and help them acquire good quality skill able to meet expectations of modern industries.

For attaining higher growth rate in **"energy sector"** IPC categorically stressed the need to control the continuing inefficiency in the power distribution system, and to curtail India's aggregate technical and commercial (AT&C) losses from the existing about **38%**. The present rate of decline in AT&C losses is a little over 1% a year. For the AT&C at 38% to go down to 15% would require an improvement of 23% which will take more than 20 years unless the energy efficiency improvement-pace is accelerated.

Section – III

The World of Energy and The World Issues

CHAPTER 6

Sources of Earth's Energy and the World Issues

Let us first recapitulate the mainpoints around energy that have emerged as the world issues before we go to analyse the world trend of production and consumption. For any action from the miniscule size to the mega one requires energy. In our world, energy exists in various forms – Electromagnetic Radiation, Light, Heat Sound, Electrical, Chemical, Nuclear, Kinetic and Potential energies. All energy is measured by the international unit, the Joule (J). Most of the earth's energy is provided by the **SUN**, in the form of Electromagnetic-Radiation. The sun radiates about 300 million million million 'J' of energy each second, out of which 100 thousand million million J of energy reaches earth per second some of which is transferred to plant and animal life, and ultimately to fossil-fuels, when burnt, produces chemical-energy which forms the main natural-source of energy on earth. The major components of the non-fossil fuel are nuclear, and renewable energy sources. The renewable energy sources include hydro-power, solar, wind, tide, geothermal, solid-biomass and animal products, biomass-gas and liquids, industrial and municipal wastes. This thesis highlights China's and India's achievements on both primary-energy/marketed-energy as well non-marketed energy sources.

Harnessing the natural forces like wind and moving water, sea level water, tidal streams, burning coal or oil, storing solar energy in photo-voltaic-cells, causing nuclear-fusion are all examples of man-made means to produce energy in the forms of electricity and light. However, all sources of the earth's energy powering the civilizations and their economies include: 1. Bio-Energy, 2. Coal, 3. Electric Power, 4. Fossil Fuels, 5. Fusions, 6. Geo-Thermal, 7. Hydrogen, 8. Hydro-Power, 9. Natural Gas, 10. Nuclear Energy, 11. Oil, 12. Renewables, 13. Solar, 14. Wind, 15. Tidal Sea-Level energy and 16. Tidal Stream-Power.

The **world issues** developed around energy are: (i) burgeoning energy demand, especially from the developing world; (ii) the fearful environmental consequences of using fossil-fuels or hydro-carbons as sources of energy; (iii) the finite nature of oil and gas reserves; (iv) the energy dilemma caused by more dependence on oil and increasing preference for natural gas; (v) the unsatisfactory nature of the international legal response to the looming shortage of sustainable energy; (vi) increasing securitization of energy; (vii) rising international diplomacy and strategies around energy; (viii) the lack of satisfactory technological, legal, economic, and social mechanisms that address this deficit; (ix) lack of energy cooperation and more of energy competition; (x) lack of analytical-compass and system to find the most efficient-energy-mix and the most appropriate fuel-substitution; (xi) increasing international prices and recurring costs per unit of energy consumed; (xii) need for new and massive capital-formation which is certain to divest, distort or derate the existing or other priority-investments; (xiii) energy infrastructure becoming a new target of international terrorism; and (xiv) the need and the impulsion to develop new international instruments for sustainable development, security and world peace.

This piece of ambitious effort hopefully ventures to emphasize first for the construction of an **integrated-knowledge-base** on all energy sources, then an **energy-analytical-compass** that the future India must have, as that together will facilitate the development of new international energy instruments. This work also seeks to advance India's objective of promoting new treaties, objective energy business models and other international energy instruments to help promote more energy-cooperation and sustainable development which can be possible by understanding more on global-energy-systems, a domain through which alone exploration of improvised ways of institutionalizing and deploying new generation technologies can be found and developed.

CHAPTER 7

Major Forms of Earth's Energy Production and Consumption

World Trends in Energy Production

The World's Primary Energy Production (coal, oil, natural gas, nuclear, hydro-electric and major renewable resources), by source, for the period 1970 to 2004 are shown below (see for a graphical presentations, Appendix-J). It may be observed that while the total energy production has almost doubled since 1970 through 2004, the source-wise production increases in 2004 over 1970 were for Coal (79.95%), Natural Gas (175.52%), Crude Oil (59.43%), Natural Gas-Plant-Liquids (218%), Nuclear-Electric-Power (2952.22%), Hydro-Electric-Power (126.58%), and Geothermal and others (298.11%). The increase in world production in respect of all sources of energy remained limited within 3 times of 1970 production-level except Nuclear **Electric-Power** whose increase was as high as 30 times.

An Analysis of World Trend with special reference to China and India

Figure 1. World Marketed Energy Consumption by Region, 2004-2030

Figure 1. World Marketed Energy Use by Fuel Type, 1980-2030

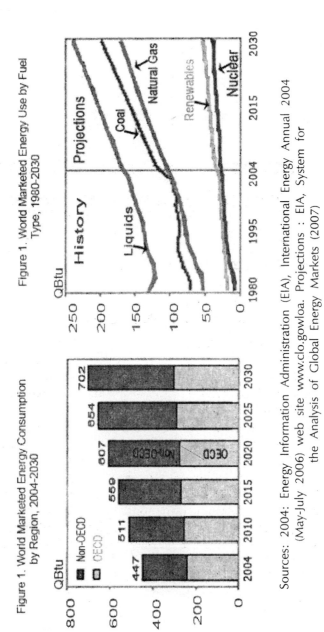

Sources: 2004: Energy Information Administration (EIA), International Energy Annual 2004 (May-July 2006) web site www.clo.gowloa. Projections : EIA, System for the Analysis of Global Energy Markets (2007)

World Primary Energy Production by Source: 1970 – 2004

[Quadrillion (10^{15}) Btu]

Year	Coal	Natural Gas	Crude Oil	Natural Gas Plant Liquids	Nuclear Electric-Power	Hydro Electric-Power	Geothermal and other	Total
1970	62.96	37.09	97.09	3.61	0.90	12.15	1.59	215.39
1975	66.20	45.67	113.08	4.12	3.85	15.03	1.74	249.69
1980	71.24	54.73	128.04	5.10	7.58	17.90	2.94	287.53
1985	82.20	64.22	115.37	5.83	15.30	20.42	378	307.13
1990	90..93	75.87	129.35	6.87	20.36	22.35	3.93	349.66
1995	88.87	80.24	133.32	8.55	23.26	25.34	4.64	364.23
2000	91.36	91.34	146.55	9.87	25.66	27.01	5.35	397.13
2004	113.30	102.19	154.79	11.48	27.47	27.53	6.33	443.10

World Trends in Energy Consumption by Energy-Type/ Country-Group

The world trend in consumption of Primary-Energy by Energy-Type (Petroleum, Dry Natural Gas, Coal, Net Hydroelectric-Power, Net Nuclear-Electric-Power, and Net Geothermal, Solar, Wind, Wood and Waste Electric-Power) for selected Country-Groups (OECD, Non-OECD and other Groups) for the period 1980 to 2004 is discussed below based on the EIA 2006 reports. China and India come under the country-group 'Non-OECD-Asia' (**Appendix-C1**).

This trend of increased oil consumption (Appendix-C1) is largely import-based and mainly shared by **OECD-Asia** (....Japan, Korea) and **Non-OECD-Asia** (.....**China, India**). In detail IEA projected Asia's growing dependence (Appendix-C1) on 'Oil-Import' (in Million-Barrels/Day increasing from year 2000 to 2030) for selected countries/ regions were for China (from 2 to 10), Japan (6-7), South East Asia (0-6), India (1-5), Korea (2-3), Pakistan (0-2) and Indonesia (0-1) to be met from Middle East (19-46), Africa (5-8), Central Asia (1-4) and Russia (4-5).

(1) Petroleum - While the world trend in consumption of petroleum in 2004 over 1980 increased by 31%, similar increase in the consumption-trends (in descending order) for the selected country-groups were: OPEC (158%), Non-OECD (55%), OECD (18%), IEA (18%), OECD-Europe (4%) and EU (3%)

Year (Thousand Barrels per Day)	1980	1985	1990	1995	2000	2004
World Total	63,114	60,085	66,546	69,912	76,688	82,595
OECD	41,763	37,481	41,480	44,752	47,909	49,510
Non-OECD	21,351	22,604	25,066	25,161	28,779	33,085
Other Groups:						
OECD Europe	14,995	12,772	13,710	14,634	15,164	15,620
OPEC	2,814	3,681	4,512	5,316	6,059	7,248
EU	14,191	11,961	12,793	13,783	14,221	14,641
IEA	39,740	35,379	39,147	42,529	45,371	47,001

(2) Dry Natural Gas – The world trend in consumption of Dry Natural Gas in 2004 over 1980 increased by 88%. However, similar increase in the consumption trends (in descending order) for the selected country-groups were: OPEC (339%), Non-OECD (148%), OECD-Europe (96%), EU (87%), OECD (54%), and IEA (53%).

Year (Trillion Cubic Feet)	1980	1985	1990	1995	2000	2004
World Total	**52.890**	**62.244**	**73.370**	**78.723**	**88.275**	**99.665**
OECD	33.448	33.014	36.823	43.432	48.683	51.479
Non-OECD	19.442	29.230	36.547	35.292	39.592	48.186
Other Groups:						
OECD Europe	9.625	10.513	11.601	13.900	16.437	18.840
OPEC	2.551	4.013	5.481	7.309	9.261	11.187
EU	9.553	10.409	11.329	13.654	15.891	17.905
IEA	31.906	31.173	34.946	41.700	46.560	48.907

(3) Coal – While the world trend in consumption of coal in 2004 over 1980 increased by 47%, similar increase in the consumption trends (in descending order) for the selected country-groups were: OPEC (800%), Non-OECD (86%), IEA (26%), OECD (14%), OECD-Europe (-29%) and EU (-32%).

Year (Million Short Tons)	1980	1985	1990	1995	2000	2004
World Total	**4,138**	**4,888**	**5,269**	**5,116**	**5,100**	**6,099**
OECD	2,225	2,526	2,551	2,318	2,467	2,532
Non-OECD	1,913	2,362	2,718	2,797	2,633	3,566
Other Groups:						
OECD Europe/ OPEC	1,275/3	1,392/5	1,298/10	973/14	910/28	900/27
EU	1,253	1,344	1,237	924	840	853
IEA	1,864	2,139	2,221	2,107	2,283	2,352

(4) Net Hydro-Electric Power – The world trend in consumption of Net Hydro-Electric Power in 2004 over 1980 increased by 59%. However, similar increase in the consumption-trends (in descending order) for the selected country-groups were: OPEC (250%), Non-OECD (132%), OECD-Europe (19%), OECD (16%), IEA (16%), and EU (8%).

Year (Billion Kilowatt hours)	1980	1985	1990	1995	2000	2004
World Total	1,722.9	1,954.9	2,148.9	2,457.3	2,647.5	2,746.9
OECD	1,079.7	1,164.6	1,179.5	1,289.8	1,330.2	1,257.1
Non OECD	643.1	790.3	969.4	1,167.5	1,317.3	1,489.8
Other Groups:						
OECD Europe/	411.0	435.0	439.2	492.4	535.7	489.5
OPEC	/25.9	/36.1	/54.4	/72.5	/82.1	/90.7
EU	281.6	286.3	262.7	304.1	331.7	302.9
IEA	1,052.8	1,128.8	1,146.8	1,251.2	1,284.5	1,219.0

(5) Net Nuclear Electric-Power – While the world trend in consumption of Net Nuclear-Electric-Power in 2004 over 1980 increased by 3.83 times, similar increase in the consumption-trends (in descending order) for the selected country-groups were: EU (3.44), Non-OECD (3.35), OECD-Europe (3.21), OECD (2.75), IEA (2.73), and OPEC (0%) –

Year (Billion Kilowatt hours)	1980	1985	1990	1995	2000	2004
World Total	684.4	1,425.5	1,908.8	2,210.0	2,449.9	2,619.2
OECD	592.7	1,192.7	1,634.6	1,943.0	2,128.2	2,220.3
Non-OECD	91.7	232.9	274.2	267.0	321.7	398.8
Other Groups:						
OECD Europe/						
OPEC	223.7/0	586.5/0	743.3/0	828.3/0	887.9/0	941.4/0
EU	210.9	566.4	720.9	819.8	875.3	935.4
IEA	588.2	1,180.8	1,608.4	1,924.1	2,104.7	2,195.4

(6) Net Geothermal, Solar, Wind, Wood and Waste Electric-Power – While the world trend in consumption of

Net Geothermal, Solar, Wind, Wood and Waste Electric-Power in 2004 over 1980 increased by 10.8 times, similar increase in the consumption-trends (in descending order) for the selected country-groups were: IEA (11.46), OECD (11.31), OECD-Europe (9.91), EU (9.84), Non-OECD (8.69), and OPEC (6.1).

Year (Billion Kilowatt hours)	1980	1985	1990	1995	2000	2004
World Total	31.1	55.5	127.0*	172.3	242.6	334.3
OECD	24.4	43.1	112.1	147.6	199.2	276.0
Non-OECD	6.7	12.4	15.0	24.7	43.4	58.2
Other Groups:						
OECD Europe/ OPEC	13.8/0	14.3/0.4	19.7/1.1	38.9/2.1	75.5/4.6	136.8/6.1
EU	13.5	13.8	18.5	37.1	72.2	132.8
IEA	23.1	40.8	106.7	141.6	191.3	264.7

An analysis of above consumption-trends, by 'Energy-Type' and 'Country-Group', over a period of 25 years (1980-2004) revealed that in the year 2004 over 1980 the highest share of world energy consumption was on account of the OPEC countries who displayed increase in consumption trends being the highest for petroleum (158%), dry-natural gas (339%), coal (800%), net hydro-electric-power (250%) and net-geothermal / solar / wind / wood / waste electric-power (610%) whereas it was the lowest for net nuclear-electric-power (0%).

The Non-OECD countries showed the 2nd highest increasing trend in consumption of most of the energy sources (petroleum by 55%, dry natural gas by 148%, coal by 86%, net hydro-electric-power by 132% and net nuclear-electric-power by 335%). The credit for a significant control in the year 2004 over 1980 in coal-consumption (-29% and -32%) by promoting higher consumption of net-geothermal/solar/ wind/wood/waste electric-power (9.91% and 9.84%) went to the OECD-Europe and EU countries respectively.

However, the IEA and the OECD countries showed spectacular increase in the use of net-geothermal/solar/wind/wood/waste electric power energy recording a growth by 11.46% and 11.31% respectively during the same period.

Consequently, total OECD energy demand increases by an average of 1.0% per year over the projection period, as compared with an average increase of 3.0% per year for total non-OECD energy demand. Countries outside the Organization for Economic Cooperation and Development (non-OECD countries) account for three-fourths of the increase in world energy use. Non-OECD energy use surpasses OECD energy use by 2015, and in 2030 total energy demand in non-OECD countries exceeds that in the OECD countries by 34%.

World Trends in Energy Consumption by 'Energy-Type' with reference to China and India

The World-Trends in Energy-Consumption by 'Energy-Type' with special reference to 'China' and 'India' is shown below:

It may be observed that **China's share** of energy-consumption in **Asia-Oceania / World** in the 25 years' period (1980 to 2004) increased in respect of 'Petroleum' from 16.45/2.80% to 27.42/7.75%; in r/o 'Dry Natural Gas' decreased / increased from 20.02/0.95% to 10.03/1.36%; for 'Coal' increased from 63.11/16.67% to 64.65/33.82%; for 'Net Hydro-Electric-Power' increased from 21.93/3.34% to 49.35/11.93%; and for 'Net Nuclear-Electric-Power' increased from 0/0% to 9.62/1.83%.

India's share of energy consumption in **Asia-Oceania / World** during the same period increased in respect of 'Petroleum' from 5.99/1.02% to 10.50/2.97%; in r/o 'Dry Natural Gas' increased from 2.02/0.10% to 8.08/1.09%; for 'Coal' increased from 11.88/3.14% to 14.99/7.84%; for 'Net-Hydro-Electric-Power' decreased/increased from 17.72/2.70% to 12.61/3.05%; and for 'Net-Nuclear-Electric-Power' decreased/increased from 3.24/0.44% to 3.02/0.57%.

(a) Petroleum Consumption - (Thousand Barrels per day)

Region/Country	1980	China	India	2004	China	India
Asia and Oceania (+*)	10,729.1	**16.45%**	**5.99%**	23,341.0	**27.42%**	**10.50%**
World Total	63,113.6	**2.80%**	**1.02%**	82,594.7	**7.75%**	**2.97%**
*(China)	1,765.0			6,400.0		
*(India)	643.0			2,450.0		

(b) Dry Natural Gas Consumption - (Billion Cubic Feet)

Asia and Oceania (+*)	2,523	**20.02%**	**2.02%**	13,472	**10.03%**	**8.08%**
World Total	52,890	**0.95%**	**0.10%**	99,665	**1.36%**	**1.09%**
*(China)	505			1,351		
* (India)	51			1,089		

(c) Coal Consumption - (Million Short Tons)

Asia and Oceania (+*)	1,092.84	**63.11%**	**11.88%**	3,190.25	**64.65%**	**14.99%**
World Total	4,137.70	**16.67%**	**3.14%**	6,098.78	**33.82%**	**7.84%**
* (China)	689.74			2,062.39		
* (India)	129.83			478.16		

(d) Net Hydro-Electric-Power Consumption - (Billion KiloWatt-Hours)

Asia and Oceania (+*)	262.70	**21.93%**	**17.72%**	664.00	**49.35%**	**12.61%**
World Total	1,722.88	**3.34%**	**2.70%**	2,746.88	**11.93%**	**3.05%**
* (China)	57.62			327.68		
* (India)	46.54			83.76		

(e) Net Nuclear-Electric-Power Consumption - (Billion Kilowatthours)

Asia and Oceania (+*)	92.73	**0**	**3.24%**	498.62	**9.62%**	**3.02%**
World Total	684.38	**0**	**0.44%**	2,619.18	**1.83%**	**0.57%**
* (China)	0			47.95		
* (India)	3.00			15.04		

Source: Derived from Energy Information Administration (EIA 2006)

Thus, China's consumption-share in all energy resources in 2004 ranged between **9.62%** and **64.65%** in Asia-Oceania and between **1.36%** and **33.82%** in the world while **India's** share remained between **3.02%** and **14.99%** in Asia-Oceania and between **0.57%** and **7.84%** in the world, consumption of coal and hydro-electricity having the highest shares in both the countries.

World Per Capita Total Primary-Energy Consumption with reference to China and India

The world per capita total consumption of primary-energy for the period 1980 to 2004 (**Appendix-A**) for the seven main regions of the world as compared with the per capita total consumption of primary-energy by China and India are shown below:

World Per Capita Total Primary-Energy Consumption by Main Regions: 1980-2004
(Million Btu)

Region	1980	1985	1990	1995	2000	2004
1. North America	286.0	267.4	277.9	279.7	286.1	280.2
2. Central and South America	39.6	38.2	40.8	45.3	49.8	50.8
3. Europe	135.7	135.1	137.3	134.8	140.8	146.5
4. Eurasia	175.7	200.4	211.2	145.7	140.4	157.2
5. Middle East	62.3	75.2	83.8	91.8	102.7	116.0
6. Africa	14.4	15.6	15.1	15.0	15.0	15.7
7. Asia and Oceania	19.9	21.8	25.0	29.9	32.0	38.5
World Total	**63.7**	**63.6**	**65.8**	**64.2**	**65.7**	**70.1**
China	17.8	20.8	23.5	28.9	30.6	45.9
India	6.1	7.7	9.5	12.5	13.5	14.5

Source: Derived from Energy Information Administration (EIA)

For a region-wise analysis per capita energy consumption are divided into: above 200 MBtu; between 100 and 200 MBtu that between 50 and 100 MBtu; and less than 50 MBtu.

It may be observed that for the period 1980 to 2004 the regions showing the highest (above 200 MBtu) and the 2nd highest (between 100 and 200 MBtu) trends in per capita energy consumption were **North America** (267.4–286.1); and **Eurasia** (140.4–211.2) / **Europe** (134.8–146.5) respectively against the **world** average low trend (63.6–70.1).

While **Asia and Oceania** region showed the lowest trend (less than 50 MBtu) in average per capita energy consumption (19.9 – 38.5), the trend of India's per capita average energy consumption during 1980– 2004 was found significantly lower (6.1–14.5) than that of China (17.8– 45.9).

In a country-wise analysis for the world (Appendix-A) it was observed that though both China and India showed a rise of 2.58 times and 2.38 times in their per capita energy consumption respectively in 2004 over 1980, analysis of their comparative position in the world trend revealed that China's place fell from 106th (1980) to just 108th (2004) while India's position in the world slipped down from 143rd (1980) to 150th (2004) as shown below:

Position in the World	1980	1985	1990	1995	2000	2004
China	106	101	14	123	123	108
India	143	137	138	151	154	150

Source: Derived from Energy Information Administration (EIA)

It was further observed that for China and India for the year 2004, among the 46 countries in the 'Asia-Oceania' Region itself the per capita energy consumption (Million Btu) of 16 countries was much higher (50.4 min. to 444.6 max.) than that of China (45.9). When compared to India (14.5), 26 countries had much higher (15.2 min. to 444.6 max.) per capita energy consumption for the year 2004.

Thus, above statistics indicate that both China and India, with developing economies geared-up at very fast pace, will generate significantly increased demands for higher energy consumption in future both in normal and under accelerated economic conditions.

Shifting Oil Trading patterns of Non-OECD members may impact India

Expectations in late 1980s/early 1990s were that the non-OPEC production in the longer term would stagnate or decline gradually in response to resource-constraints. The relatively low-cost of developing oil resources within OPEC countries (especially those in the Persian Gulf region) was considered such a vast advantage that non-OPEC production potential was viewed with considerable pessimism. In actuality, however, despite several periods of relatively low-prices, the non-OPEC production rose every year since 1993, adding more than 6.9 million barrels per day between 1993 and 2003.

The non-OPEC supply became increasingly diverse over past three decades, and growth in non-OPEC oil production played a significant role in the erosion of OPEC's market-share, which fell from 52% in 1973 to 39% in 2003. North America dominated non-OPEC supply in the early 1970s, the North-Sea and Mexico evolved as major producers in the 1980s, and much of the new production in the 1990s came from the economies of South America, West Africa, the non-OPEC Middle East, and China.

Non-OPEC supply from proven-reserves increased steadily, from 48.9 million barrels/per day in 2003 to 72.6 million-barrels/per day (mb/pd) in 2030, as shown on p.159, as high prices attract investment in areas previously considered uneconomical. As higher oil prices assumed to continue, oil production in the non-OECD Europe and Eurasian region may exceed 14.0 mb/pd in 2015, based in large part on the potential investment outlook for the Caspian-Basin region, where long term production-potential is still regarded with considerable optimism. Caspian-output may more than double to 4.2 mb/pd in 2015 and may increase steadily thereafter, although there is still considerable uncertainty about export routes from the Caspian-Basin region. Exploration and test-well activity have pointed to some production-potential for Bangladesh and Myanmar (formerly Burma), but significant output is not expected until after 2010.

OIL PRODUCTION TREND (OPEC & Non-OPEC)
(Non-OPEC Share increasing @ 2.3%)

TREND OF OIL IMPORT
(OECD & Non-OECD)
[OECD-23.8% increase & Non-OECD 82.4% increase]

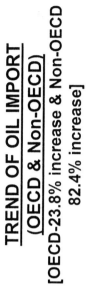

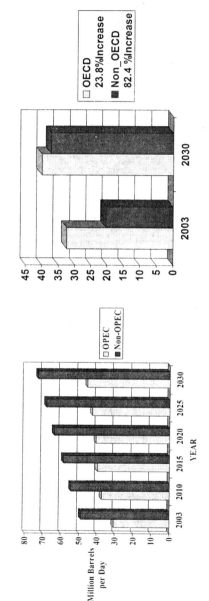

Source: Derived from Energy Information Administration (E1A)

Because oil is fungible and traded in world commodities markets, there is much uncertainty associated with projections of future patterns of oil trade; however, anticipated changes in the world's oil-trading-patterns, as shown on p.159, particularly, the shifting regional dependence of importing regions on producing-regions, may impact geopolitical ramifications. In 2003, the OECD economies imported 17.9 mb/pd of oil per day from OPEC producers, of this 11.3 mb/pd came from the Persian Gulf region. Oil movements to OECD economies represented 57% of the total petroleum exported by OPEC member nations and 50% of all Persian Gulf exports.

By the end of the projection period, OPEC exports to OECD economies in the reference case are estimated to be about 3.2 mb/pd higher than their 2003 level, and almost 42% of the increase is expected to come from the Persian Gulf region. The significant shift expected in the balance of OPEC export shares between the OECD and non-OECD economies is a direct result of the economic growth anticipated for the non-OECD nations, especially non-OECD Asia. OPEC petroleum exports to non-OECD economies increase by 13.6 mb/pd over the projection period, with more than 85% of the increase going to the non-OECD economies of Asia. **China**, alone, is likely to import about 8.4 mb/pd from OPEC in 2030, 69% of which is expected to come from Persian Gulf producers.

World Trends in Energy-Consumption by 'End-Use' sector

The pattern of energy consumption by residential, industrial, commercial and transportation sectors as per EIA, is primarily guided by combination of various factors, such as availability of energy resources and level of economic activity in any region, demographic, social and   political factors.

The OECD nations in total used more energy in 2003 than did the non-OECD nations, in **residential sector,** however, more rapid growth of residential energy consumption is projected for the non-OECD and it is likely

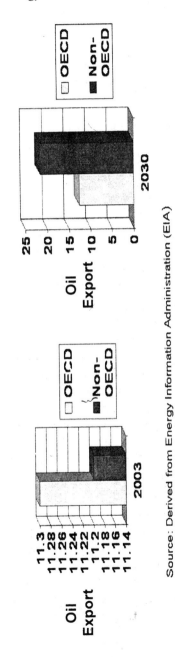

SHIFT IN SHARE OF PERSIAN GULF OIL EXPORT
(MILLION BARRELS PER DAY)

Source: Derived from Energy Information Administration (EIA)

to surpass OECD nations by 2010. Strong economic growth linked with large and growing population in the non-OECD countries (80 percent of the world's population) results in improved standards of living and higher demand for household appliances. Even relatively small changes in per capita consumption will have a profound impact on total residential energy use in the non-OECD economies, though residential energy use per capita in 2003 was about 6 times higher in the OECD countries than in the non-OECD countries.

Commercial sector energy consumption is on rise in both OECD and Non-OECD countries but the share of OECD countries remains high in the projection period (2003- 2030). The largest increases in commercial electricity demand are projected for the nations with rapidly growing economies, particularly China and India, as their burgeoning economies foster increases in demand for services.

Industrial Sector is the largest of the end-use sectors, consuming 50% of delivered energy worldwide in 2003, and industrial energy use is projected to grow more rapidly than energy use in the other end-use sectors. Worldwide, the energy-consumption in the industrial sector is estimated to increase by an average of 2.4% per year between 2003 and 2030, as compared with 1.0% average annual growth in the world's population. Industrial energy consumptions are estimated to increase in all the countries and regions, however, its estimated growth rate in the OECD region (a 1.2% average per year) is slower than for the non-OECD region (a 3.2% average per year).

The OECD economies generally have more energy-efficient industrial operations and a mix of industrial output that is more heavily weighted toward non-energy-intensive sectors than do the non-OECD countries. In the United States, the manufacturing share of total economic output has declined steadily over the past two decades, while the output share for service industries (included in the commercial sector) has increased.

Additionally, within the U.S. manufacturing sector, a smaller share of output has been produced by the heavy, energy-intensive industries (such as steelmaking). Similar developments are expected for the other OECD economies, as increasing international trade fosters a shift toward a less energy-intensive mix of industrial activity. Many of Japan's heavy industries are reducing their output as demand for energy intensive materials increasingly is met by imports from China and other Asian countries.

Energy demand in the **transportation-sector** is estimated to grow substantially (OECD @ 0.9% and non-OECD countries @ 2.3% every year), but the total share of OECD is expected to continue to remain higher than the non-OECD countries. However, the gap between consumption in the non-OECD and OECD economies narrows down substantially over the projection period. The major hurdle facing China's and India's projected increases in the transportation energy demand is the need for increased infrastructure development.

CHINA'S ENERGY CONSUMPTION TREND (SECTOR WISE)

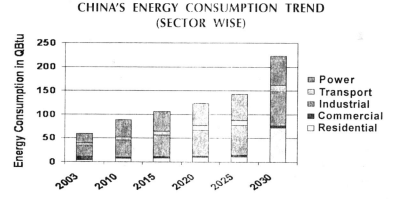

Energy and Economic Growth in the context of World Trends in Energy Consumption

The world economic growth is expected to increase at an average annual rate of 3.8% (period 2003-2030) with strong growth for worldwide energy demand in spite of considerable increase in oil prices. Countries outside the Organization for Economic Cooperation and Development (non-OECD countries) account for three-fourths of the increase in world energy use and non-OECD energy use surpasses OECD energy demand by 34% during 2030. Much of the growth in energy demand among the non-OECD economies occurs in non-OECD Asia, which includes China and India where demand in the region nearly triples over the projection period.

In contrast, for the OECD—with its more mature energy-consuming nations—energy use grows at a much slower average rate of 1.0 per cent per year over the same period. Energy demand growth averages 3.7% per year for non-OECD Asia (which includes China and India), 2.8% per year for Central and South America, 2.6% per year for Africa, 2.4% per year for the Middle East, and 1.8% per year for non-OECD Europe and Eurasia. The increases result from projections of strong regional economic growth.

For all the non-OECD regions combined, economic activity—as measured by gross domestic product (GDP) in purchasing power parity terms—expands by 5.0% per year on average, as compared with an average of 2.6% per year for the OECD economies. The OECD nations, for the most part, are more mature energy consumers with well-established infrastructures, and their economies generally are moving away from energy-intensive industries toward services. GDP in China and India combined was about 91% the size of U.S in 2003, their combined GDP on a purchasing power parity basis is projected to be almost double that of the United States in 2030.

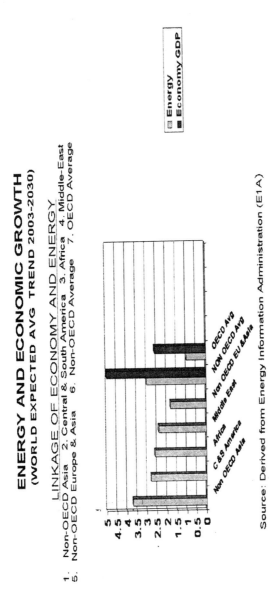

ENERGY AND ECONOMIC GROWTH
(WORLD EXPECTED AVG TREND 2003-2030)

LINKAGE OF ECONOMY AND ENERGY

1. Non-OECD Asia   2. Central & South America   3. Africa   4. Middle-East
5. Non-OECD Europe & Asia   6. Non-OECD Average   7. OECD Average

Energy
Economy GDP

Source: Derived from Energy Information Administration (EIA)

Section – IV

Development-Management of Energy Resources in China

CHAPTER 8

Management of Coal in China

China is the largest producer and consumer of coal in the world. Coal makes up 69% of China's total primary-energy consumption. China holds an estimated 126.2 billion short-tons (bst) of recoverable coal-reserves, the 3rd largest in the world behind the United States and the Russia. Many of China's large coal-reserves have yet to be developed. Northern-China contains most of easily accessible coal and almost all of its large state-owned mines. Coal from southern-mines tends to be higher in 'Sulphur' and 'Ash', and therefore unsuitable for many applications. China's coal-consumption in 2003 was 1.53 bst or 28% of the world total. In 2004, China consumed 2.1 bst of coal, representing more than 33% of the world total and a 46% increase since 2002. Coal consumption has been on the rise in China over the last five years, reversing the decline seen from 1997 to 2000.

China's coal-industry traditionally consists of large state-owned, local state-owned, and thousands of town/village based coal-mines where inefficient management, insufficient investment, outdated-equipments, and poor safety-environment prevent full-utilization of coal-resources. The

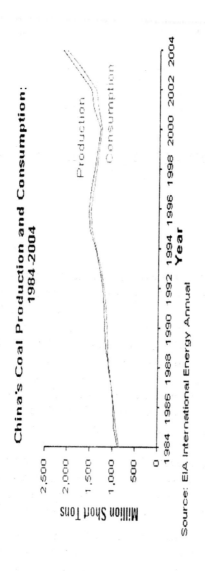

China's Coal Production and Consumption: 1984-2004

Source: EIA International Energy Annual

goal of consolidating the coal-industry is to increase total coal-output, attract greater investment and new coal technologies, and improve the safety and environment of coal-mines.

Besides, China's coal-consumption for electricity-generation (about 39% of total) tripled between 1971 and 1988, from 67 million-tonnes (MT) to 228 MT, to 488 MT in 1996 and 597 MT in 2003 which would increase much higher by 2030 which, in the present condition, suffers from slow uneconomic transport-system, due to geographical reasons. While majority of coal-mines are concentrated in north-China, the greatest demand for coal originates in the cities and provinces along the south-eastern coast making internal-shipment/rail-transport slow, difficult and costly. Although infrastructure (rail, roads and ports) for coal-transport improved significantly in the past ten years, it still remains inadequate to meet current demand, leaving aside future demand. However, the completion of the Shuo-huang railway (the second dedicated coal-line) and the Huanghua coal-terminal in 2003, will provide upto 60 MT/per-year of new coal-transport-capacity. Coal being the main-fuel for China in the foreseeable future, it is expected that high coal-usage will continue but with expected much increased efforts/investments to improve coal-quality.

According to one industry report (2005), China had 28,000 coal-mines, of which 2,000 were state-owned. Independent analysts estimate that China has closed down between 20,000 and 50,000 small coal-mines over the past several years. Operation of state-owned mines shifted in 1998 from the central government's Ministry of Coal to the provincial, regional or municipal governments. Poor environmental health and safety performance of these mines and over-supply in the domestic market prompted the central government to earmark 23,000 of these mines for closure in 1999.

In Feb. 2006, the NDRC (National Development and Reform Commission) developed a plan to restructure China's coal-sector to consolidate coal-industry into 6/7 giant conglomerates in China's main coal-producing provinces by 2015. Under the NDRC's directives, the Chinese government plans to aggregate the coal-industry into large state-owned holding companies and raise capital through international stock offerings, much like the creation of CNPC and Sinopec in oil sector, out of state assets and to attract foreign investments, new/high-efficiency technologies, technology of environmental-benefits and coal-liquefaction, coal-bed methane production, and slurry pipeline transportation projects.

Such firms are seeking to pursue foreign capital through international stock-offerings, the China-National-Coal-Import-Export-Corp., is the primary Chinese agency for foreign investors in the coal-sector. Areas of interest already shown by foreign investors include: technology of environmental benefits, coal-liquefaction, coal bed methane production, and slurry pipeline transportation projects.

CHAPTER 9

Management of Oil in China

China is the world's 2nd largest consumer of oil after the United States, and the 3rd largest net importer of oil after the U.S. and Japan, an important factor in world oil-markets. Together with its strong economic growth, China's demand for energy is surging rapidly.

China also produces a significant amount of oil and contains sizeable proven oil-reserves. According to *Oil and Gas Journal (OGJ)*, China had 18.3 billion barrels of proven oil reserves as of Jan. 2006. EIA estimates that China will produce 3.8 Million-barrels/per day (Mmbbl/d) of oil in 2006, slightly higher than the previous year. Of this, 96% is expected to be crude-oil. EIA estimated that China has consumed 7.4 Mmbbl/d of oil in 2006, representing nearly half a million barrels per day increase from 2005. For 2006, EIA data forecasts that China's oil-consumption will increase by 0.5 Mmbbl/d and its increase in oil demand will represent 38% of the world total increase in demand.

China's largest oil-producing fields are mature. Roughly 85% of Chinese oil production capacity is located onshore.

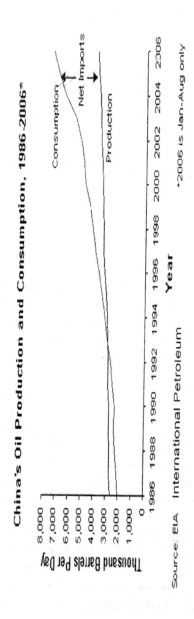

China's Oil Production and Consumption, 1986-2006*

Source: EIA International Petroleum

*2006 is Jan-Aug only

With increased production from the mature oil-fields China's oil-exploration activities now focus on developing new/ untapped-reserves in its western interior provinces and offshore-fields. China's largest oil-producing field, CNPC's Daqing field in north-eastern China, accounts for more than 900,000 bbl/d, or 1/4th of China's total crude-oil production. Daqing is a mature oil-field, and production levels have been reduced since 2004 while CNPC works to extend the life of the field.[1] New oil discoveries in the Shengli field in north-eastern China (operated by Sinopec) supplies more than 500,000 bbl/d. CNOOC also produces more than 500,000 bbl/d from its offshore oil fields in the Bohai Bay and South-China Sea.

Chinese Major Oil Fields by Production (January 2006)

China National Petroleum Corp. (CNPC)/PetroChina		China Petroleum and Chemical Corp. (Sinopec)		China National Offshore Oil Corp. (CNOOC)
Field	Production (bbl/d)	Field	Production (bbl/d)	Total Offshore
Daging	9,29,268	Shengli	5,35,531	5,19,108
Liaohe	2,56,991	Sinopec Star	78,567	
Xinijang	2,22,524	Zhongyuan	67,092	
Changging	1,62,422			

Source: *Oil and Gas Journal, 2006*

China's petroleum industry underwent major changes over the last decade. In 1998, the Chinese government reorganized its state-owned oil and gas assets into two vertically integrated companies: the 'China National Petroleum Corporation' (CNPC) and the 'China Petroleum and Chemical Corporation' (Sinopec), each operating through a range of local subsidiary companies. CNPC and Sinopec operate virtually all of China's oil refineries and the domestic

---

1. Country Analysis Brief (www.eia.doe.gov)

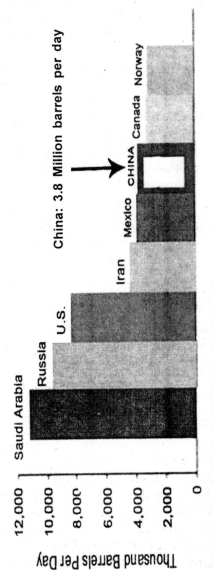

Top World Oil Producers, 2005

China: 3.8 Million barrels per day

Source: EIA International Petroleum Monthly

pipeline distribution network. The other major state-sector company is the 'China National Offshore Oil Corporation' (CNOOC), which handles offshore exploration and crude-oil production. CNPC, Sinopec, and CNOOC were formed with Initial-Public-Offerings (IPOs) of stock between 2000 and 2002.[2] Many foreign companies have been contracted to undertake oil-exploration and production activities in China. According to Chinese law, China's national oil-companies are entitled to take a majority (51%) stake in any commercial discovery, although they can choose to take a minority stake if they wish.

The intention behind the corporate restructuring and IPOs was to make these state-owned firms work more like the integrated International-Oil-Companies (IOCs) elsewhere. In 2000, both CNPC and Sinopec offered its IPO of a minority 15% stake in its operations on both the Hong Kong and New York stock-exchanges.[3] In Feb. 2001, CNOOC held its IPO of a 27.5% stake in its operations. It is worth noting that although CNPC, Sinopec, and CNOOC were formed with Initial-Public-Offerings (IPOs) of stock yet in all of these stock-offerings, only minority stakes were sold and the IPOs did not offer foreign companies a major voice in corporate-governance enabling the Chinese government maintaining a majority stake and control in all the state-owned holding companies.

China maintains domestic price-ceilings on finished petroleum-products which, despite several decisions to increase domestic prices over the last couple of years, have not kept pace with the price-increases in international markets. The Chinese government provides refiners with subsidies to ease the gulf between low domestic-rates and high international-prices. The eventual goal is to eliminate subsidized-prices, but given the dependency of vulnerable segments of the Chinese population on cheap-fuels,

---

2. China Country Analysis Brief (www.eia.doe.gov)
3. China Country Analysis Brief (www.eia.doe.gov)

particularly in agriculture, it will likely take at least several years to accomplish this goal.

Recently, offshore oil-exploration in China has been the greater focus of the Oil-Majors. CNOOC has initiated several Production-Sharing-Contracts (PSCs) with the International Oil Companies for exploration and development in the Bohai Bay region. Conoco-Phillips holds the largest acreage in the area, with total discovered reserves estimated at 732 million barrels. Conoco-Phillips has a 49% stake in the Bozhong and has produced 30,000 bbl/d of crude oil from its Peng Lai field since 2002, which it expects will eventually produce 140,000 bbl/d. Other companies involved in oil-exploration and production activities in the Bohai Bay region are Kerr-McGee, Apache, Chevron, and Royal Dutch Shell. Some independent analysts estimate that the Bohai Bay area holds more than 1.5 billion barrels of recoverable oil reserves.[4] CNOOC holds a 51% stake in the CACT Operators Group, which produces 110,000 bbl/d from five offshore-fields in the South-China Sea. Several other oil exploration and production projects are underway in the South-China Sea and Pearl River Delta area. CNOOC also established (Dec. 2005) a joint-venture with Husky Energy, Devon Energy, and Kerr-McGee for deepwater oil and gas exploration, declaring its major priority, in the South-China Sea. CNOOC is also involved in large-scale oil-exploration activities in the East-China Sea in spite of territorial disputes with its neighbours.

China, expecting its growing future-dependence on oil-imports, has been acquiring interests significantly in exploration and production **abroad**. CNPC has acquired exploration and production interests in 21 countries spanning four continents. CNPC announced (2005) its intentions to invest a further $18 billion in foreign oil and gas assets between 2005 and 2020. In Sudan, CNPC has invested more than $8 billion in the country's oil-sector, including

---

4. China Country Analysis Brief (www.eia.doe.gov)

investments in a 900-mile pipeline to the Red-Sea. CNPC also finalized (Oct. 2005) the purchase of Petro-Kazakhstan, whose assets include 11 oil-fields and licenses to 7 exploration-blocks complemented by the 600-mile Sino-Kazakh oil-pipeline to deliver 200,000 bbl/d of crude-oil to China. CNPC's other overseas-investments (2005) include Encana's oil-gas assets in Ecuador and Petro-Canada's oil-gas assets in Syria. CNPC has acquired stakes in oil fields and production companies in Kazakhstan, Venezuela, Sudan, Iraq, Iran, Peru and Azerbaijan.[5] Sinopec acquired a 97% stake in Udmurtneft which produces 120,000 bbl/d of crude-oil and holds 1 billion barrels of proven reserves in Russia. Sinopec also signed (Oct. 2004) a Memorandum-of-Understanding (MOU) with the Iranian government to acquire a 51% stake in the large Yadavaran oil-field, which could produce 300,000 bbl/d. Sinopec also acquired a 40% stake in Synenco Energy in Canada expecting the project to produce a total of 100,000 bbl/d of synthetic crude-oil by 2010.

CNOOC purchased (2005) Repsol-YPF's oil-fields in Indonesia, making CNOOC the largest operator in the offshore Indonesian oil sector. CNOOC also acquired (Jan. 2006) a 45% stake in an oil and gas field in the Niger-Delta. CNOOC has also reached smaller deals for oil-exploration and development rights in Equatorial Guinea and Kenya, among other countries. Taken together, above activities represent only a sample of China's international partnerships and foreign-acquisitions making their total contribution to Chinese oil-imports (2005) by nearly 300,000 bbl/d, or 8.5% of total oil-imports by China. China's oil imports will rise by an amount nearly equal to Saudi Arabia's total current oil production capacity.[6]

---

5. Impact of China's energy security by Dr Swaran Singh
6. OKSANA ELKHAMRI, Pacific Northwest Center for Global Security (Volume 2 / Issue 3) Spring 2006

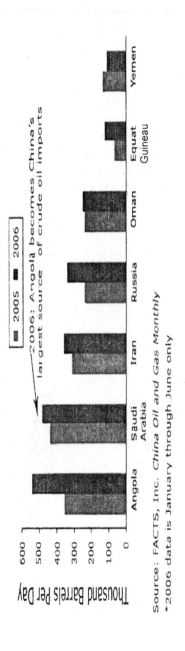

Top Sources of China's Crude Oil Imports, 2005 and 2006*

2006: Angola becomes China's largest source of crude oil imports

Source: FACTS, Inc. *China Oil and Gas Monthly*
*2006 data is January through June only

China also began receiving (May' 2006) crude-oil imports from its first **transnational oil-pipeline** which spans 620 miles, connecting Kazakhstan with Xinjiang Uygur to transport 200,000 bbl/d of crude-oil, with plans to double the capacity by 2010. Half of the imported oil comes from Kazakhstan and half from Russia. Russia's Far-East project, expected to be completed by 2008, may also be a source for China's enhanced crude-oil-imports in future. China's National Development and Reform Commission (NDRC) approved (April 2006) a feasibility-study to construct a new crude-oil-pipeline from Myanmar to China. As Myanmar does not produce significant amounts of crude-oil, the pipeline is envisioned as an alternative transport-route from the Middle East and Africa that would bypass the choke-point of the **Strait-of-Malacca.**

A major issue for the Chinese oil-sector is the **lack of adequate refining-capacity** suitable for heavier Middle-Eastern crude-oil, which makes up a large share of Chinese crude-imports. China's recent attention has been on building **more new refining-facilities** and upgrading existing plants enabling processing of heavier/more-sour grades of crude-oil from Middle-Eastern countries. China has 6.2 Mmbbl/d of crude-oil refining-capacity (Jan. 2006) with Sinopec and CNPC. The expansive sector is undergoing modernization and consolidation, with dozens of small refineries being closed and larger refineries expanding and upgrading their existing facilities with more emphasis on increased capacity-utilisation. According to BP Statistical-Review of World Energy, capacity-utilization of Chinese Refineries increased from 67% (1998) to 94% (2004).

China's Major Oil Refineries

China National Petroleum Corp. (CNPC)/PetroChina		China Petroleum and Chemical Corp. (Sinopec)		West Pacific Petrochemical Corp.	
Refinery	**Capacity (bbl/d)**	Zhenhai	403,000	Dalian	160,000
Dalian	410,000	Ningbo	320,000		
Lanzhou	250,000	Maoming	270,000		

Fushu	200,000	Nanjing	270,000		
Heilongjiang	160,000/ 120,000	Guangzhou	260,000		
Liaoyang	200,000	Shanghai	226,000/ 176,000		
		Zibo	210,000		
Total:	24,15,000		30,95,000		1,60,000
Total China:	62,46,000				

[Source: *OGJ*; FACTS, Inc. *China Oil and Gas Monthly*]

China's national oil-companies are currently planning or building several new refineries and upgrading existing plants. PetroChina increased (July 2006) the capacity of its Dalian refining-center from 210,000 bbl/d to 410,000 bbl/d, making it the largest refinery in China. Sinopec (July 2006) also set up a new 160,000-bbl/d refinery at Hainan. Sinopec also increased (May 2006) the capacity of Guangzhou refinery from 154,000 bbl/d to 260,000 bbl/d.

The NDRC approved (April 2006) a joint-venture-refinery (PetroChina-Kuwait Petroleum Corporation) in Guangzhou with a capacity of 3,00,000 bbl/d. CNPC is also building (Aug. 2005) a 2,00,000-bbl/d capacity refinery in Dushanzi. Sinopec (July 2005) also signed an agreement with Exxon-Mobil and Saudi-Aramco to expand the capacity of its Quongang refinery in Fujian from 80,000 bbl/d to 2,40,000 bbl/d. CNOOC, which has historically focused on offshore-exploration and development, has shiftingly signed (Dec. 2005) an agreement with Royal-Dutch-Shell to construct a joint 2,40,000 bbl/d crude-oil refinery and a 2.3 Mmt/y petrochemical-facility complex in Guangdong province. As China seeks to bring additional refining facilities online to meet growing demand for finished petroleum products, BP forecasts that the country will increase refining capacity by 1.8 Mmbbl/d between 2004 and 2008, a 32% increase in total capacity.

CHAPTER 10

Management of Natural Gas in China

Historically, 'Natural Gas' has not been a major fuel in China, but its share in the country's energy-mix is increasing. *Oil and Gas Journal (OGJ)* estimates (Jan. 2006) that China's domestic proven reserves of natural gas stood at 53.3 trillion cubic-feet (Tcf). Other sources have put reserves much higher. Cedigaz estimates (Jan. 2006) that China held 83 Tcf of proved natural gas reserves. EIA estimated that China consumed 1.3 Tcf of natural gas in 2004, almost doubling the level of natural gas consumption from five years prior.

In 2004, natural gas accounted for only around 3% of total energy-consumption in China which is expected to rise in future and expected to be double by 2010.[1] Until recently, natural gas was used primarily as a feedstock in chemical fertilizer production and an energy source at oil and gas fields. The **natural gas sector in China** is dominated by the three large state-owned oil and gas holding companies:

---

1. China Country Analysis Brief (www.eia.doe.gov)

CNPC, Sinopec, and CNOOC. CNPC, China's largest natural gas producer, operates primarily through its chief subsidiary PetroChina. However, all the three companies operate through numerous local subsidiaries. China's largest reserves of natural gas are located in western and north-central China. Several recent discoveries of natural gas promise a significant increase in China's natural gas production in the coming years.

Sinopec discovered (2006) **three new natural gas-fields** in north-east China holding an estimated 2.1 Tcf of recoverable reserves. Sinopec confirmed (2006) a much larger discovery at the Puguang natural gas-field in the south-western province of Sichuan holding a proven recoverable reserves of 8.9 Tcf.[2] PetroChina discovered (2005) an additional 3.5 Tcf of recoverable natural gas reserves at the existing Daqing oil and gas field in northeast China's Heilongjiang province. CNOOC and Husky-Energy announced (June 2006) a new natural gas discovery with estimated possible reserves of 6 Tcf in the South-China Sea. The largest reserve is the Sulige-field in the Ordos-basin in the Inner Mongolia Autonomous Region with proven recoverable reserves of 18.9 Tcf. Another large natural gas field, the Kela-2 field in the Tarim basin, holds proven reserves of 8.9 Tcf. CNPC (including PetroChina) reported that at the end of 2005, the company held total proven recoverable natural gas reserves of 81.6 Tcf.[3] For **transportation of natural gas** China has a fragmented system of domestic-pipelines and distribution-networks which forced China's natural gas consumption to remain limited to local natural gas producing regions which lay in remote basins in the western part of the country.

China has undertaken efforts to **increase its natural gas transport infrastructure** and improve its distribution-networks connecting to eastern population centers due to

---

2. China Country Analysis Brief (www.eia.doe.gov)
3. China Country Analysis Brief (www.eia.doe.gov)

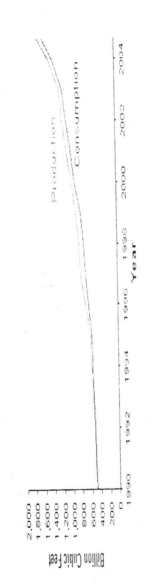

China's Natural Gas Production and Consumption, 1990-2004

Source: 1990-2004: EIA: 2005: Facts. Inc *China Oil and Gas monthly*

growth in its natural gas demand in recent years, complemented by new natural gas discoveries. The NRDC, CNPC, Sinopec and the PetroChina have planned to build a cross-country natural gas pipeline network. In addition, China is also planning to **establish trans-national natural gas pipelines** with several neighbouring countries. China's another international pipeline-project plans to link the Russian natural gas grid in Siberia to China via a pipeline from the Kovykta natural gas fields with a capacity of 2.9 Bcf/d (China would consume 1.9 Bcf/d).

With rising consumption of natural gas in China amid uncertainties surrounding the potential of piped Russian natural gas, **LNG** has increasingly been considered by Chinese companies. CNOOC in a joint venture with BP built China's first LNG import terminal in Guangdong province, which received its first 60,000 ton shipment of LNG in May 2006. The facility has a capacity to handle 3.7 million tons/year (Mmt/y) of LNG, with a plan to double the capacity in the future. CNOOC awarded a 25-year, 3.3 Mmt/y LNG supply agreement to Australia's North-West Shelf consortium to supply the new import terminal. CNOOC is currently **building** another LNG import terminal in Fujian province with a capacity of 3 Mmt/y to receive LNG from BP's Tangguh consortium in Indonesia. CNPC, Sinopec, and CNOOC are all considering a dozen of new LNG facilities in China.

One major hurdle for natural gas projects in China is the lack of a unified regulatory system. Currently, natural gas prices are governed by local regulations. The Chinese government is in the process of drafting a new legal framework for the country's natural gas sector, but the process has been slow, and there are still considerable uncertainties regarding price-regulation and taxation issues dealing with natural gas sales.

CHAPTER 11

Management of Electricity in China

China's electricity-generation continues to be dominated by fossil-fuel sources, particularly **coal**. The Chinese government has made the expansion of natural gas-fired power plants a priority. In 2004, China had total installed electricity generating capacity of 391.4 Gigawatts (GW), 74% of which came from conventional thermal sources. In 2004, China generated 2,080 billion kilowatthours (Bkwh) and consumed 1,927 Bkwh of electricity. Since 2000, both electricity generation and consumption have increased by 60%. According to one industry-study conducted in 2005, over 120 GW of generating capacity is currently under construction in China.[1]

China, before bringing reformation in its power-sector in 2002, faced many problems viz., serious oversupply problem in the 1990s due to demand-reductions from closures of inefficient state-owned industrial-units; forced shut-down

---

1. China Country Analysis Brief (www.eia.doe.gov)

of smaller thermal-power plants; imposition of moratorium on construction of new power plant till 2001; approval to dozens of major new power-projects since 2003; surging demand surpassing completion-schedules of new generating stations; resultant highly increased demand for petroleum products mainly to provide off-grid backup-diesel-generators by the commercial/industrial enterprises; inter-province grid-connection for power-transmission being insufficient and unplanned creating both surplus-capacity vis-à-vis capacity-shortage due to lack of a national power-grid network; all resulting in loss of reliability in the electricity supply-system of the country.

To reform its electricity-sector China established the State-Electricity-Regulatory-Commission (SERC) in 2002 which is responsible for the overall regulation of this sector. The monopoly of 'State-Power-Corporation' (SPC) was completely reorganized by the Chinese government into separate business units for generation, transmission, and services. China's electricity-generation sector, after the reform, is dominated by five different state-owned holding-companies, namely China-Huaneng-Group, China-Datang-Group, China-Huandian, Guodian-Power, and China-Power-Investment. These five holding companies manage more than 80% of China's generating-capacity. Much of the remainder is operated by Independent-Power-Producers (IPPs), in partnership with the privately-listed firms of the state-owned companies. China's electricity transmission and distribution sector is now dominated by two new companies, the Southern-Power-Company and the State-Power-Grid-Company.

The Chinese government aims to merge SPC's 12 regional-grids into 3 large Power-Grid-Networks, namely a northern-grid, a north-western-grid and a southern-grid to be operated by State-Power-Grid-Company and Southern-Power-Company. Chinese government plan to achieve an integrated National-Electricity-Grid by 2020. The deregulation followed by other reforms have opened the electricity sector also to foreign-investment.

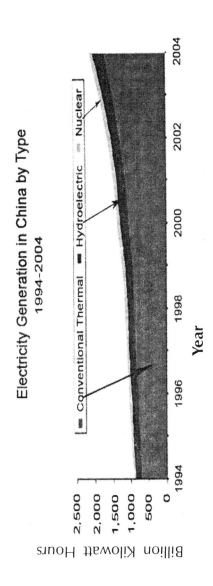

Electricity Generation in China by Type
1994-2004

Conventional Thermal   Hydroelectric   Nuclear

Billion Kilowatt Hours

2,500
2,000
1,500
1,000
500
0

1994   1996   1998   2000   2002   2004

Year

Source: EIA International Energy Annual

In China's power-generation sector the conventional thermal-sources are expected to remain the dominant fuel for electricity-generation in the coming years, with many power-projects under construction or planned that will use coal or natural gas. The Chinese government is also planning to shut-down or modernize many small and inefficient power plants in favour of medium-sized (300 to 600 MW) and large (1000 MW and more) units.

China's 11th Five-Year Plan (2006-2010) calls for the country to increase the share of natural gas and other cleaner-technologies in the country's energy-mix. The first natural gas fired plant in Beijing started operations in July 2006 with a capacity of 150 MW. To achieve this objective further China's Huaneng-Power-International commissioned (July 2006) a new natural gas-fired Power-Plant in Shanghai with a capacity of 1,200 MW, making it China's largest natural gas-fired Power-Plant. Construction is also underway at the 2,000 MW Huizhou Power-Plant near Shenzhen that will use 560,000 metric tons of LNG per year from the new Guangdong terminal. In Guangdong, 6 other 300-MW gas-fired Power Plants are under construction. Some more existing coal and oil-fired Power Plants (1.8 GW) are also being converted to run on natural gas. Several companies are working to open additional larger natural gas-fired generators in Beijing.

China, in 2004, was the world's second-largest producer of hydroelectric-power behind Canada. In the same year, China generated 328 billion kwh of electricity from hydro-electric sources, representing 15.8% of its total generation which is certain to increase in view of many large-scale hydroelectric-projects planned or under-construction in China. The largest power project under construction is the Three-Gorges-Dam, which includes 26 separate 700-MW generators, for a total of 18.2 GW. After completion in 2009 it will be the largest hydroelectric-dam in the world. Though the Three-Gorges-Project already has several units in operation, the complete project is expected to be in operation by 2009. Another large hydropower-project to be set up by Yellow-River-Hydroelectric-Development-Corporation involves construction of 25 generating stations (15.8 GW) over a series of dams to be made on the upper portion of the Yellow-River involving three different provinces namely, Shaanxi, Qinghai, and Gansu.

CHAPTER 12

Management of Nuclear Power in China

China is also actively promoting nuclear power as a clean and efficient source of electricity-generation. China's total installed capacity for nuclear power-generation increased from 2 GW at the beginning of 2002 to 15 GW as of mid-2005. [1] Although it makes up only a small fraction of China's installed generating capacity, many of the major developments are taking place in the Chinese electricity sector recently involving nuclear power. The Chinese government policy emphasizes nuclear power-generation as a source of clean electricity generation and a means of reducing dependence on fossil fuels. China plans a total of 27 GW of additional nuclear generating capacity to be completed by 2020.

As of mid-2006, China has 8 new nuclear power plants under construction, the biggest of which is a 6-GW nuclear-complex at Yangjiang in Guangdong province which is set to

---

1. China Country Analysis Brief (www.eia.doe.gov)

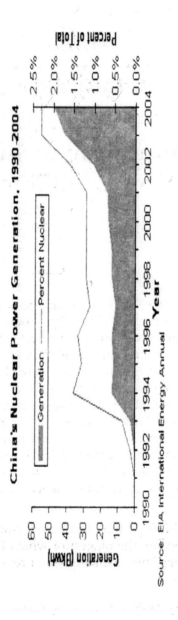

China's Nuclear Power Generation, 1990-2004

Source: EIA, International Energy Annual

begin commercial operation by 2010. The 1st generation-unit (1-GW) of the Lingao nuclear power plant began operation in May 2002 followed by the 2nd unit (1-GW) in Jan. 2003. At the Qinshan nuclear power plant the 1st generation-unit (600-MW) began operation in Feb. 2002, the 2nd unit (600-MW) in Dec. 2002. At Yangjiang a new nuclear-complex (6-GW), and a second generating facility at Daya-Bay have also been planned.[2]

EIA and independent sources forecast that China will add upto 27 GW of new nuclear-energy capacity by 2020, but even with this expansion, nuclear power will only represent less than 5% of its total installed electricity generating capacity.[3] It may be worth observing that while China's natural gas use will grow, rising electricity-demand will also force continued growth in consumption of **coal** as well as expansion in **nuclear** and **hydro-electricity** production.

Consequently, China is also expected to account for one-quarter of the world's CO_2 emissions over that period. Although China is presently a net coal-exporter, it may become a net-importer of coal as early as 2015. China's electricity needs also are motivating its future nuclear power development. China has the largest planned increase in nuclear power over the next two decades, with plans to add from 24 to 32 numbers of nuclear-plants by 2020—a quadrupling of current capacity.

---

2. China Country Analysis Brief (www.eia.doe.gov)
3. China Country Analysis Brief (www.eia.doe.gov)

Section – V

China's Strategic Energy Management

CHAPTER 13

China's Strategic Energy Management

The trends of increase in the Primary-Energy Production of China (and India) for the period from 1980 to 2004 is shown below. It may be observed that while China's production as %age of world production increased from 6.30% (1980) to 12.63% (2004) the same for India marginally increased from 1.08% (1980) to 2.49% (2004) only.

Primary Energy Production of China and India, 1980-2004:
[Quadrillion (10^{15}) Btu]

Year	China	World Total	China (as % of World Total)	India	India (as % of World Total)
1980	18.122	287.559	6.30	3.101	1.08
1985	24.303	307.160	7.91	5.266	1.71
1990	29.385	349.663	8.40	6.821	1.95
1995	35.463	364.226	9.74	9.484	2.60
2000	36.680	397.129	9.24	9.831	2.48
2003	48.647	421.714	11.54	10.646	2.52
2004	55.948	443.100	12.63	11.055	2.49

Source: Derived from Energy Information Administration (EIA)

China, the second-largest energy consumer in the world after the United States, has traditionally been largely self-sufficient in energy-supplies, a legacy from the autocratic Maoist-era of the 1950s and 1960s. Large domestic-supplies of coal dominated its domestic energy-use, and coal continues to account for two-thirds of China's overall consumption. But China's highly accelerated economic growth since early 1980s together with Government's determination to sustain that growth amply fuelled its oil-demand, and the government's decision to expand the use of natural gas will boost its future gas consumption.

The whole world is amazed to see the economic growth-rate and expansion in the energy supply network of China. The Delivered Energy-Consumption and Projections (Quadrillion Btu-QBtu) for China, as shown below, by 'End-Use-Sector' for the period 2010-2030 evidences this observation:

Projection of Energy-Consumption for China by End-Use-Sector (2003-2030)

Sector	Act-ual	Projections — CHINA					Average Annual % Change
(Quadrillion Btu)	2003	2010	2015	2020	2025	2030	
Residential Sector	3.8	7.6	8.7	9.6	10.8	12.3	4.5%
Commercial Sector	1.4	2.2	2.5	2.8	3.2	3.6	3.5%
Industrial Sector	22.9	36.3	45.2	54.1	62.7	72.6	4.4%
Transportation Sector	4.4	6.6	7.8	9.2	10.9	12.9	4.1%

Source: Derived from Energy Information Administration (EIA)

The EIA's projections of consumption-requirements of energy by China (Appendix-B1)) for the period 2010 to 2030, based on the consumption-pattern 'End-Use-Sectors-wise' of 2003, revealed that China's energy requirements would increase by 3.24 times form **3.8 to 12.3 QBtu** (Industrial Sector); by 2.57 times from **1.4 to 3.6 QBtu** (for Commercial-

Sector); by 3.17 times from **22.9 to 72.6 QBtu** (Industrial Sector); and 2.93 times from **4.4 to 12.9 QBtu** (Transportation-Sector). In the residential and commercial sectors about 50% of this increase would be for 'electricity'; in Industrial Sector 50% of the increase would be for 'coal' while in Transportation-Sector almost the entire increase would be for 'Oil' (Appendix-B1).

The Delivered Energy Consumption and Projections (Quadrillion Btu-QBtu) for China by 'Fuel-Type' for the period 2010–2030 is shown below:

Projection of Energy-Consumption for China by Fuel-Type (2003-2030)

Fuel-Type	Actual		Projections For CHINA				Average Annual % Change:
(Q Btu)	**2003**	**2010**	**2015**	**2020**	**2025**	**2030**	**2003-2030**
Oil	10.8	15.7	19.1	22.8	26.5	30.7	3.9%
Natural Gas	1.2	3.1	4.0	4.9	6.0	7.1	6.8%
Coal	13.2	22.2	26.6	30.5	34.5	39.3	4.1%
Electricity	5.7	9.5	12.0	14.5	17.3	20.4	4.8%
Heat/ Renewables	1.6	2.0	2.5	3.0	3.4	3.9	3.2%
Total Delivered Energy	**32.5**	**52.6**	**64.1**	**75.7**	**87.6**	**101.4**	**4.3%**
Electricity- Related Losses	13.0	24.4	27.7	30.9	34.1	37.7	4.0%
TOTAL:	**45.5**	**77.0**	**91.8**	**106.6**	**121.7**	**139.1**	**4.2%**
%age of Electricity Related Losses	28.57%	31.69%	30.17%	28.99%	28.02%	27.10%	

The EIA's consumption-projections of energy by China (Appendix-B1) for the period **2010** to **2030**, based on the consumption-pattern 'Fuel-Type' of 2003, revealed that China's energy-requirements, excluding losses, would increase by 2.84 times form **10.8 to 30.7 QBtu** (Oil); by 5.92 times from **1.2 to 7.1 QBtu** (Natural Gas); by 2.98 times from **13.2 to 39.3 QBtu** (Coal); and 3.58 times from **5.7 to 20.4 QBtu** (Electricity). In the total increase in all delivered-energy 38.78% share would be for 'Coal'; 30.28% share would be for 'Oil'; and 20.12% share would be for 'Electricity'. Due to electricity-related losses (**28.57%** in 2003) the production levels would have to be increased accordingly.

China, having well considered its rising demands particularly for oil and gas adopted many nationalist, diplomatic-steps and shrewd-strategies viz., increasing import-dependence, resorting to selective exports, a going-out business-policy to acquire foreign supply-nodes, and inviting foreign-firms to explore and enhance domestic production, as discussed below.

China has been Asia's largest oil producer since the mid-1960s, in recent years producing well over 3 MMBD. Most production has been onshore, dominated by several large north-eastern fields, mainly at Daqing, Liaohe, and Shengli. Production rose strongly from the late 1960s to the early 1980s with the development of these fields, and by the mid-1980s, China was a net oil-exporter, mainly to Japan.

However, oil-demand accelerated during the 1980s and early 1990s while oil production lagged, as the large traditional fields matured and gradually went into decline. Demand doubled between 1984 and 1995 from 1.7 to 3.4 MMBD and has continued to grow strongly since, rising to nearly 6 MMBD by early 2004. China became a net importer in 1993, and by 2003 it surpassed Japan to become the world's second-largest oil consumer behind the United States and the fifth-largest importer. China now imports roughly one-third of its oil. China's leadership has responded to this historic shift with both vigorous domestic-reforms and aggressive global-energy security-policies. Efforts are under way to maintain oil production in the traditional north-eastern fields while boosting production in western China, where prospects for growing production are better—the so-called "stabilize the East, develop the West" policy.

The IEA 2006 forecasts that China's oil-imports will rise five-fold by 2030, from slightly under 2 MMBD in 2002 to 10 MMBD, when imports will account for 80% of China's total oil needs. The DOE's Energy Information Administration; the Asia-Pacific Energy Research Centre (an arm of the Asia-Pacific Economic Cooperation (APEC) forum); and the East-West Center Energy Program have also come to very similar conclusions. China's leadership now faces the long term realization that oil import dependence is unavoidable. Moreover, as in the rest of Asia, China will become heavily dependent on the Persian Gulf for future supplies, and its oil will increasingly have to transit a series of vulnerable maritime choke points. The East-West Center forecasts that by 2015, 70% of China's oil imports will come from the Middle East. Other significant shares of China's oil imports will come from Russia by pipeline and rail, from Central Asia by pipeline, and from Africa.

In China's 10th Five-Year Plan (2000-2005) building a national **Strategic-Petroleum-Reserve** (SPR) was focused. The work in the first of these facilities, located in Zhenhai, is completed recently with a capacity to store 32 million barrels (Mmbbl) of oil. The NDRC has selected three other sites to have Strategic-Oil-Reserves: Dalian (20 Mmbbl), Huangdao (25 Mmbbl), and Daishan (25 Mmbbl). There have been contradictory news-reports regarding the overall capacity of the total SPR network, the anticipated storage-tanks, filling-rate, and numerous other project-details. Government policies aimed at **substantially increasing the use of natural gas**, accentuated China's import-dependence and long term energy security concerns. China presently uses very little natural gas, accounting for only 3% of overall domestic energy consumption. However, the government has embarked on an aggressive policy to increase gas use to help replace coal for energy generation, diversify overall energy use, and provide cleaner-burning fuel for environmental needs. Current plans call for gas to make up 8% of total energy demand by 2010. In order to boost gas use, the government is accelerating domestic natural gas exploration and development and expanding the national pipeline system to transport more gas from fields in north, central, and western China to the major cities around the east coast. A major 2,500-mile west-east pipeline is being built to move natural gas from the sparsely populated Xinjiang Uyghur Autonomous Region to Shanghai. The government is also working to develop gas markets by creating more effective regulatory structures and increasing flexibility in the gas pricing system.

Over the long-run, although natural gas is an important element of China's overall energy and environmental needs, it will also add to energy security concerns. China does have significant domestic gas reserves and recent exploration has been quite successful, but beyond 2010 demand is likely to outrun domestic production, and a growing share of gas needs will have to be met through imports. The DOE (USA) forecasted that imports will account for 40% of China's gas needs by 2025.[1] For China, imported gas-supplies will be needed both in the form of LNG and via long-distance pipeline. Significant LNG supplies will be available in the Pacific region from Australia, Indonesia, Malaysia, Brunei, and East Timor, but China will also need to have a significant portion of LNG needs supplied from Russia's Sakhalin Island projects, as well as a high volume from the Persian Gulf from huge projects in Qatar, Iran, Oman, and probably Yemen. China is also likely to import gas via pipeline from Russia's East Siberian Irkutsk region, which appears to have large gas reserves and where a large regional gas pipeline scheme is being planned. Consequently, a significant portion of LNG will have to be transported largely from the same volatile regions as oil imports, namely the Persian Gulf and Russia.

China's energy sector is developing in spite of constraints and limiting-factors

Some of the main constraints and limiting-factors checking a faster and expected growth of China's energy sector, need a discussion here to show that if China's strength of will removes or even minimises the effects of these limiting factors, the growth in its energy sector will be higher than before.

---

1. EIA International Energy Outlook 2006 page 44

(i) Geographical-constraints in energy-distribution is a limiting factor in China

China suffers from a geographical mismatch between its coal-producing and coal-consuming regions. In China energy resources, production-centres and distribution-centres are located widely dispersed from region to region, with nearly 67% of coal-reserves situated in north/north-western China, while oil/gas-reserves are concentrated principally in the north-east/east/far-west and in off-shore regions. Northern-China is the most energy-rich region, followed by the south-west (due to hydro) and the north-west. Chinese coal-industry's major problem remains in the main coal-producing-regions, in the centre-north and north-east of the country, are at a considerable distance from some of the principle coal-consuming-provinces in the east and south-east of the country. Net coal-imports, from other provinces, are highest in the coastal provinces such as Jiangsu (65 million tonnes), Zhejiang (45 million tonnes), Guangdong (42 million tonnes) and Shanghai (41 million tonnes), all of which, apart from Jiangsu, produce relatively small amounts of coal themselves (less than 10 million tonnes).

By contrast, the net coal-exporting provinces such as Shanxi, Inner Mongolia, Henan and Heilongjiang, (all major coal-consumers) are at significant distances from the coast. Each year about 620 million tonnes of coal are transported by rail over an average distance of 580 kms. China's 9th Five-Year Plan (1996-2000) targeted the development of "coal-by-wire", the construction of thermal-power plants near mine-mouths with the electricity distributed to the main consumer demand-centres on the coast by high-voltage, long-distance transmission-lines that would transmit power to the high demand centres along the coast. However, given the very serious water-shortage in the whole of northern-China, which affects region's economic and social-development, this strategy will perhaps need a re-consideration. Whether, further establishment of very-large thermal-power plants in these very dry regions, can be justified on a broader economic and social basis, remains an issue.

With coal accounting for a very large %age of freight, the inadequate transportation-network to meet the level of demand has had major implications for China's coal-industry Significant stockpiles that have been built up at the mines, have then been forced to curtailing of production. Indeed, in the past it was often the lack of rail-transport capacity, rather than lack of demand for coal, which acted as a break on production and encouraged a number of coastal power-stations to turn to the international market for supplies. Some estimates have put the cost of these bottlenecks at as much as US$ 100 billion per year in opportunity costs due to the fact that materials are unable to reach manufacturing facilities.[2]

China's strategy for energy-development was based on three main geography-based approaches: coal be the main energy-source in north-east regions; nuclear power be the main focus of energy-development in western-regions; and hydro-power will provide most energy-supplies to southern-regions. Thus, the geographical constraints in China will remain a limiting factor, in the optimization of distribution of coal and supply of power.

(ii) Problem of capacity-distribution and energy-mixing in power-sector

Several units of 300/600 MW are now being constructed, 71.8% of the installed-thermal-capacity is coal-fired and less than 300 MW in size. Small-size plants, combined with inconsistent fuel-quality and low-load-factors due to low plant availabilities or lack of fuel, mean that the average thermal-efficiencies may range from 27% to 29%, compared to around 38% in OECD countries. With the smaller plants consuming 20-40% more fuel than larger plants, it is estimated

---

2. International Private Power Quarterly, Fourth-Quarter 1998

that some 300 million tonnes of coal could be saved by raising the efficiency of boilers and other coal fired plant by 30-35%.[3]

China too suffers from power shortages and have led to nation-wide boom in power plant construction; however due to improper centralized control may lead to surplus power in the grid. **GAIZHI**, the Chinese term meaning "transforming the system " also applied to the Chinese electric power sector by way of unbundling the electricity companies of single entities into three separate elements viz. Genco, Disco and Transco responsible for generation, distribution and transmission of electricity. These were implemented during April 2002 to break monopoly, introduce competition, improve efficiency, reduce cost/reasonable pricing mechanism, optimize resources allocation and formally to build up a healthy power market system. The Chinese electricity sector is experiencing difficulties in implementing these reforms, basically to remove the hurdle of supply demand imbalance.[4]

(iii) Inadequate transport-network and infrastructure

The inability of the transport-system to meet demand has been the major-constraint in the supply of coal within China. Inadequate rail-capacity to support the level of coal production leads to accumulation of coal-stockpiles at mines. Railways are a major part of China's transportation-system and coal is a major commodity of the rail system. Administration of the rail system has shifted from the central ministry and is handled by 12 regional administrators. The length of railway track grew from 21,800 kilometres to 56,678 kilometres between 1949 and 1996, with electrified-track covering 10,082 kilometres of this distance. There were plans to extend the railway system to 70,000 kilometres by the year 2000. Every province including Tibet is being linked to the rail system. Of the railway line added since 1949, 75% has been built to the west of the north-south Beijing-

3. Report of Coal Industry Advisory Board CIAB, IEO 2006, page 25
4. China's Energy Security by Zha Dojang, Survival, Vol 48 No 1 Spring 2006

Guangzhou artery for defence-reasons[5]. The system which serves the industries and mines in the eastern-half of the country is severely overburdened.

Similarly, the road-transportation carried about 20% of all freight in 1995, with most activity being concentrated in the coastal-areas. The Chinese Government recognized the limitation of the existing-infrastructure and has given priority to increasing the capacity and efficiency of the nation's transportation-system. Investment in the transport-sector has increased to 2.6% of GDP since 1991.[6]

(iv) Generating-capacity and electricity-output are unevenly distributed between various networks and regions due to inadequate transmission-grids

China has 15 semi-autonomous power-grids, with a grid-connected capacity of nearly 224 GW. Although they are inter-connected, there is little inter-change of power as there are only a few interconnection-points. Investment in power-transmission as %age of total-investment in thermal-power, hydraulic-power and power-transmission (excluding nuclear and others) dropped from 24% in 1980 to 17% in 1993. The rapid increase in generating-capacity has resulted in high failure rates for the existing-network and in some cases an under-utilisation of the existing generating-capacity. For example, power-stations in the Shentou area (Shanxi Province), which have a total-capacity of 2,300 MW, can only transmit 1,500 MW to end-users. **The State-Power-Corporation planned to invest about US$ 14.5 billion for upgrading the transmission-networks in 280 cities including proper formation of National Power Grid by 2020.** The generating-capacity and electricity-output are unevenly distributed between the various networks and regions, with the north and east providing the most capacity and output. Indeed, one of the objectives of the **18,200 GW** three Gorges hydro-electric-project, scheduled to enter service by 2010, is to

5. Coal in the Energy Supply of China CIAB page 43
6. Coal in the Energy Supply of China CIAB page 42

provide a national-grid-network.[7]

China, **in addition to** vigorously working on primary-energy/marketed-energy, also has been seriously endeavouring to increase its domestic production **in the other areas:** solar energy, geothermal-energy, wind energy, tidal-energy and wave-energy, as discussed below.

Solar Energy – It is estimated that two-thirds of the country receives solar radiation energy in excess of 4.6 kWh/ m^2/day; the western provinces are especially well endowed. By 2002, 7 million Chinese households situated in isolated areas did not have access to electricity as there was no grid-connection in these areas. China is working with the World Bank/Global Environment Facility (GEF), rectifying this situation to install 10 MW of PV in Solar-Home-Systems (SHS). To provide power to isolated areas, China is instituting, a massive and globally an ambitious electrification programme, based on renewable energy technologies and valued at more than 1.8 billion RMB. China is also implementing a massive "Township-Electrification-Programme, a part of China's National-Strategic-Programme' aiming in the first-phase installing power-systems in 1,061 townships (covering about 1 million people). Majority of its solar-systems are PV/ PV-diesel/ PV-wind hybrid; the second phase of the Programme (2005–2010) plans to electrify a further 20,000 villages. Private enterprises (Shell and Sun Oasis collaboration) have also been involved in bringing power to the villages. After completion of this programme, it is believed that China will have the greatest number and density of installed hybrid village power systems in the world.

It is reported that the country is the world's largest manufacturer of Domestic Hot Water (DHW) systems and also the largest user. Private survey indicates that solar water heaters installed in China cover an area of about 26 million m^2. China's 'State Economic and Trade Commission' plans for

---

7. Coal in the Energy Supply of China CIAB page 71

renewable energy to supply 2% of total energy supply by 2015, incorporating an average annual 17% growth for solar thermal systems

Geothermal Energy – China, following its fast economic growth and increasing environmental concerns, increased utilization of geothermal-energy by 12% per annum during 1990s. Studies identified more than 3,200 geothermal features in China, of which some 50 fields have been investigated and explored. High-temperature resources are mainly concentrated in southern Tibet and western parts of Yunnan and Sichuan Provinces, whereas low-medium temperature resources are widespread over the vast coastal area of the south-east, the North China Basin, Songliao Basin, Jianghan Basin, Weihe Basin, etc. The primary development has been in the growth of geothermal energy used directly. By 1998 there were more than 1,600 sites being used for installation centres for fish-farming, irrigation, earthquake-monitoring, however, the main emphasis has been on the expansion of installations for space-heating, sanatoria and tourism.

The development of geothermal power-generation has been, by comparison, relatively slow, owing to the large hydro-electric resources in those provinces with high-temperature geothermal-resources (Tibet and Yunnan). The largest power-complex is located at Yangbajing (Tibet). China's aggregate capacity is approximately 30 MWe, generating 100 GWh annually.

Wind Energy – In China, wind-power has been used for water-pumping for many hundreds years. By 1960s the traditional multi-bladed mechanical-windmills were overtaken by the advent of low-cost diesel engines. China again turned to wind-power to power its enormous electricity-requirement and installed (10th Five-Year Plan: 2001–2005) wind-turbines on a massive scale (1,192 MW) increasing use of renewable energy resources to account for 5% of country's total-output. The World Bank estimated that a total of 18,000 MW new capacities (small hydro, wind, biomass, solar and geothermal) would be necessary, following

China's rapid economic growth, over a period of 10 years to maintain the level of 5%. It has been estimated that China's potential could be as high as 160, 000 MW as its southern and eastern coastal areas being well blessed with wind energy. In addition to grid-connected or stand-alone wind turbines, China's Township-Electrification-Programme is also installing hybrid PV-Wind systems in an effort to electrify the large areas of the country without access to power.

Tidal Energy – The south-eastern coastal areas of Zhejiang, Fujian and Guangdong Provinces are considered to have substantial potential for tidal-energy. China's utilization of tidal-energy with modern technologies began in 1956 for pumping irrigation-water, thereafter for power generation. In 1958, 40 small tidal-plants (12 KW) were built for generating electricity. By 1980 these were supplemented by much larger stations (of which the 3.2 MW (Jiangxia) and the 1.3 MW (Xingfuyang) schemes were the largest. Since 1970s emphasis has been placed on optimizing the operations of existing plants to improve their performance. Additionally, a feasibility-study for a 10MW intermediate-level experimental tidal-power-station has been undertaken.

Wave Energy – Since 1980s, China's research on wave-energy concentrated mainly on fixed and floating/oscillating water-column-devices/pendulum-devices. By 1995, China's Guangzhou Institute of Energy Conversion (GIEC) successfully developed a symmetrical turbine wave-power generation-device (60 KW). Since then over 650 units have been deployed in the past 10 years, mainly along the Chinese coast. There are many projects currently supported by the State Science and Technology Committee aimed to develop onshore wave-power stations along the Chinese coast.

China's energy focused on renewable sources in 11th Five-Year Plan

China's top economic planning body, the National Development and Reform Commission (NDRC), announced a plan to raise consumer electricity rates by the equivalent of 2.5 US cents per kilowatt-hour. A tiny fraction of the additional charge, or 0.1 cent per kilowatt-hour, will be used to develop renewable energy, a senior be used to cover the portion of the costs of renewable-energy development that are higher than the average for conventional energies. During the gathering of the State Energy Leading Group, the highest authority in China on energy issues, Premier Wen Jiabao stressed that renewable energy is strategically important. He urged all government departments concerned to take effective measures to accelerate the development of renewable energies, so as to "lift the share of quality, clean energies in the total energy-mix". According to statistics, US$38 billion was invested in renewable-energy development worldwide in 2005. China topped the list with a commitment of $6 billion, which did not include its spending on large hydro projects. According to the Medium and Long-Term Programme for Renewable Energy Development, prepared by NDRC, renewable energies are expected to account for 16% of the country's total energy-mix by 2020. The Renewable Energy Law will deal with basic and strategic energy development issues in China. It will rely on economic leverage to regulate the energy sector, making sure that extravagant users of energy pay a higher price, and encourage the prospecting and extraction of energy reserves and the development of renewable and new energies. The so-called "green GDP" factors now have a considerable bearing on the government's assessment of an official's performance. China's long term energy conservation and renewable energy development blueprint will generate an investment worth hundreds of billions of yuan within next few years.

China, the world's second-largest energy consumer after the United States, plans to reduce its energy costs per unit GDP growth by 2010 from the current level, aimed at an energy-saving and environmentally-friendly society, said the proposal of the 11th Five-Year Programme (2006-2010) detailed recently by the central government. Companies, state-owned or private, domestic or foreign, are also eager to embrace renewable energy projects, for reasons similar to those mentioned above, or out of a belief that the energy sector is a gold mine, or will be in the future. A major barrier that has prevented renewable energies from being developed faster is weakness. China has shown limited interest in independent technology development. To date, most renewable-energy equipment or components used in China for wind-power, biomass or solar energy have been imported, resulting in high costs.

Beijing pledged to stage a Green Olympics, which would be more environmentally friendly than any previous Games. The 2008 Beijing Olympic Games were expected to recruit a diverse selection of renewable-energy technologies. Its main venue, the Olympic Green, had 20% of its power supplied by wind-generated electricity. The plan is to increase the share of renewable energy in the energy mix from current 7% to 12% in next 15 years time as per 11th Five-Year Plan. For example, the country is now promoting new technologies and materials in building construction, in an attempt to cut energy usage such as heating by 50 percent within the next five years. China's 11th Five-Year Plan also stipulated that the industrial sector must cut energy use by 20%. The emission-levels of major-pollutants will be cut by 10% and the forest coverage rate will be increased to 20%.

A medium-sized company producing energy-saving electric bulbs in South China's Guangdong Province said they foresee tremendous business opportunities, since the government is pushing ahead with energy conservation projects. China plans to reduce its energy cost per unit of GDP growth by 2010 from the current level, aimed at an energy-saving and environmentally-friendly society, as per the 11th Five-Year programme (2006-2010).[8] China is putting effort and money into research and development (R&D) to

---

8. Fair Trading Issues. (www.china.org.cn)

speed up its ambitious **coal-to-liquid (CTL) Fuel-Projects,** intended to convert its abundant coal resources into liquid fuel. China's largest coal producer, the state-owned Shenhua Group, has joined hands with Sasol to set up two CTL plants in Northwest China. Sasol, based in South-Africa, is the world leader in producing fuel from coal. The multinational has produced fuel in South Africa equivalent to more than 1.5 billion barrels of oil. Therefore, biological fuel costs and the possibility of a decline in oil prices will be the main curbs to the development of biofuels.[9]

China's environmental problems may affect its future energy security strategy

China's rapid economic growth over the last two decades has also brought with it several **energy related environmental problems.** China's major environmental issues include: air pollution (carbon-dioxide, sulphur-dioxide particulates) from more dependence on coal, acid rain; water shortages, particularly in the north; water pollution from untreated wastes; deforestation; estimated loss of one-fifth of agricultural land since 1949 due to soil erosion and economic development; desertification; and trade in endangered species. Many of China's cities are among the most polluted in the world. In fact seven of the world's ten most polluted cities are in China. China is the world's second-largest source of carbon-dioxide emissions behind the United States. According to EIA study the Energy-Related Carbon Dioxide Emissions (2003E) in China were 3,541 million metric tons (2.7 metric tons per capita), owing to Coal (81%), Oil (17%), and Natural Gas (2%). EIA forecasts predict that China will experience the largest growth in carbon-dioxide emissions between now and the year 2030 due to continued higher coal-consumption of low quality. In long run these may prove damaging human health, overall air and water quality, agriculture, and ultimately its economy. According to one estimate the total cost of air and water pollution damage in

---

9. Asia Times at www.atimes.com China Business, 21 Sep 2006

China was US$ 54 billion, or nearly 8% of GDP in 1995[10]. China is a **non-Annex-I country** under the United Nations-Framework-Convention on Climate Change, meaning that it is not bound to any GHG emissions reduction targets set under the Kyoto-Protocol. However, China has taken steps to improve environmental conditions in the country through its new **Law on Renewable Energy** (Jan. 2006) which seeks to promote cleaner-energy-technologies, with a goal to increase the use of renewable energy from nearly 3% in 2003 to 10% of the country's electricity consumption by 2010. For these reasons the future energy policy and strategies of China will encourage more production and increased import of more efficient and clean-energy; and be constrained by the investment-requirements on improved/cleaner technology and also remain under INCREASING pressure due to the International Agreements of many organizations on environment to which China is a party. China's 11th Five-Year Plan (2006-2010) calls for a 20% reduction in energy-consumption per unit of GDP by 2010 and an estimated 45% increase in GDP by 2010.

The plan states that conserving resources and protecting the environment are basic goals, but it lacks details on the policies / reforms necessary to achieve these goals. For China, the goal of sustainable-development is already under emphasis as reflected in its White-Paper on Agenda-21 which states, 'Because China is a developing country, the goals of increasing social productivity, enhancing overall national strength and improving people's quality of life cannot be realized without giving primacy to the development of the national economy and having all work focused on building the economy.[11] It may be conclusively observed from above that these developments, namely burgeoning energy-requirements and import-dependence to fuel its own future economy associated with the growing sense of insecurity, encouraged and compelled China to take up "energy" as

---

10. Coal in the Energy Supply of China CIAB page 53
11. http://www.acca21.edu.cn/chnwp2.html

one of its highest agenda which its Government markedly, stubbornly and aggressively pursued altogether as a separate area of management.

Section – VI

Development-Management of Energy Resources in India

CHAPTER 14

Management of Coal in India

Globally 'coal' supplies around 23% of world primary-energy and contributes 60% to electricity-production. In India the share of coal-fired electricity out of total electricity generated was 70% and that in China was 80%. Around 70% of global steel-production consumes coal as the most important fuel. India and China rely heavily on coal both for electricity-generation and steel-production. The largest consumers of coal in the world are the United States, China, EU15, India and Russia, which together comprise around 70% of total coal consumption.[1] For India, 'coal' also plays an integral role in its economic and social development and a crucial role in sustainable development as it is the most widely used energy-source for production of electricity, steel, cement, bricks, fertiliser, chemical, paper and many other medium and small-scale industries; and coal reserves are abundant hence providing an accessible and affordable energy-source; coal-mining is a major source of direct/indirect employment, especially in India where it is essential

---

1. Coal in the Energy Supply of China CIAB page 33

for alleviating high-levels of rural unemployment and poverty; the taxes and royalties on these mines are an important source of government revenue contributing to the provision of economic and social infrastructure of the country.

The gross reserve of coal is 200 BT of which about 70 BT will be economically recoverable, a pinch of nature requiring this energy-source to be raised to the maximum level of efficiency and effective-use. India is the world's 3rd largest coal-producer behind China and the U.S. India's coal-consumption increased from 140 million short tons-mst (1984) to 478 mst in 2004, expected to be growing to 775 mst by 2020. For India the increased growth in coal-consumption is a result of its higher rates of economic growth and increasing rates of electrification. Global energy-needs are projected to continue to grow at an average annual rate of 2% to 2020. Much of the increase in global energy use is expected to occur in developing countries, India and China particulary, due to high energy-intensity of output coupled with strong economic growth and increased rates of electrification. Coal is projected to play an important role in meeting this growth in energy demand. The IEA projects that 70% of the increase in coal-demands to 2020 will come from non-OECD countries, mainly from China and India for power-generation.

Production trend of coal – The primary-energy sources in India experienced a relatively slow-growth in the 1990-1995 period from 189.17 to 219.24 MTOE (annual average growth-rate of only 3.2%), where Coal and Lignite accounted for nearly 63% of total primary-energy, as shown below. In India, **Coal** is the major-source of primary-fuel mainly for the power, steel, cement and brick-making sectors. The electric power-stations consume nearly 75% of the product and steel-industry roughly 15%. Cement and Brick industry is the other major consumer.

India's Primary sources of commercial energy (MTOE)

Year	Lignite	Coal	Oil	N-Gas	Hydro	Nuclear	Total
1990-91	6.91	(106.63)	53.73	15.42	5.96	0.52	189.17
(% share)	(3.65)	(56.37)	(28.40)	(8.15)	(3.15)	(0.28)	(100)
1991-92	7.83	115.29	54.37	15.98	6.05	0.46	199.97
(% share)	(3.91)	(57.65)	(27.19)	(7.99)	(3.03)	(0.23)	(100)
1992-93	8.14	119.86	56.37	15.98	5.82	0.46	206.83
(% share)	(3.94)	(58.05)	(27.25)	(7.73)	(2.82)	(0.22)	(100)
1993-94	8.87	124.02	57.52	15.98	5.86	0.46	212.72
(% share)	(4.17)	(58.30)	(27.04)	(7.51)	(2.76)	(0.22)	(100)
1994-95	9.41	128.52	58.00	15.98	6.88	0.46	219.24
(% share)	(4.29)	(58.62)	(26.45)	(7.29)	(3.10)	(0.21)	(100)

Reorganization of coal-sector

The coal-industry in India was nationalised, in response to poor environmental and safety records of privately-run-mines and to develop coal mining for industrialization and economic growth, through Coal-Mines (Nationalization) Act, 1973 with formation of 'Coal-India-Limited' (CIL), which together with its subsidiaries contributes nearly 90% and 73% of total production of coal and lignite respectively. In 1993, limited private participation was permitted in the coal-sector, essentially in captive-mining for self-use.

For enhancing coal-production the Government of India denationalised (Feb. 1997) the coal-industry after 25 years of nationalisation experience to invite private-investment. For bringing further reformation and advancement in coal-sector an Expert Committee on coal recommended that the coal blocks held by Coal India Limited (CIL) which CIL cannot bring into production by 2016-17, either directly or through joint ventures, should be made available to other eligible candidates for development and bringing into production by 2011-12. This required amendment in the Coal-Mines (Nationalization) Act, 1973 to facilitate (a) private participation in coal mining for purposes other than those specified and (b) offering of future coal blocks to potential entrepreneurs.

Accordingly, the Coal-Mines-Nationalization (Amendment) Bill 2000 was introduced in Parliament for bringing in suitable legislative amendments to permit private-sector entry into coal-sector. Now, foreign direct investment (FDI) in coal mining has been allowed and coal mining by joint venture companies is permitted. However, its passage is still awaited. An increase in productivity is expected.

Deficient issues relating to coal industry

India's coal industry's contribution to economic development has two dimensions, one associated with coal-mining, the other with coal-use. Sectors in electricity-generation, iron and steel, cement and brick-making are highly dependent on coal which are vital for economic development. Coal mining activities provide export-earnings for domestic economies and also generate employment in mining and dependent services.

Although there are over twice as many underground mines as open cast mines, over 80% of coal-production in India is from opencast mines, generally in the central-south and east of the country. There are 561 coal-mines in India, but only a few of these mines have large-scale operations (over 10mt/Year in production). Underground mining methods are limited to conventional board and pillar, with limited use of modern long-wall techniques. India's coal has twice the ash-content of U.S. coal, resulting in serious environmental and health consequences for its population. Currently, about 53% of India's total energy (and 70% of India's electric power-generation) is derived from coal.[2]

In India coal mining is still a labour-intensive industry, around 50 lakh are employed in China and 5 lakh in India. China's coal-sector has the highest labour-intensity (5,000 workers per million tonne of coal mined) while for India it is 2,171 workers. India's coal-industry also generates income

---

2. EIA, IEO 2006 page 55

and employment in other ancillary and regional industries that are dependent on coal mining.

India's coal-sector has a low productivity level (0.55 ton output per man-shift) and also lack mechanisation for want of investment which considerably impeded the production rise. In a conventional thermal power plant, only 35% of the coal's energy is converted into electricity. But if the coal is first gasified and then used in a combined cycle power plant, the efficiency of energy conversion can rise to 40-45%, the same input of coal will produce far more electricity. A movement toward energy independence would demand accelerated work in operationalizing the production from coal sector through integrated gasification and combined cycle route.[3] The contribution of coal to future energy market and security in India is threatened by its ageing coal-capacity, liberated electricity-markets that favours new-capacity-developments with low-costs and new-technology and the unaccounted electricity losses ranging between 30 and 40%.

Access to affordable energy is a driving-force behind economic development. For India which has a relatively high dependency on energy intensive production, such as metals and manufacturing, its economic growth is more closely linked to energy-consumption from coal which is accessible and affordable. However, to prevent the exhaustion of finite energy resources and meet environmental expectations, requirements for sustainable-development, economic growth must become less reliant on energy-consumption from finite energy resources like coal.

In India modern-energy is inaccessible by a larger section of population due to inadequate distribution-infrastructure and economically-unaffordable prices. So, coal-fired power is a competitive electricity-technology, due to low-cost of coal. However, the affordability of coal in the future will depend on policies designed to internalize both positive and negative externalities such as environmental-impacts, energy

---

3. *The Hindu*, August 14, 2005

security and energy-safety, improvised measures on efficiency and productivity, and technology upgradation and modernization. In the short to medium-term, despite improvements in technology, deployment of alternative energy-technologies at mass scale will not be competitive with the existing conventional-technologies such as those for coal, thus, making the reliance of electricity more on coal than from the new energy sources. For future India, alleviating energy-poverty by ensuring energy availability / accessibility/affordability will be a prime agenda-item where 'coal' will remain the best fuel to provide affordable, safe and reliable electricity because coal is widely available, can be easily and safely transported, compared with oil or gas, and is and will continue to be a relatively low-cost energy supply-source.

Need for More Efficient Development and Utilization of Coal Resources

The Department-of-Energy (USA), in partnership with several other U.S. Government agencies, has been working with the Government of India on several projects to support efficient development and to increase the use of India's domestic coal-resources. In April 2006, India became a partner in the Future-Gen international partnership which will work to create a zero-emissions coal-fired power plant that will produce hydrogen and sequester CO^2 underground, enabling greater use of coal in an environmentally sustainable way. Several high-priority projects have since been identified including pursuing investment opportunities and information exchanges in the areas of coal mining and processing, coal-mine-safety, coal-mine-methane, and coal-gasification. In the area of coal-based power-generation, a proposed strategic partnership has been established between India's National-Thermal-Power-Corp. and the U.S. Department of Energy's National-Energy-Technology-Laboratory to collaborate on advanced research and development of clean and efficient power-generation.

CHAPTER 15

Management of Oil in India

Oil and gas together provided (1990-1995) nearly 34% of the total primary-energy. The total oil-reserve in the country is 765 MT only. The domestic production being inadequate, nearly 40% of the country's consumption is imported. The table below gives the volume of import and production of crude:

India's Crude-Oil Import and Production (MT)

Year	Import	Production	Total
1990-91	20.70	33.02	53.72
1991-92	23.99	30.35	54.34
1992-93	29.25	26.95	56.20
1993-94	30.82	27.03	57.85
1994-95	27.35	31.23	59.58

Source: CMIE

Note: India also exports small amount of oil to neighbouring countries.

The Digboi oil-field (discovered in 1890) in Assam, provided India with its first and only commercial oil production for more than 60 years and still producing but at less yield. Since 1960 numerous onshore discoveries have been made in the western, eastern and southern parts of India. The production of oil is picking up after a fall in 1992-93 due to ethnic-troubles in the oil-field region in eastern India.

In 1974 the outstanding offshore oil-field Bombay-High oil/gas-field was discovered. In 2001 this one field provided almost 35% of national oil output. India's self-sufficiency in oil had declined considerably from the mid-eighties when it reached 70%. The domestic refinery-capacity is insufficient and petroleum products like kerosene, diesel and LPG are imported.

The disproportionate demand of the middle distillates is being discouraged, with little effect, through hiking of petroleum prices. The price structure is administered by the government for providing heavy subsidies to kerosene being used extensively by rural people for lighting and cooking and diesel for mass transport and agriculture. With increasing demand and rise in international oil-price India's import-bills are becoming seriously burdensome exceeding US $ 10 billion/year. Oil conservation efforts are there but the impact is not very significant. Oil production has been privatized but the expected growth is yet to be seen. Decontrol of prices by withdrawing the administered price mechanism is also being considered to curb both demand and import.

Consumption of petroleum-products increased at the rate of 3.8% per annum during 2003-04. In 2003-04, excluding exports, India consumed 116.01MMT of crude oil products including refinery-fuel. Domestic production of crude-oil was between 30.3 MMT and 33.86 MMT. 72.2% of consumption was met through imports. In 2003-04, the proven reserve to production (R/P) ratio was only 22. In January 2005, India signed a long term deal for 7.5 million metric tons/annum LNG with Iran. The oil-sector remains largely in the hands of the Central Public-Sector-Units (CPSUs). The exception is in refining where some 26% of capacity is now in private hands. In 1987, India allowed private participation in refining through joint ventures, which was eventually de-regulated in 1998. The country's largest refinery, a 27 MMTPA facility at Jamnagar, Gujarat is run by a private-sector company. Parallel marketing of LPG and kerosene was permitted in 1993. Under the scheme, imports of these products were decanalized and private parties were allowed to import and market these at market-determined prices. Over the years parallel marketers have developed facilities for imports, storage tanks and LPG bottling plants as well as setting up their own distribution and marketing networks. Despite one of the most liberal exploration licensing regimes, India has failed to attract any oil majors to explore in India.

Exploration-blocks were put on offer under the New Exploration-Licensing-Policy (NELP) in 1999, under radically different terms and conditions in order to try and attract private investment. NELP, so far, has not been very successful in attracting investments in a massive way. So far, India has offered only 110 oil and gas blocks and 16 coal-bed-methane blocks for exploration in its attempt to raise domestic energy production to reduce import dependence.

An indication of global interest in India's energy deposits, is illustrated by major firms snapping up seismic-data worth Rs. 200 million ($4.5 million) for 55 oil and gas blocks and 10 coal-bed-methane blocks offered for exploration on 22nd February, 2006.[1] This is expected to translate into aggressive bidding for the blocks offered under the sixth round of the New Exploration-Licensing-Policy (NELP) and third round of coal-bed-methane exploration. Of the 55 oil and gas blocks offered in the sixth round of NELP, 24 are in the deep sea, six in shallow offshore and 25 are on land blocks. Since India's major energy imports are in the form of crude-oil, the specific issues relating to oil need special attention. The choices available to increase oil-security must include: establishment of a strategic oil-reserve; diversification of sources of oil imports; investment in equity oil abroad; and enhancement of domestic supply.

---

1. *The Economic Times*, 28th Feb 2006.

Notwithstanding above, according to (http://petroleum. nic. in) *India Hydrocarbon Vision-2025* (Ministry of Petroleum & Natural Gas, GOI) as against India's estimated crude requirement (MMT) which is estimated to increase from 122 (2001-02) to 190 (2011-12) and further to 364 (2024-25) the present domestic crude production is only 33 MMT, the gap will have to be met through imports and increase in domestic production.

CHAPTER 16

Management of Natural Gas in India

The 'natural gas' though a primary-energy source in India experienced a relatively slow-growth in the 1990-1995 period increasing very marginally from 15.42 MTOE (8.15%) in 1990-91 to only 15.98 MTOE (7.29% of total primary-energy). Natural gas production in India had both fall and rise in the first half of the nineties. The country's estimated reserve is 707 BCM. Until 1997, public sector firms concentrated mainly on oil and gas exploration. Progressive liberalization of exploration and licensing policies have attracted some private and foreign firms. Despite this the success of the explorations has been marginal in enhancing oil reserves. However, some sizeable gas reserves amounting to 680 MTOE (176 MTOE claimed by Reliance and 504 MTOE claimed by Gujarat's State-Petroleum-Corporations (GSPC)) has been recently reported[1].

---

1. Energy and Sustainable Development in India page 48, 2005/06, *Helio International* and *The Economic Times*, 28th Feb 2006

'Natural Gas' is a clean, efficient and a viable source of energy which is currently used abundantly in transportation, in power-sector and as a cooking-gas too. Compressed natural gas and also a mixture of petrol and alcohol ('gasohol') are being tried in vehicles on a purely experimental basis to reduce pollution in cities. Importing natural gas through pipelines may be cheap, but it does not provide energy security to India. We have huge reserves in the Krishna-Godavari basin which needs to be explored to provide cheap and environmental friendly natural gas.

According to (http://petroleum.nic.in) *India Hydrocarbon Vision-2005* (Ministry of Petroleum & Natural Gas, GOI) as against India's requirement (MMSCMD) of Natural-Gas which is estimated to increase from 151 (2001-02) to 313 (2011-12) and further to 391 (2024-2025) the present domestic crude production is only 65 MMSCMD, the gap will have to be met through imports, increase in domestic production and by switching to liquid fuels.

India's collaboration and research has a long way to go

The Department of Energy (USA) has been working with India to help them develop their domestic natural gas resources that can offer near-term alternatives. India has discovered a significant reserve of natural gas off its east-coast but lacks adequate infrastructure to move this gas to major national markets.

Another important area for future domestic natural gas production is from coal-bed-methane (CBM). India is believed to have significant resources of CBM that could make important contributions to meeting future energy needs. This is an opportunity for the U.S. private sector, which has extensive experience in the area of CBM development, to engage in this key energy source. India's Ministry of Coal and Ministry of Petroleum and Natural Gas with the U.S. Trade and Development Agency (USTDA) and the U.S. Environmental Protection Agency are working together to establish a CBM Clearinghouse Information Centre, an initiative under the Methane to Markets Partnership. This Centre would promote the development of CBM projects and CBM resources by collecting data, conducting training, facilitating technology transfer, and providing consulting services. USTDA has provided a $506,000 grant to Reliance Industries Limited to partially fund the cost of technical assistance to develop CBM resources at Reliance's Sohagpur field.

The U.S. Department of Energy is also working with India on ongoing research and development of the first hydrate drilling offshore India which is expected to accelerate efforts to develop methane-production from hydrates in both the countries, potentially providing a significant increase in the quantity of domestic natural gas availability in the Indian market. DOE has provided specialized-equipments and research-scientists to detect and evaluate gas hydrates in cores. DOE and the Directorate General for Hydrocarbons are in discussions to develop an MOU to exchange information and analyses, conduct joint studies and projects, and exchange scientific and technical personnel in order to increase understanding of the geologic occurrence and the potential for methane production from natural gas hydrates in both India and the United States.

Accelerating Energy Sector Regulatory-Reform is essentially needed

In order to meet India's growing demand for energy, significant new investment is needed. Necessary legal and regulatory framework must also be in place to attract the needed capital. India has recently enacted a Petroleum and Natural Gas Regulatory Board Act which seeks to promote competition, open access and greater transparency in gas pipeline transportation. India is considering a number of regulatory issues and processes that it will have to address to develop a full 'Regulatory-Scheme' that will be attractive to the potential investors. India's effort to establish an appropriate regulatory regime is also being supported by a USTDA grant to the Government of India for a limited feasibility study of a national pipeline grid and to explore the possibility of providing further technical assistance in the area of gas sector regulation.

CHAPTER 17

Management of
Electricity in India

In India's energy sector the area of highest concern and thrust is electricity generation. Based on the IEA projections the energy required for electricity generation for the period 2003 to 2030 is graphically shown on P-234.

The **electric-power** situation in India appears dismal. The annual growth-rate in the eighties was more than 7% but it has declined to 5% in the nineties (1990-1995). The source-wise installed-capacity for electricity-generation is also shown below:

India's Electricity-Generation Installed-Capacity (MW)

Year	Hydel	Thermal	Nuclear	Total
1990-91	18,753	45,768	1,565	66,086
1991-92	19,194	48,086	1,785	69,065
1992-93	19,574	50,749	2,005	72,330
1993-94	20,366	54,347	2,005	76,718
1994-95	20,829	58,110	2,225	81,164
	(25.67%)	(71.60%)	(2.74%)	(100%)

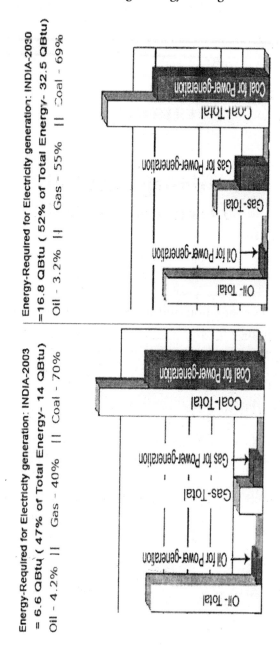

Energy-Required for Electricity generation: INDIA-2003
= 6.6 QBtu (47% of Total Energy- 14 QBtu)
Oil - 4.2% || Gas - 40% || Coal - 70%

Energy-Required for Electricity generation: INDIA-2030
=16.8 QBtu (52% of Total Energy- 32.5 QBtu)
Oil - 3.2% || Gas - 55% || Coal - 69%

Over the last 25 years, India's power-capacity has risen at the rate of 5.87% per annum. The total supply of electricity has risen at the rate of 7.14% over the same period. In 2004-05 the average Plant-Load-Factor (PLF) was 74.8%. Power-shortage and low-quality of power continue to plague the country. For the country as a whole, the aggregate technical and commercial losses, which include theft, billing and collection inefficiency, transmission and distribution losses, exceeds 40%[6]. In the 8th Five-Year Plan (1992-97) the capacity addition has been only 18,000 MW against a downsized target of 26,000 MW. There is shortage both in peak-power and also in energy reaching 23% and 7% respectively last year. The demand in evening peak-hours cannot be met because of low hydro-installation whose share is steadily falling over the years. The Economic Survey, 2005-06, has revealed that the power-shortage that occur around 12% in peak and 8% on average is equivalent to Rs. 15,000 crore of foregone generation and associated GDP loss of Rs. 3,00,000 crore.

The 9th Plan had a priority on 'Hydel' but the Central and State sectors failed to secure loans from international funding agencies, because of their financial weaknesses as the State-Electricity-Boards incurring heavy losses for almost free distribution to agricultural loads and Central Sector (accounting for more than 30% of installation) failing to collect payments from SEBs for the electricity sold. The government's invitation to foreign investors on very liberal terms did not bring good response.

To enable robust growth, the Government of India has taken a number of policy initiatives and has put in position an enabling legal framework. These include the Electricity Act 2003, National Electricity Policy, Tariff Policy, Accelerated Power Development and Reform Programme (APDRP), the 50,000 MW Hydro Initiative, the 100,000 MW Thermal Initiative, Ultra Mega Power Projects plan, rural electrification

6. Energy and Sustainable Development in India page 27,2005/06, Helio International and The Economic Times, 28th Feb 2006

schemes under Rajiv Gandhi Gramin Vidyutikaran Yojana and various other plans and policies. The State utilities are being unbundled and corporatised for better performance and accountability. Power Regulatory Commissions have come out with notifications for open access and trading has emerged as a substantial market activity. CERC has come out with 'Staff Consultation Paper' on the establishment of a Power Exchange. [7]

The operation of the power system has been transformed with the Availability Based Tariff (ABT) regime and system discipline has been ensured. Grids of various regions viz. North-East, East, North and West have been interconnected and are now operating in synchronous mode and Southern Region is connected through an asynchronous HVDC network. Establishment of inter-regional links and development of national grid has become a reality. Inter-regional power transfers are on the increase. This will facilitate not only exchange of power from surplus region to deficit region but also enable trading and development of electricity market, including merchant power plan. The Ministry of Power has set a target of adding a 100,000 MW of generation-capacity by 2012. This capacity-addition programme includes the 41,110 MW proposed to be added in the 10th Five-Year Plan (2002-07). During 2004-05, the Central-Electricity-Authority completed preparations of the pre-feasibility reports of 162 schemes with an aggregate installed capacity of over 47,000 MW under the 50,000 MW 'Hydro-electric' initiatives.[8]

The country has a large **hydro-electric** potential estimated at 84,000 MW at 60% load-factor. Less than $1/4^{th}$ of that has been tapped. Large hydro-projects are also being stiffly opposed by environmentalists all over the country. Electrical

---

7 . An address by T. Sankaralingam, Chairman and Managing Director, NTPC, New Delhi, 19 September 2006

8. Energy and Sustainable Development in India page 27 (2005/06, Helio International and The Economic Times, 28th Feb 2006

energy conservation measures are being adapted and energy audit is being enforced. However, independent experts are of the opinion that the power scene will not brighten up unless the government expresses a strong political will.

The economic growth of India will continue to be hampered as long as the country's power-supply constrains its industrial development and the financial losses of the power-sector remain a burden on public-sector finances. India's power-sector is plagued by capacity-shortages, resulting in frequent blackouts, and deteriorating physical and financial conditions. Industry-surveys consistently rate power-supply as one .of the most critical constraints. With responsibility for electricity supply shared constitutionally between the central government and the states, the Government of India has placed increased emphasis on improving the efficiency of supply, consumption, and pricing of electricity. This can only be achieved by reforming power sector management and financing at the state level.

The source of the state-power-sectors' ailments is poor operational-efficiency of the State-Electricity-Boards (SEBs), which form the foundation of India's power-system. Due to subsidized-tariffs; low investment in transmission and distribution systems; inadequate maintenance; and high levels of distribution losses, theft, and uncollected bills, the SEBs are continually in severe financial-distress and have been unable to provide quality-supply and efficient-service to their customers. Commercial losses of SEBs and State-Generating-Companies, which together generate almost 70% of India's electricity supply and provide most of the distribution to consumers, reached about US$3 billion in 1997-98, or about 1% of India's GDP, and continue to rise.

In most of India's states, the power-sector is a major drain on already limited state budgets. Although publicly reported total energy-losses are about 21% nationwide, closer examination of the losses of SEBs shows that there is often significant under-reporting. The sector's heavy reliance on increasingly tight state budget resources has been the key obstacle to expanding access to electricity to consumers and upgrading systems. SEB losses and power subsidies are also a major drain on state budgets. In India power-sector reforms are critical for providing the impetus to states' economic growth and for redirecting public spending to priority areas. The financial weakness of the SEBs has also been one of the major stumbling blocks in achieving financial closure of Independent-Power-Producers (IPPs). Nationwide, the shortfall in energy supply is conservatively estimated at 11% and 18% during peak-hours, although among states the variation is substantial.

The Government of India, with World Bank assistance, has been encouraging the states to undertake in-depth power-sector reforms. This involves separating the state government from power-sector management, establishing independent regulatory framework for the sector, reducing subsidies and restoring the creditworthiness of the utilities through financial restructuring and cost-recovery based tariffs, and divesting existing distribution assets to private operators.[9] The Economic Survey for 2005-06 informs that despite various reformist measures, the power sector is in mess. The growth rate of power generation has slowed down to 4.7% in 2005 from 6.5% in 2004. The commercial loss of SEBs has gone up to Rs. 22,569 crores in 2005-06 from Rs. 22,558 in 2004-05.[10]

9. The Economic and Political Weekly Oct 2002.

10. Energy and Sustainable Development in India page 29 (2005/06, Helio International and The Economic Times, 28th Feb 2006)

CHAPTER 18

Management of Nuclear
Power in India

The release of atomic energy has not created a new problem. It has merely made more urgent the necessity of solving an existing one.

— Albert Einstein (1879 - 1955)

Nuclear power contributes a very nominal percent of energy to the total energy-mix. India's current civilian nuclear programme has an installed capacity of 3,850 megawatts electric (MWe) which is expected to reach 20,000 MWe by 2020.

The landmark deal between India and US has made nuclear-energy, the future energy for the power-sector of India. The target of 20,000 MWe of nuclear power generation capacity suddenly appears to be feasible and achievable. The Indo–US deal is likely to reduce India's dependence on hydrocarbon. With the reserves of coal and hydrocarbons coming down, nuclear-energy seems to be the answer for the power sector. It is also preferred as it is environmentally viable and leads to energy security.

Nuclear Power in India: An Inevitable Option for Sustainable Development

India is the world's largest democracy with a population of about 1.045 billion and low per capita income. In recent years, it has witnessed an impressive growth rate in GDP. The development aspirations of its populace demand that this growth rate be sustained for long enough so as to enable them to have a decent quality of life. This requires matching growth in the availability of energy. To jump start the nuclear power programme, two Boiling Water Reactors were set up at Tarapur near Mumbai in the late 1960s. These reactors are still in operation. In a similar manner, in parallel with the indigenous self-reliant three-stage programme, we are planning to set up Light Water Reactors. The ongoing construction of two 1000 MWe units at Kudankulam in technical cooperation with the Russian Federation is a step in this direction.

Electricity generation in the fiscal year 2001-02 was about 515 billion kWh from electric-utilities and about additional 120 billion kWh were generated by captive power- plants. On a per capita basis, this works out to be 610 kWh per year. In the OECD countries, the corresponding figure is about 10,000 kWh. India's population is expected to rise to 1.5 billion by the year 2050. If the population needs per capita electricity consumption of about 5000 kWh per year, India has to plan to have total electricity-generation of about 7500 billion kWh per year. This is about 12 times the generation in the fiscal year 2001-02. In India, the Central-Electricity-Authority (CEA) undertakes periodic Electric-Power-Surveys (EPS) to make projections of the energy requirements of the country. These estimates guide the planning process for capacity addition in the country. As per CEA's 16th Survey-Report (Jan. 2001) the projected energy-requirement should increase from 5,29,014 million kWh in 2001-02 to 13,17,644 in 2016-17.[11]

Electricity generation of this magnitude calls for a careful examination of all issues related to sustainability, including diversity of energy supply sources and technologies, security of supplies, self-sufficiency, security of energy-infrastructure,

---

11. www.cscap.nuctrans.org/Nuc-Trans/locations/india/india.htm

effect on local, regional and global environments and demand side management. The concept of sustainability calls for the exploitation of available resources to improve the quality of life of people without harming the interests of future generations and degrading the environment beyond the inherent corrective-capability of natural processes. In this context, it need to be considered that in India, more than 70% of power-generation is through the burning of coal having ash content in the range of 35 to 50%. With an estimated coal reserve of 221 billion tonnes only and extremely limited availability of oil and gas, coal will continue to be the mainstay of power generation in India for a long time.

India has a large hydro-potential and only a part of this potential has been exploited. All issues related to exploitation of this resource need to be addressed and the full hydro-potential needs to be harnessed expeditiously. Displacement of people in a country with a high population density is a major issue and is particularly acute in case of hydro power development. Renewable resources are very important, as they are geographically dispersed. They should be tapped to meet the energy demands of small communities. Unfortunately, at the present level of technology, renewables cannot be used for central power stations and remain very expensive due to high capital costs and their low availability factor. Renewable energy sources have additional problems arising from seasonal variations. In above background the importance of nuclear power appears as a viable future promise.

The programme-profile of India's Department of Atomic-Energy envisages the use of domestic uranium-resources in Pressurized-Heavy-Water-Reactors (PHWRs), followed by the recycling of spent-fuel in Fast-Breeder-Reactors. PHWR technology is already in the commercial domain, with a good record of safe operation of nuclear power-reactors. Nuclear power is a well-established technology in India which can contribute to both the development of a large fraction of world population and also to the protection of the global-environment. Given the uranium and thorium resources of the country, this has inevitably to take place through the use of Fast-Breeder-Reactors and Thorium-Reactors which can tap the full energy potential in nuclear-fuel materials through the use of recycling technologies.

Nuclear Power Programme

The first stage of the nuclear power programme, comprising setting up of Pressurised Heavy Water Reactors (PHWRs) and associated fuel cycle facilities, is already in the commercial domain. The technology for the manufacture of various components and equipment for PHWRs in India is now well established and has evolved through active collaboration between the Department of Atomic Energy (DAE) and the industry. Twelve PHWRs are operating and six PHWRs comprising a mix of 540 and 220 MWe rating are under construction. As we gain experience and master various aspects of the nuclear technology, performance of our plants will continuously improve. The average capacity factor of the plants operated by the Nuclear Power Corporation of India Limited (NPCIL) has steadily risen from 60% in 1995-96 to 85% in the year 2001-02.

The second stage envisages the setting up of Fast Breeder Reactors (FBRs) backed by reprocessing plants and plutonium-based fuel fabrication plants. In order to multiply the fissile material inventory, Fast Breeder Reactors are necessary for our programme. A higher power-generating base through Fast Breeder Reactors is also needed to establish the use of thorium on a large scale in the third stage of our programme. A 40 MWt Fast Breeder Test Reactor (FBTR) has been operating at the Indira Gandhi Centre for Atomic Research (IGCAR), Kalpakkam, since attaining first criticality on 18 October 1985. FBTR uses a unique and indigenously developed mixed uranium carbide-plutonium carbide fuel, which has functioned extremely well upto the current burn-up of about 100,000 MWd/t. The FBTR has provided valuable experience with liquid metal Fast Breeder Reactor technology and the confidence to set up a 500 MWe Prototype Fast Breeder Reactor (PFBR). The PFBR design is now ready and, with several full-scale components already manufactured by Indian industry, is well poised for start of construction. Pre-project activities are already in progress at Kalpakkam near Chennai.

The third stage will be based on the thorium-uranium-233 cycle. Uranium-233 is obtained by irradiation of thorium in PHWRs and FBRs. An Advanced Heavy Water Reactor (AHWR) is being developed at Bhabha Atomic Research Centre (BARC) to expedite transition to thorium-based systems. The reactor physics design of AHWR is tuned to generate about 75% power from thorium.

Status of Nuclear Technology in India

Nuclear power technology in India has reached a state of maturity and the Department of Atomic Energy continues to take steps to further its development. These steps are aimed at further improving the safety and availability of operating stations, reducing the gestation period of plants under construction by using innovative management techniques, cost optimisation and development of new reactor systems. For example, repair technologies have been developed to improve the availability factor of nuclear power plants. Some of the repair jobs completed successfully include *en masse* replacement of coolant channels, endshield repair, and calandria inlet manifold management.

Indian industry is geared to manufacture equipment needed for the setting up of nuclear power plants. Plants for the production of heavy water, fabrication of fuel and mining of uranium are under the direct control of the Department of Atomic Energy and their performance during recent years has been excellent. Heavy water plants are working at full capacity and continuously implementing measures to conserve energy. India's experience in managing the back-end of the fuel cycle is also noteworthy. Fuel reprocessing started in India early in the programme based on indigenous efforts.

At present, India has three reprocessing plants to extract plutonium from spent fuel, the first at Trombay, the second at Tarapur and the third at Kalpakkam. With total protection of the environment as an overriding consideration, management of the radioactive waste in the fuel cycle has received high priority in India's nuclear programme right from its inception. Facilities for managing intermediate and low-level wastes have been set up and are operating successfully alongside every nuclear facility in the country. To treat high-level waste from reprocessing plants, a waste immobilisation plant has been set up at Tarapur incorporating hi-tech features such as complete remote operation and maintenance. A facility for interim storage of vitrified waste has also been built nearby. For ultimate disposal of high-level waste, research on setting up an underground waste repository is in progress. The third stage will be based on the thorium-uranium-233 cycle. Uranium-233 is obtained by irradiation of thorium in PHWRs and FBRs. An Advanced Heavy Water Reactor (AHWR) is being developed at Bhabha Atomic Research Centre (BARC) to expedite transition to thorium-based systems. The reactor physics design of AHWR is tuned to generate about 75% power from thorium.[12] With regard to the new reactor systems, IGCAR is working on the design and technology development of fast reactors, while BARC is working on the Advanced Heavy Water Reactor and other technologies for thorium utilisation. To summarize, India has developed expertise in every aspect of nuclear technology and is presently undergoing a major expansion of its nuclear power programme, both in terms of the commercial deployment of present-day technologies as well as bringing in newer technologies. The necessary industrial and R&D infrastructure is in place to facilitate this process. Recently India became an active member of an

12. World Nuclear Association Annual Symposium 4-6 September 2002 – London by World Nuclear Association 2002 on Nuclear Power in India: An Inevitable Option for Sustainable Development of a Sixth of Humanity by Dr. Anil Kakodkar

international consortium to launch a multi-billion dollar experimental fusion reactor **International Thermonuclear Experimental Reactor (ITER)** project in the France's southern region of Cadarache.[13]

The unit energy costs of nuclear power are comparable to power from coal at locations away from coal pits. Nuclear Power Corporation, which builds, owns and operates nuclear power stations, is a triple A-rated company and has been highly commended for its excellent commercial performance, both in building power plants as well as in their operation. High capacity factors, low fuel transportation cost, low discount rates and reduced capital costs are factors, which make nuclear power more attractive, and conditions in India have become more favourable in terms of these parameters over the years. Further, with its low variable costs, nuclear power improves its relative economics with years of operation of the power plant.

Considering that India has a mature technology base and that the economics of nuclear power are favourable in several parts of the country, DAE formulated a programme for increasing installed nuclear-capacity to set up about 20,000 MWe installed-capacity by the year 2020. India's **present** 2,720 MWe nuclear power plants includes 14 reactors at 6 sites (Tarapur, Rawatbhata, Kalpakkam, Narora, Kakrapar and Kaiga); **on-going** 3,960 MWe nuclear power plants includes 8 reactors at 4 sites (Tarapur, Kaiga, Rawatbhata and Kudankulam); and **future** nuclear power plants include one AHWR having a rating of 300 MWe and a mix of 500 MWe FBRs, 680 MWe PHWRs and 1000 MWe LWRs so as to reach a total of about 20,000 MWe by the year 2020.

Thus, when compared with the options of power-generation with coal or hydro, India's fuel-resource position convincingly calls for the development and deployment of a nuclear power programme to meet the long term energy-needs in a sustainable manner. The technology resources

---

13. The Hindu, 22nd Nov 2006

needed to pursue the nuclear power programme are in place for the programme being pursued at present, and also to be pursued in near future. For programmes beyond this, research and development is in full swing and it is being ensured that human resources to pursue these aims will be available as and when needed.

Section – VII

India's Strategic Energy Management

CHAPTER 19

India's Strategic Energy Management

There is no security on this earth, there is only opportunity.
— General Douglas MacArthur (1880-1964)

India is now the sixth largest energy consumer in the world. India being one of the fastest growing economies in the world, growing at over 8% since the country's economic and financial crisis of 1991, has a fast growing energy demand fueled by fast-increasing industrialisation and urbanisation. Parallel to this, India's energy demand has to rise much hight than the EIA's projections (2010-2030: average @3.2% annually) which, combined with limited domestic energy-reserves (except coal), will place India before many crises: shortages of resource, capacity and infrastructure; colossal size of energy inefficiency and losses; import-dependence; technology-upgradation and modernisation; effective and integrated network of all energy related regulatory-frameworks; nationwide energy-database and management information system; social and managerial problems; sporadic strength and stability of political will to be followed by unpredictable threats and insecurities as well as the new political developments specially at international level.

India needs a priority and massive increase in investments in its energy sector because its economic growth has to take place at an expected level of over 8% per annum for planned development. There has been a global interest in India's energy sector ever since the process of liberalization to invite foreign-investment was initiated by the Government of India in 1991. India's enormous potential for energy production and consumption has enhanced investment prospects in this field. On the other hand there are related apprehensions being voiced by several NGOs relating to the inevitable increase of environmental problems including population displacements. Future massive expansion in India's energy sector would depend both on emergence of appropriate capital-markets globally and materialization of a neo-innovative politics/diplomacy nationally. This is true for new production-capacity, both conventional and renewable, as well as measures directed at improving energy-efficiency in various user-sections and in the energy sector itself.

Projection of Energy-Consumption for India by End-Use-Sector (2003-2030)

The Delivered Energy-Consumption and Projections (Quadrillion Btu-QBtu) for India by 'End-Use-Sector' for the period 2010-2030 is shown below:

Sector	Actual	Projections For — INDIA					Average Annual % Change
(Quadrillion Btu)	2003	2010	2015	2020	2025	2030	2003-2030
Residential Sector	1.7	2.6	2.9	3.2	3.5	3.8	3.1%
Commercial Sector	0.4	1.0	1.2	1.4	1.6	1.8	5.4%
Industrial Sector	5.7	7.1	8.4	9.9	11.5	13.0	3.1%
Transportation Sector	1.4	1.8	2.1	2.4	2.7	3.0	2.9%

The EIA's projections of consumption-requirements of energy by India (Appendix-B2) for the period 2010 to 2030, based on the consumption-pattern 'End-Use-Sectors-wise' of 2003, revealed that India's energy-requirements would increase by 2.24 times form 1.7 to 3.8 QBtu (Industrial Sector); by 4.5 times from 0.4 to 1.8 QBtu (for Commercial-Sector); by 2.28 times from 5.7 to 13.0 QBtu (Industrial Sector); and 2.14 times from 1.4 to 3.0 QBtu (Transportation-Sector). In the Residential and Commercial sectors about 47.4% and 83.3% respectively of this increase would be for 'electricity'; in Industrial Sector 35.4% and 29.2% of the increase would be for 'oil' and 'coal' respectively while in Transportation-Sector almost the entire increase would be for 'Oil'.

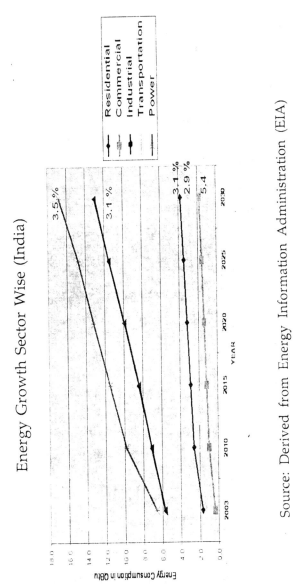

Energy Growth Sector Wise (India)

Source: Derived from Energy Information Administration (EIA)

Projection of Energy-Consumption for India by Fuel-Type (2003-2030)

The comparison [both graphical and quantitative, in (Quadrillion Btu - QBtu)] between 'Delivered Energy-

Consumption' (Year: 2003) and 'Requirement-Projections' (Period: 2010   2030) for India by 'Fuel-Type' for the period 2010-2030 are shown below:

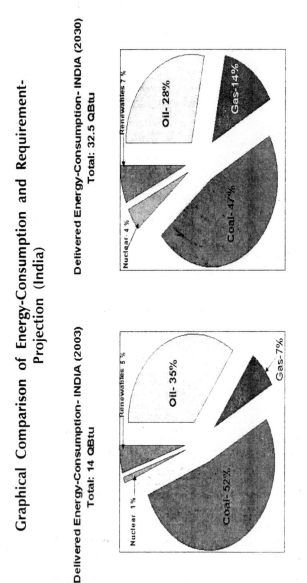

Graphical Comparison of Energy-Consumption and Requirement-Projection (India)

Source: Derived from Energy Information Administration (EIA)

Quantitative Comparison of Energy Consumption and Requirement Projections (India)

Sector	Actual	Projections For — INDIA					Average Annual % Change
(Quadrillion Btu)	2003	2010	2015	2020	2025	2030	2003-2030
Oil	4.6	5.9	6.7	7.3	8.1	8.9	2.5%
Natural Gas	0.6	0.8	1.0	1.3	1.7	2.1	4.9%
Coal	2.2	2.9	3.4	3.9	4.3	4.7	2.7%
Electricity	1.8	2.9	3.6	4.3	5.0	5.9	4.6%
Heat / Renewables	0.0	0.0	0.0	0.0	0.0	0.0	16.5%
Total Delivered Energy	9.2	12.5	14.6	16.8	19.2	21.6	3.2%
Electricity-Related Losses	4.8	6.9	7.9	8.9	9.8	10.9	3.1%
TOTAL:	14.0	19.4	22.5	25.7	29.0	32.5	3.2%
Electricity Related Losses	34.29%	35.57%	35.11%	34.63%	33.79%	33.54%	

Source: Derived from Energy Information Administration (EIA)

The EIA's projections of consumption-requirements of energy by India (Appendix-E) for the period **2010 to 2030**, based on the consumption-pattern 'Fuel-Type' of 2003, revealed that India's energy-requirements, excluding losses, would increase by 1.93 times form **4.6 to 8.9 QBtu** (Oil); by 3.5 times from **0.6 to 2.1 QBtu** (Natural Gas); by 2.1 times from **2.2 to 4.7 QBtu** (Coal); and 3.3 times from **1.8 to 5.9 QBtu** (Electricity).

In the total increase in all delivered-energy 41.20% share would be for 'Oil' alone; 27.31% share would be for '**Electricity**'; and 21.76% share would be for '**Coal**'. Due to electricity-related losses (actual being **34.29%** in 2003, higher by 5.72% than that of China) the production levels, as a result the consumption-level requirements would also have to be increased accordingly.

The energy experts view that India's energy security dilemma can be best approached through analysis of India's **energy-mix** with its integrated-energy policy. However, before that India's vigorous endeavouring and achievements in fields other than primary-energy/marketed-energy need to be discussed first which include: Solar Energy, Wind Energy, Tidal-Energy, Wave-Energy, Ocean-Thermal-Energy, as below.

Solar Energy – India has a good level of solar-radiation, receiving the solar energy equivalent to more than 5,000 trillion kWh/yr. Depending on the location, the daily solar-radiation incidence ranges from 4 to 7 kWh/m^2 with the hours of sunshine ranging from 2,300 to 3,200 per year. Solar-thermal and solar-photovoltaic technologies are both encompassed by the Solar-Energy-Programme that is being implemented by the MNES. The Programme plans to utilise India's estimated solar-power for potential of 20 MW/km^2, and 35 MW/km^2 solar-thermal. The country has also developed a substantial manufacturing capability, becoming a lead producer in the developing world.

The Ministry of Non-Conventional Energy Sources (MNES), working with the Indian-Renewable-Energy-Development-Agency (IREDA) continues to promote the utilization of all forms of solar-power as part of the drive to increase the share of renewable-energy in the Indian market where showroom-cum-sales/service-centres (Aditya-Solar-Shops) are being established nationwide. The development programmes include both Solar-Thermal and Solar-PV. The Solar-Thermal Programme covers solar-water heating, solar-cooking, solar-dryers, solar air-heating and solar-buildings. Out of these solar air-heating technology has been applied effectively to various industrial and agricultural processes (e.g. drying/curing, regeneration of dehumidifying agents, timber-seasoning, leather-tanning) and also for space-heating.

The Solar-Photovoltaic-Programme (SPV) aims particularly at rural/remote areas. By end-2002 more than 1.03 million SPV systems representing 107 MWp were deployed (of which 46 MWp were exported). SPV technology has been applied to home-lighting, street-lighting, solar-lanterns, water-pumping, telecommunications, stand-alone power plants and others. The development-programmes were continued during the 10th Plan (2002–2007). The MNES has the objective to provide solar-lighting to 5,000 villages in 10th Plan and to 80,000 villages by 2010. The Solar-Grid Power-Programme comprises two components: the Solar Thermal Power Programme and the Solar PV Power Programme. By 2004, 31 projects (aggregate capacity, 2.5 MW only) were installed in 10 States and 3 Union Territories. Seven more projects (totalling 550 kW) are under construction. India has a plan to set up a 140 MW Integrated-Solar-Combined-Cycle-Power Plant in Mathania (Rajasthan).

Wind Energy – The Indian Wind-Power programme was initiated in 1983-84. The Ministry of Non-conventional Energy Sources (MNES) publication (1983), **'Wind Energy Data-Handbook'** serves as a data-source. The extensive Wind-Resource-Assessment (1985), helped beginning of concentrated-development/harnessing of renewable energy sources, more specifically, of wind energy, has now become the world's largest such programme. The published wind-data, contained in **'Handbook-on-Wind Energy-Resource-Survey'**, will facilitate research and development of Wind Energy Technology in India. An **'Indian Wind-Atlas'** has also been proposed.

The Indian wind-resource is estimated at 20,000 MW (at the micro-level) but studies have revised this to over 45,000 MW (at 50 m-hub height).[1] Potential locations with abundant wind have been identified in the 10 states (Andhra Pradesh, Gujarat, Karnataka, Kerala, Madhya Pradesh, Maharashtra, Orissa, Rajasthan, Tamil-Nadu and West-Bengal). It has been estimated that the 10 states have an exploitable technical potential of 13,000 MW. In terms of currently installed wind-turbine-capacity, India ranks 5th in the world behind Germany, USA, Spain and Denmark. By 2003, commercial installed-capacity had grown to 1,870 MW of which Tamil-Nadu alone possessed 53%. For Lakshadweep and Andaman and Nicobar-Islands Hybrid-Projects (wind-diesel) are being developed.

---

1. Renewable EnergyAccess.com

Tidal Energy – The main potential-sites for Tidal-Power generation are Gulf-of-Kutch, Gulf of Khambhat (Gujarat) and Gangetic-Delta in the Sunderbans area (West-Bengal). The tidal-ranges of the Gulf-of-Kutch and the Gulf-of-Khambhat are 5 and 6 m, the theoretical-capacities are 900 MW and 7,000 MW, and the estimated annual output of 1.6 and 16.4 TWh/Year respectively. In the Sunderbans area setting up of a 3 MW Tidal-Power Plant is also under consideration.

Wave Energy – The Indian Wave-Energy-Programme started in 1983. Researches conducted by the Indian Institute of Technology/Department of Ocean-Development (GOI) identified the OWC as most suitable for Indian conditions. A 150 kW pilot OWC was commissioned (1991) at Vizhinjam-Harbour (Kerala). The scheme operated successfully, producing data that were used for the design of a superior generator and turbine. An improved power module was installed at Vizhinjam in April 1996 that in turn led to the production of new designs for a breakwater comprised of 10 caissons with a total capacity of 1.1 MWe. The National Institute of Ocean Technology succeeded IIT and continues to research wave-energy including the Backward-Bent-Duct-Buoy (a variant of the OWC design).

Ocean Thermal Energy Conversion – Having an extremely long-coastline, a very large EEZ-area and suitable oceanic-conditions, India's potential for OTEC is extensive. Conceptual studies on OTEC plants in the islands of Lakshadweep and Andaman-Nicobar and off the Tamil-Nadu coast were initiated in 1980. In 1984 a preliminary design-study for a 1 MW 'Rankine-Cycle floating-plant' was conducted. The National Institute of Ocean Technology-NIOT (formed in 1993) signed (1997) an MOU with Saga University (Japan) for the joint-development of a 1 MW plant near the port of Tuticorin (Tamil-Nadu).

In 2001, Department-of-Ocean-Development (GOI) conducted a study to determine the actions required to maximise the country's potential from its surrounding ocean and prepared a Vision-Document and a Perspective-Plan-2015 (forming part of the 10th Five-Year Plan) in which all aspects of the Indian Ocean will be assessed (forecasting of monsoons, modeling of sustainable-uses of coastal-zone, mapping of ocean-resources, etc.).

It has been postulated that most of India's future OTEC-plants, fully-commercial, will be 'closed-cycle floating plants' in the range of 10-50 MW (with a possibility to increase to 200–400 MW). India's NIOT is working with Saga University (Japan) for the development of OTEC technology and scaled-up plants. Reasons for delayed development of OTEC technology is attributed to plant's mechanical-problems and availability of ocean's weather-window.

India's New Energy Policy is an 'INTEGRATED ENERGY POLICY'

The colossal import-bills of crude-oil prompted the government and the industry to focus on integrated Energy Policy and Energy Security. India set up an Energy-Coordination-Committee (ECC) in 2005 to formulate an Integrated-Energy Policy to explore ways for fuel-substitution, alternative-technologies, and for exploiting synergy for energy-system-efficiency in areas of both production and consumption. If the energy system is to be efficient, policies have to look at it as an integrated-system as with five separate Ministries (Coal, Petroleum Natural Gas, Atomic-Energy, Power, and Non-Conventional Energy Sources) policies are not always consistent; and opportunities for inter-linkages, synergy and optimal solutions do not emerge. For the first time in independent India, the Draft Report of the Expert-Committee on Integrated-Energy Policy has tried to address the country's energy-issues from a holistic prospective and tried to evolve an Energy Policy on an integral-basis. [The previous two major policy-statements (the Fuel-Policy-Committee, 1974 and the Working-Group of Energy Policy, 1979) were mainly policy-recommendations, most of which were not implemented.]

The Expert-Committee on Integrated-Energy Policy observed (Draft-Report, 2005) that: in order to ensure sustained growth of 8% through 2031, India would need to grow its primary energy supply 3 to 4 times and electricity supply 5 to 7 times in comparison to today's consumption; and by 2031-32 power generations' capacity would have to increase to 7,78,095 MW. India would require, meeting this vision, to pursue all available fuel-options and energy forms, both conventional and non-conventional, as well as new and emerging technologies and energy sources. Assuming an 8% growth rate, the Expert-Committee made ten different projections, as shown below, with varied energy-mix combinations for the year 2031-32.

In all the projections, the share of coal ranged between 65% and 42%, share of oil varied between 34% and 28%, gas had a share ranging between 12% and 7% while nuclear-energy's share could rise up to a maximum of 6%.

Indian Scenario for Fuel-Mix in Year 2031-32 (Unit: MMTOE)

Energy-Source	Coal Dominant Case	%	Renewable Dominant Case	%
Oil	467	28%	406	29%
Natural Gas	114	7%	163	12%
Coal	1082	65%	659	42%
Hydro	5	0%	50	4%
Nuclear	3	0%	89	6%
Solar	-	0%	-	0%
Wind	1	0%	0	1%
Fuel-Wood	-	0%	-	5%
Ethanol	-	0%	-	0%
Bio-diesel	-	-	-	1%
Total	1672	100%	1383	100%

Source: Planning Commission, 2005. [Assumption: 8% GDP growth]

It may be observed that 'coal' shall remain India's most important energy source until 2031-32 and possibly beyond. The U.S. Department of Energy expects Indian coal consumption to rise by 70% over the next 25 years to meet demand for electricity that is expected to rise by 150%. India will need to take a lead in seeking clean-coal-technologies and new coal-extraction technologies such as in-situ gasification in order to tap its vast coal-reserves that are economically unviable with conventional-technologies. The committee has concluded that imported-coal is far more cost-competitive than imported-gas for power generation. This preference for coal over gas is likely to continue for a while.

Thus, in future 'Coal' will remain the most important energy-source for many industries in India. Although India's abundant coal-reserves (200 BT) cover all ranks from lignite to bituminous, they tend to have a high-ash content and a low calorific-value and only about 70 BT will be economically recoverable, a pinch of nature requiring this energy-source to be raised to the maximum level of efficiency and effective-use. The low quality of much of its coal prevents India from being anything but a small exporter of coal (traditionally to the neighbouring countries of Bangladesh, Nepal and Bhutan) and conversely, is responsible for sizeable imports (around 13 million tonnes/yr of coking coal and 12 million tonnes/yr of steam coal) from Australia, Canada, China, Indonesia and South Africa. India's import-bills on coal-import will continue in future unless there comes a technological and a foreign-market break-through together with many other measures as discussed in Para 8.1.

'Oil' is another major import concern for India. Oil demand in India grew by over 6% annually during the past decade, more than three times the world average, but at the same time oil production rose barely from 700 to 800 MBD. Consequently, imports jumped from 500 MBD to 1.3 MMBD, or from 42% to 62% of total consumption. Roughly half of India's current oil-imports come from the Middle East. Over time, India's import dependence will grow due to limited prospects for new oil exploration and production. Both the U.S. Department of Energy and the IEA expect Indian oil demand to be among the fastest-growing in the world at nearly four percent annually by 2025. Combined with essentially flat or declining oil production, imports will account for 85% of total oil-demand by 2025, most of which will have to come from the Middle East, Central-Asia, and Africa.

India has historically been self-sufficient in 'Natural Gas', but limited domestic gas-resources and rising demand will lead to change in the future. Gas makes up only about 7% of India's energy-consumption, but demand is expected to continue increasing making India a major importer in the form of LNG and possibly pipeline supplies. The DOE estimates Indian gas-consumption to triple from 0.8 trillion-cubic-feet (TCF) in 2001 to 2.5 TCF by 2025, driven by the demand for electricity and the need to substitute for dirty coal. At the same time domestic gas production is likely to rise more slowly to only 1.5 TCF, meaning that 40% of India's gas needs are likely to be imported by 2025. India is already moving to develop the infrastructure to boost imports.

India's first LNG import terminal, Petronet, a joint-venture between India's state oil and gas companies ONGC, GAIL, and IOC, along with Gaz-de-France, began operation in late 2003 and is importing gas from Qatar. Another Shell-sponsored terminal was planned for 2005 in Gujarat to bring LNG from Oman. In all, the government has approved plans for 12 possible import terminals in the future. It is also possible that India will be importing gas by pipeline in line with a series of proposals to bring gas from Turkmenistan, Iran, Pakistan, and Bangladesh, all of which have potential large exportable supplies. ONGC has recently made history by receiving the first shipment of oil at Mangalore port from Sakhalin-I field in Russia as part of its equity share in the project. India is also likely to take part in the exploration and production of crude and natural gas from the Sakhalin III field in far east Russia.[2]

India needs to take advance diplomatic measures, as each of these proposals has serious geo-political problems,

2. The Hindu, 2nd Dec. 2006

and the outlook for pipeline-supplies will depend on resolving key regional-geopolitical rivalries and constraints. The large majority of India's future gas-imports will necessarily come from the Persian Gulf, with lesser amounts possible from Central Asia and neighbours, Pakistan and Bangladesh. Whether be it Nuclear, coal or gas based plant, power-generation for future India will need a thorough examination of all alternatives to determine a right capacity-distribution and fuel-mix, as discussed below.

Non-OECD India (as well as China) needs to develop reliable electricity supplies progressively

World's total net-electricity-consumption is projected to grow steeply at an average rate of 2.7% per year, from 14,781 billion kilowatthours (bkwh) in 2003 to 21,699 bkwh in 2015 and to 30,116 bkwh in 2030, increase shared by **Non-OECD countries (71%)**, specially **China** and **India**, as shown overleaf, and OECD countries (29%). The OECD-countries' electricity-sector is well-established, and equipment-efficiency gains are expected to temper growth in electricity-demand. In addition, slower population-growth is expected for the OECD-economies than for the non-OECD economies; and some European countries, as well as Japan, are expected to see their populations decline. Residential electricity-consumption-growth in the non-OECD Asia is by far the fastest in the world, at 6.5% per year, driven by population-growth and rising living standards. In 2030, residential-electricity-consumption in the region may total 3,016 bkwh, nearly four-times its 2003 level. In the commercial and industrial sectors also, electricity-consumption in 2030 may grow strongly, at an average-annual-rates of 4.8% and 4.0% to 1,291 and 5,653 bkwh, respectively. The continuing challenge for the **non-OECD economy** will be to develop reliable electricity-supplies steadily and avoid shortages or excess capacity as per the report of IEO 2006.

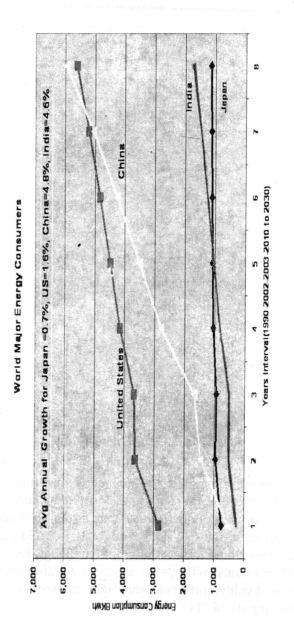

World Major Energy Consumers

Avg Annual Growth for Japan =0.7%, US=1.6%, China=4.8%, India=4.6%

Energy Consumption BKwh

Years Interval(1990 2002 2003 2010 to 2030)

Source: Derived from Energy Information Administration (EIA)

Re-Structure of Energy Sources in India

The strategic-goals for **Energy-Independence** by **2030** would call for a shift in the structure of energy sources. First, fossil fuel imports need to be minimized and secure access to be ensured. Maximum hydro and nuclear power potential should be utilized, apart from the use of coal and gas based thermal power generation. The most significant aspect, however would be that the power generated through renewable energy technologies has to be increased to 25% against the present 5%. It would be evident that for true energy independence, a major shift in the structure of energy sources from fossil to renewable energy sources is mandated.[3]

India should ensure efficient mixing of fuels as the right choice of fuel-mix is very vital for the production of electricity and its supply based on actual requirements which vary from region to region and as a function of available natural-resources, energy security concerns, and market-competition around and among the alternative means of fuel-choices. Electricity suppliers must decide how much capacity of each generation technology to build, and then they must decide when to use the different types of capacity, balancing the costs and flexibility of the different technologies in their generation fleets. Base-load systems usually are operated over the longest periods and produce the most electricity per unit of installed capacity. For example, in the United States coal-fired steam plants represent 35% of the country's installed capacity but 52% of its total electricity-production. In contrast, natural gas and oil-fired units represent 43% of U.S. capacity but only 18% of production.

The **Fuel-mixes** for electricity production of USA, OECD Europe, Japan, China and India are shown overleaf. High oil prices forced switching from oil-fired generation to natural gas and nuclear power and reinforced the coal's

---

3. Former President of India Dr. A.P.J. Abdul Kalam's address at the inauguration of the Bio-Diesel Conference towards Energy Independence at Rashtrapati Nilayam, Hyderabad on 09-06-2006

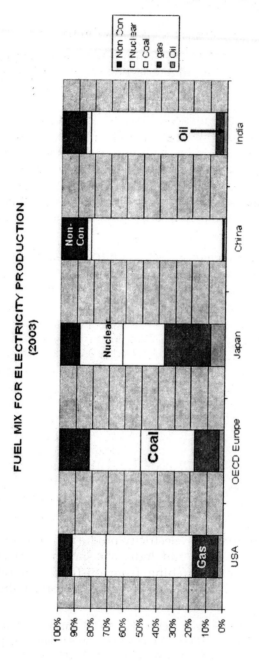

FUEL MIX FOR ELECTRICITY PRODUCTION (2003)

Source: Derived from Energy Information Administration (EIA)

vital-role in world power-generation. Similarly, the relatively higher fossil-fuel prices of recent years are raising renewed interest in nuclear power and making renewable-energy sources more competitive economically.

India's Energy Security Strategy

India's growing dependence on imported-oil supplies has recently catalyzed an aggressive strategy to secure supplies overseas. India seems to be emulating China in its overseas energy security strategy. ONGC of India is beginning to stake out new overseas oilfield-investment plans through its international subsidiary ONGC Videsh Ltd. India's largest oil-stake to date is its 25% share in the Greater-Nile-Oil-Project in Sudan in partnership with China's CNPC and a 20% share in ExxonMobil-led Sakhalin project. ONGC is also moving rapidly in West Africa with the purchase of a 50% stake for $600 million in Angola's Greater-Plutonia offshore project.

ONGC is also beginning to source large supplies of LNG from the Persian Gulf through deals, coming online with Qatar and Oman. ONGC also signed a preliminary deal with Iran to buy LNG. ONGC Videsh Ltd. Acquired an equity stake in a large gas discovery offshore Burma and also bid for Cairn Energy assets in Bangladesh; has been awarded exploration blocks in Syria; and has been negotiating with Iraq, Libya, Kazakhstan, and the United States for exploration blocks. With more than 50% of its total oil-supplies now sourced from the Middle East, India has announced plans for a strategic oil stockpile, but it has not moved very far in doing so yet.

In the field of 'ENERGY', policymakers, regulators, consumers and producers in India are in an impasse facing uncertainties in policy-formulation and investment-decisions where increasing energy demand outstripping the reliable sources of supplies; technology is advancing at an unprecedented rate; environmental-regulations have grown costly and complex; energy-companies confronting greater competition to meet the increased energy demands of our growing population and economy; growing uncertainties about the stability and security within the global energy market; increasing expectations of the Indian people for a much higher growth-rate requiring a stable, low-cost, and secure supply of energy.

The demand for energy is growing to increase significantly in future where the GDP of India is expected to grow to US$ 2 trillion by 2020 from the current level of US $ 500 billion, with 70% oil import and 75% usage of coal for power-generation, the economic and ecological distortion caused is huge. Thus, there is a need to shift from these energy sources. The answers to these are natural gas, nuclear power, renewable-energies and bio-fuels, all have huge potentials in India. For utilization of these new energy sources huge investments are required. There is also a need for private participation in this sector with the help of the government.

A proper response to these uncertainties is the development and implementation of a sound, unified, integrated Energy Policy and Strategy for India. This strategy will deliver to consumers a ready, reliable and environmentally responsible supply of affordable energy-resources and energy-related services from a broad range of energy providers. The new Energy Policy should be based on the objectives of equity, security, efficiency, and environmental-protection developed on a sound, integrated, reliable, environmentally responsible energy strategy where all the energy sources are optimally used.

A country's desire for peace and rapid development, however, cannot by itself be a guarantee of its security and prosperity. The centre of gravity in world affairs is slowly but noticeably moving towards Asia, which has the fastest-growing economies, the fastest-rising military expenditures and the areas with the most serious potential for crisis. Asia, at the centre of the global-war on international terrorism, will determine the new world order. In a world in which rapid economic growth has usually been set in motion through political autocracy, India presents itself as a democracy-based economic model of modernization.

In a world characterized by rapid economic change and uncertainty, India has to make the best use of her available resources and opportunities to promote the well-being of its people through economic and social modernization and technological developments. India is pursuing a pioneering political-system of modernization via democracy. Political asymmetries are striking in Asia, a continent whose significance in international relations has already begun to rival that of Europe. As a part of Asia, while China is committed to pursuing political-autocracy and market-capitalism, India has demonstrated that democratic-politics and market-economics can blend nicely for developing nations and that they need not follow the model set by South Korea, Taiwan, Thailand and other states which first achieved impressive economic growth under authoritarian rule before moving to democracy under pressure from their burgeoning middle classes.

Future conflict between countries will be driven not by ideology but by competition over scarce and depleting natural-resources. The likelihood and seriousness of resource-wars has to be seen in the context of the growing inter-state economic competition in the world. The Information-Revolution and Globalization has brought fundamental changes in polity, economy and security but not in the nature of international-relations or in the makeup of the international-systems. For example, the rapid pace of technological–developments is itself a consequence of nations competing fiercely and seeking relative advantage in an international system based not on collective security but on national security. What have altered are the forms and dimensions of conflict.

Nothing better illustrates the dangers of resource-wars than the emerging situation in Asia, where high economic growth-rates have fuelled concern and competition over raw materials and energy resources. Energy has become critical to continued economic expansion in Asia and the spectre of inadequate energy supply has intensified geopolitical rivalry among outside powers in oil-rich Central Asia, the Caspian Sea basin and West Asia. India's energy vulnerability is greater than that of China's, which has in recent years become an oil-importer. India's increasing concern over energy security arises from its fast-rising dependence on oil and petroleum products imported by sea from the Gulf region. That concern has underscored the importance of protecting sea-lines vital to India's economic and strategic interests.

Overall, India's energy-future looks dependent mainly on high consumption of domestic coal, on high-volume imports of coal, oil and gas. It may, however, be possible for India to stem its ballooning energy-deficit through a strategy that should combine and integrate the following **thirteen essential fronts:**

(i) Capital Formation to meet Planning Commission's projections for 1997-2012

To meet the Planning Commission's projection of 7.4% economic growth in the period 1997-2012, there has to be a commensurate growth in commercial energy sources which would require a fresh capacity-addition of 100,000 MW and an investment of US$ 160 billion. Vast capital-investments in all forms of energy–fossil-fuels, nuclear-energy and renewable-energy, will be required to fuel the Indian economy during the early decades of the 21st century in all phases of the energy sector, from production, generation, storage, transmission, distribution to improved end-use efficiency. This calls for massive-investments in infrastructure from public, private-sector and joint-partnerships both at domestic and international levels. The investments would also need the policy-makers to work towards creating an attractive environment with appropriate policy, legislative and regulatory framework for more private investments and foreign-direct-investments. This will make the energy sector a driver of economic resurgence.

(ii) More Aggressive Search for Oil and Gas is a Must for India

The second pillar of this strategy will be to encourage a more aggressive search for oil and gas finds in India by providing incentives for exploration to foreign and Indian companies. Overall recovery-rates from drilling, so far averaging only about 30%, has to be increased. With the entry of more foreign companies, India's traditional and conservative regulatory and working environment has to be made more liberal, facilitating and professional. Indian government should now offer more attractive business-terms for exploration.

India is geographically diverse, from the desert of Rajasthan, to offshore basins, and to island chains, therefore a more coordinated and fertile environment for oil and gas exploration will be required. The western part of Rajasthan adjacent to Pakistan looks very promising after Britain's Cairn-Energy reported several oil-discoveries in 2004 in that region. The biggest find, the one in Jan. 2004, was at Mangala, estimated to contain at least 500 million barrels of recoverable reserves. Commercial production at this field was slated to begin by 2007, with an expected volume of more than 100,000 barrels per day.

(iii) Building commercially competitive Nuclear Power Plants is India's Necessity

The third pillar of the energy security strategy has to be a greater emphasis on generating commercial nuclear power to produce more electricity with less pollution. India's heavy dependence on coal for generating electricity has contributed to high levels of carbon emissions. In fact, India has one of Asia's highest levels of carbon-intensity. As a non-Annex-I country under the UN-FCCC, India is not obligated to reduce its emissions of carbon/GHG. Yet, if India is to meet its energy security-needs in a more environmentally friendly way, it will increasingly have to turn to the GHG-free commercial nuclear power. India, despite having one of the world's oldest commercial Nuclear Power programmes, still remains more attracted to coal and natural gas for electricity generation mainly because of high costs involved in building Nuclear Power Plant. So, the challenge for India is to make nuclear power economically more viable and commercially more competitive.

The problem of safe-disposal of Spent-Fuel has to be managed yet more safely and innovatively though India, however, intends to recycle Spent-Fuel as new fuel for its next-generation of commercial Nuclear Power Plants, known as Fast-Breeder-Reactors to potentially support an electricity-generating capacity as large as 500,000 megawatts. Commercial nuclear power can make significant contribution to meeting India's growing electricity needs while helping to reduce carbon/GHG-emissions.

Even though the Nuclear Suppliers Group (NSG) promises India greater access to nuclear-technology, the American, French and Russian nuclear-firms who are keen to enter India's commercial nuclear power sector will take many years to materialize. Through Fast-Breeder-Reactor, India can recycle the Spent-Fuel from its natural uranium-fuelled plants. India's three stage nuclear power programme based on Close nuclear fuel cycle will ensure long term objective of utilizing the vast Thorium resources for power generation with complete control on the knowledge of reprocessing the spent nuclear fuels as stated by Shri Anil Kakodkar, Chairman, Atomic Energy Commission.[4]

(iv) Overland Pipelines for import of Oil and Natural Gas and Building up Strategic Highways

The fourth pillar of India's search for energy security has to be the building of Bilateral-Energy-Cooperation with neighboring nations to facilitate plans for regional natural gas and oil-pipelines, including from Burma, Bangladesh, Iran and Turkmenistan. An overland-pipeline through Pakistan to import natural gas from Iran's huge South-Pars field to India, could be a major foreign-exchange earner for

---

4. The Hindu, 21st Sept. 2006

Pakistan. If Pakistan earns upto $735 million/year as transit-charges, it also accepts an economic-anchorage. However, two offshore routes bypassing Pakistan have also been technically analyzed by international firms at the behest of the Indian and Iranian governments. While debate over the overland-pipeline proposal raged inconclusively, India in the meantime entered into a major LNG import-contract with Iran. India's deal (2005) with Iran, a 25-year contract, is the biggest deal to annually import 7.5 million metric-tons of LNG from Iran starting from 2009.[5]

The Burmese military junta's decision to start building a pipeline to India's North-East underscores the potential of bilateral energy-cooperation in southern Asia. Once Burma's international isolation eases and Western petroleum firms exploring oil and gas there, it is conceivable that Burma could become an important source of energy supply at least to India's eastern states. So also can Bangladesh. Bangladesh also can earn substantial foreign-exchange by selling its natural gas (western firms like Shell and Unocal estimated the reserves at 38 trillion-cubic-feet) to India and by large transit-fees from a pipeline running across its territory from Burma to India.

Though Bangladesh has agreed in principle to permit the construction of a pipeline from Burma through its territory to India, its actual construction being still far off, its surprising refusal to sell gas to India, is certainly based on politics, not economics, warrants India to take special diplomatic-efforts as it cannot economically and indefinitely persist with its reluctance to commercially tapping its gas-reserves, and further, as it has the choice to chart a stronger economic development for a better future for its large, growing population through sale of its gas, with India signing a free-trade agreement with Thailand, followed by such accords with Sri Lanka and Nepal, Bangladesh cannot keep itself isolated from the regional-cooperation trends. **China's great western development** effort is one of the major dynamics of contemporary China, which have some kind of analogy with

5. www.geopoliticalreview.com/archives/000662india_iran_oil.php

the opening of north American west in the second half of nineteenth country to improve the economic growth by utilizing the uniqueness of geographical regions. Applications of modern transportation technology in difficult terrains, backed by strong fiscal health of China, have led to build up of costly road and railway networks and harbours. [6]

These networks of transportation will be the bearers of Chinese goods, natural resources along with the Chinese influence. Network does not define the clear intention but merely acts as a multipurpose conduit with feature of flexibility and interoperability to ascertain the results as per the Matrix of relationship among the nations in the regions forming different nodes of the network. Network also exhibits a feature of interdependence of various nodes and India's participation will definitely increase the degree of interdependence with stabilization effect in the region. China has always had better sense than India of the link between geography and strategy. The contrast is striking. After Independence, India allowed its existing border infrastructure to degrade and consciously chose not to develop additional connectivity on its northern borders.

Beijing, on the other hand, was determined to build first class strategic transport links between its eastern seaboard and the remote regions of western China, including Tibet and Xinjiang. Having consolidated its internal access, China sought to extend it to the border regions near Kashmir in the west to Arunachal Pradesh in the east with Nepal in the middle. India should find ways to leverage the current positive ties with China to develop greater connectivity between Kashmir on the one hand and Tibet and Xinjiang on the other. Such a creative approach, which might involve developing bus services between Demchok in Ladakh and Mansarovar as well as the revival of old trade routes between Leh and Tibet, would transform the fortunes of J&K and bring peace and prosperity to the Himalayan region that has suffered so much because of territorial disputes involving India, China and Pakistan.[7]

---

6. The China Quarterly, 2006 by John W. Garver

7. Indian Express: "Diplomacy takes a high road", 26 March 2006

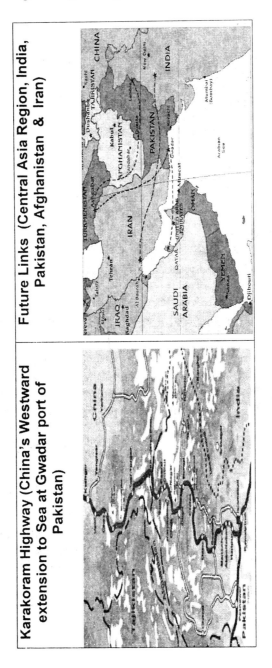

Karakoram Highway (China's Westward extension to Sea at Gwadar port of Pakistan)

Future Links (Central Asia Region, India, Pakistan, Afghanistan & Iran)

The reliable and easy accessibility to Leh and further will open the corridor to Central-Asia regions to India which is in the national interest of India in long term to meet its strategic and commercial objectives.

The **Asian-Highway** (AH) project is a cooperative-project among countries in Asia and the United Nations Economic and Social Commission for Asia and the Pacific (ESCAP) to improve the highway systems in Asia. It is one of the three pillars of Asian Land Transport Infrastructure Development (ALTID) project, endorsed by the ESCAP commission at its forty-eighth session in 1992, comprising Asian-Highway, Trans-Asian-Railway (TAR) and facilitation of land transport projects. A budget and a timeline for construction was to be announced during 2006-07.[8] India's active participation in this future project will strengthen the ties with other countries of the region with strategic interest besides meeting the commercial interest.

(v) Aggressive acquiring of foreign ownership-rights is an obligation

The fifth pillar of India's energy security-strategy would be for its large petroleum companies, five of which figure on the **Fortune 500** list, to acquire ownership-rights over oil-reserves in other parts of the world more aggressively. China has been aggressively pursuing this path, entering into major deals in Central-Asia and Africa. India's state-owned firms like the Oil and Natural Gas Corporation (ONGC) and Gas Authority of India Limited (GAIL) have now started buying equity in oil and gas reserves in other parts of the world. Example is that of ONGC's investments in Iran.

Building a sensible strategy for energy security demands a comprehensive, integrated approach encompassing military, diplomatic, economic and political levers. A pragmatic foreign policy that seeks to engage other states while determinedly pursuing national interests is a necessary component of any energy security plan.

---

8. From Wikipedia, the free encyclopedia web-site

(vi) Justification for India's assertive maritime role has emerged

In addition to countering land-based threats, India has to support its maritime security in the Indian Ocean region. India is a peninsular country with a long coastline and vast exclusive economic zone (EEZ). The movement by sea of 95% of its external trade and 84% of its oil makes India's maritime interests particularly susceptible. While military-threats from across land-borders can be anticipated, threats from the seas are less predictable because of the flexibility, mobility and stealth of naval forces. Threats from the sea can materialise in days or even hours, but building a strong navy is a task of many decades. It is central to India's energy security interests that its navy plays a greater role in the Indian Ocean region, which is critical for oil and trade for much of the world. In the years to come, the concentration of remaining oil reserves in the Persian Gulf area would make the Indian Ocean region even more important. In recognition of that need, India needs to continue and further expand its naval role having already illustrated by its US encouraged naval escort of commercial ships passing through the Strait-of-Malacca which helped India's naval presence gaining rapid acceptance and legitimacy in South-East Asia.

Further, India may also face competition from China in the Indian Ocean region. China appears to be positioning itself along the vital sea-lanes from the Persian Gulf to the South-China Sea. It has helped Iran upgrade its Bandar-e-Abbas port. It is building a deepwater naval-base and port for Pakistan at Gwadar. It has begun military cooperation with Bangladesh and it has strategically penetrated Burma, positioning itself in the Coco Islands, at Hainggyi port and elsewhere along the Burmese coastline. China's new strategic focus on the seas, in return, is influencing India's long term security planning. Thus, China's growing oil-import-needs and extending its strategic and military influence on sea-routes act as sufficient justification for

India's assertive maritime role when already, the rising oil-imports by China and India have sharpened their mutual competition over energy resources and also pushed up international oil and gas-prices.

(vii) Energy Pricing needs re-consideration to develop Relative-Pricing-System

Based on purchasing power parity comparisons, the Indian consumer pays the highest tariffs in the world for its energy supplies/services. Petroleum products are priced at international parity without any competition among incumbents and then loaded with taxes and levies. Access to petroleum-products including subsidized kerosene meant for the Public-Distribution-System is limited. Relative-Pricing-System can play a very important role in the choice of fuel-mix and energy-form. In addition, a relating-pricing is supposed to be the most vital aspect of an Integrated-Energy Policy in order to be effective both in promoting the most efficient-fuel-choices and facilitating the most appropriate fuel-substitution.

(viii) Promotion and Performance-Measurement of Energy-Efficiency Technologies

Indian industry has not shown much enthusiasm in investing in cleaner-energy and on energy-saving technology. Probable reasons are the low-level of per-capita energy-consumption and carbon-emissions, relatively low price of energy compared to investment cost in energy-saving process and cleaner-energy system. Though awareness for the need about energy-saving-technologies is increasing in India yet a lot of efforts are to be planned and monitored to harvest the investments already committed/to come in the area of cleaner energy.

The 8th Five-Year Plan (1992-97) made a provision of Rs. 1,000 crore for energy-efficiency to provide projected energy-savings of 5000 MW and 6 million tonnes in the electricity and petroleum sectors respectively. However, this money was not explicitly spent for this purpose. The 10th Five-Year Plan (2002-07) suggested demand-side management in 'transport-sector' and proposed benchmarking in the 'hydro-carbon-sector' against the rest in the world with the target for energy-savings as 95,000 Million-Units.

Performance-Reviews and follow-ups, need to be done effectively, will need a parallelly and professionally developed plan for Management-Information-System necessitating generation, preservation and reporting of both normative and actual data as defined and required in each such schemes to enable correct and timely assessment and evaluation of the actual savings realized against the targets set by the Government.

(ix) Promotion of Research and Development on Energy

The Energy related R&D did not get the resources it needed. The Expert-Committee strongly felt the need to focus on research on energy-generation, distribution and conservation. International-Energy-Agency addressing Delhi-Sustainable-Development-Summit (2006) commented that to meet the energy demand and stabilize CO_2 concentrations, unprecedented technology changes must occur in this century as no single technology or policy can do it all.

The Expert-Committee recommended a comprehensive R&D plan to make India self-sufficient by making breakthroughs in clean-energy by recommending five technology-approaches: (i) Coal-Technology (recovering coal-bed-methane and mine mouth methane; in-situ coal-gasification; carbon-capture and sequestration; and integrated gasification combined cycle-IGCC); (ii) Solar-Technology (a technology approach should be initiated to bring down the cost of solar photovoltaic or solar thermal by a factor of five as soon as possible and by improving the efficiency using Nano Technology); (iii) Bio-fuels-Technology (a bio-fuel mission to plant Jatropha or other appropriate oil plants on half a million hectare of wasteland within two years should be undertaken); biomass-plantation and wood-gasification, and community biogas-plants that all run on commercial basis; (iv) Nuclear-Technology including Fusion-

Power and (v) Battery and Hydrogen-Technology (a development-oriented coordinated research). [9]

The Expert-Committee has also recommended the formation of a National-Energy-Fund (NEF) by imposing a tax of 0.1% of the turnover of all energy-firms whose turnover exceeds Rs. 100 crores a year. As per 2004-05 turnovers, this will collect Rs. 500 to Rs. 600 crores per year and will increase overtime. In order to encourage the firms to do their own R&D a rebate of up to 80% of this tax may be given to firms for R&D carried out by them.[10] An Independent Board should govern the funds with representatives from the Department of Science and Technology (DST), Planning-Commission and Energy-Ministries. However, the majority of representatives should be outside experts. The idea is to support all stages of R&D from basic research to diffusion with appropriate policies, resources and institutions.

(x) Potentials of Energy-Conservation in India

India has a huge potential for energy-savings. A study done for the Asian-Development-Bank in 2003 estimated an immediate market potential of energy saving of 54,500 Million Units and a peak savings of 9,240 MW, totaling an investment potential of Rs. 14,000 crore. The cost-effective saving potential is at least 10% of the total generation through Demand-Side-Management. Additional savings are possible by auxiliary reduction in generation plants.

For energy-conservation the Expert-Committee suggested that: (i) programmes and standards on energy-efficiency and conservation be established and enforced; (ii) the Bureau of Energy Efficiency (BEE) should develop such standards for all energy intensive industries and appliance and develop

---

9. Planning Commission (GOI), Draft Report of the expert committee on IntegratedEnergyPolicy, NewDelhi Dec2005http://planning commission.nic.in/reports/genrep/intengpol.pdf

10. http://planningcommission.nic.in/reports/genrep/intengpol.pdf

modalities for a system of incentives/penalties for compliance / non-compliance and the standards be of levels equal to current international norms; (iii) the BEE should be made autonomous and independent of the Ministry of Power, to be funded by a contribution from all energy Ministries or from a tax on fuels and electricity and an adjusted tax on fuels for generating electricity, the BEE staffing should be substantially strengthened; (iv) the existing national energy efficiency organizations like the Petroleum Conservation Research Association (PCRA) should be merged with BEE to ensure that BEE is responsible for energy efficiency for all sectors and all end uses.[11]

(xi) Projection and Revision of energy-estimates must consider 'Energy–Intensity'

The major source of uncertainty in long term projections is the relationship of energy-use to GDP over time (called, Energy-Intensity). Energy Demand and Economic Growth are linked, but the strength of link varies among regions over time. For the OECD countries, history shows the link to be relatively weak, with energy demand lagging behind economic growth. For non-OECD countries (particularly China and India but excluding non-OECD Europe and Eurasia), energy demand and economic growth have been closely correlated for much of the past two decades. Economic growth only recently (that is, within the past decade or so) began to outpace growth in energy-use among the emerging economies of the world. The trend of energy-intensity in respect of USA, China and India are shown overleaf, based on the data from IEO 2006.

The 'Living-standards' of individuals strongly influence the link between economic growth and energy demand. Advanced economies with high living-standards have a relatively high level of energy-use per capita, but they also tend to be economies where per capita energy-use is stable or changes very slowly. In the OECD economies, there is a

11. http://planningcommission.nic.in/reports/genrep/intengpol.pdf

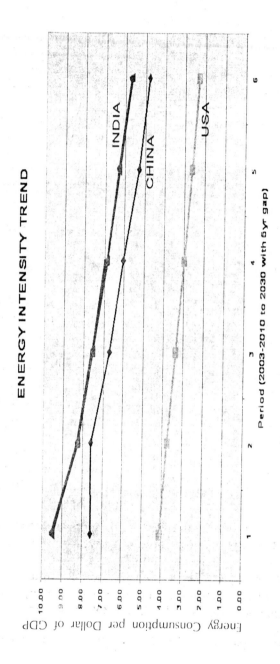

Source: Derived from Energy Information Administration (EIA)

high penetration rate of modern appliances and motorized personal transportation equipment. To the extent that spending is directed to energy consuming goods, it involves more often than not purchasing of new-equipment (more-efficient) to replace old-one (less-efficient) resulting in a weaker-link between income and energy demand. The pace of improvement in energy-intensity may change, given different assumptions of macroeconomic growth over time. Faster growth in income leads to a faster rate of decline in energy-intensity.

Therefore, for energy-planning to be more intensive and effective in the dynamic and multi-dimensional economic-context of India, if energy-intensity and similar more criteria (in quantitative, qualitative and monetary-terms) are analysed based on fuel-type/sector/ region/ area/time-period, considering those criteria in the projection and revision of energy-estimates will be useful, inter alia, for determination of energy-substitution decisions, best fuel-mix, investments, new-capacity and also in management of demand-supply.

(xii). India's 11th Five-Year Plan (2007-12) will need a marathon exercise to curtail the present (38%) aggregate technical and commercial (AT&C) losses

India's Planning Commission (IPC) through its approach-document (14 June 2006) to the 11th FYP (2007-12) proposed many reforms to achieve an average growth-rate of 8-9% in the 11th Plan, against only 7% in 10th Plan, stressing that India's economic-fundamentals have improved to the point where they have the capacity to make a decisive - impact on common people's economic-welfare if only accompanied with completion of the reform-agenda after evolving a political consensus.

The approach-document to the 11th Plan focused to draw a noticeable attention on the need to curtail the present level of **energy-inefficiencies.** For attaining higher growth-rate in **"energy sector"**, IPC categorically stressed the need to control the continuing inefficiency in the power-distribution-system, and to curtail India's "aggregate technical and commercial" (AT&C) losses from the existing about 38%. The present rate of decline in AT&C losses is a little over 1% a year. For the AT&C at 38% to go down to 15% would require an improvement of 23% which will take more than 20 years unless the energy-efficiency improvement-pace is accelerated.[12]

(xiii). Regional Co-Operation Towards an Asian Energy Community: An Exploration

The quantum of energy loss by India-China is so much that:

(i) A mere 10% saving in India's and China's energy consumption is more than the total power generation of Australia and a 20% saving can generate enough electricity to feed complete Middle East.

(ii) A mere 16-18% saving in India's energy consumption alone is equivalent to the total generating capacity of Pakistan, Bangladesh and Sri-Lanka or Pakistan, Afghanistan, Kyrgyzstan, Tajikistan put together. It indicates that effective energy saving measures in India and China will not only achieve its own requirement but also ensure availability of scarce energy resources in its surroundings .

Currently other regions of the world such as Western Europe and North America are seeking to improve energy market efficiency and secure cost-effective energy supply through energy market integration and system interconnection. However, the countries in the Asian region are depriving themselves of such opportunities primarily due to their isolated and, in some cases, fragmented energy systems.

However, the Asian economies are gradually waking to the possibility of creating an energy consortium with the neighbouring countries, if not with the rest of the Asian region. The Asian economies are lagging far behind the US

12. http://www.thehindubusinessline.com/2006/07/05/stories/htm

and the EU in both demand side measures and strategic reserves to fall back on. One of the target areas of Asian energy cooperation could be to build an **Asian Strategic Petroleum Reserve** (SPR) and to create an **Asian Emergency Response System**. An Asian SPR would be like a global energy security insurance policy. The Asian SPR would be a safeguard against OPEC's ability to raise oil prices and would prevent any market failure, by enabling governments to provide supply liquidity in an emergency situation. [13]

13. Research and Information System for Developing Countries - http://www.ris.org.in

Section – VIII

Securitization of 'ENERGY': Its Need and Implications

CHAPTER 20

Securitization of 'Energy': Its Need and Implications

To conquer the enemy without resorting to war is the most desirable.
The highest form of generalship is to conquer the enemy by strategy.

—Ancient Chinese Warlord

Origination of the concept of "securitization"

Historically the concept of safety and security, in its simplest form, co-exists with human beings. In its original form, the concept is natural, logical and desirable. However, with the growth of civilization, the scope, application and implication of this concept, were extended to include border, territory, region, population and nation to support the human-policy of protecting and preserving its past, of ensuring favourable actualization of its present; and of assuring its future-welfare, as contributed by 'political-science'; and borrowing, lending and adding asset and derivatives as contributed by 'economics, finance and insurance'. But, in a broader sense, issues relating to securitization or national-security might be extended from just population, nation and vast national-systems of critical importance with a view to including the whole range of measures affecting the economic and social welfare of a population or a nation, as well as provision against aggression from abroad or subversion from within but that is very selectively applied. The concept was extended to treat "energy" as a 'commodity of national importance/security' and might have securitized by some countries to maintain and pursue both sustainable and ambitious development.

Securitization-concept gathered inconsistent offensive-meanings/mechanism and got selective but multi-dimensional extensions in political science

Internationally, use of the term 'securitization' remained normally dormant and un-invoked unless the safety of a nation was thought to be under threat, internally or externally, due to military-action, man-made mass-disturbance, natural-disaster, illegal-immigration, maligned interference, and even justified imposition. Only some countries, such as the United States and Russia, formalized the highest level of consideration of such problems in national-security-council. Generally, invocation of national-security is often regarded in national constitutions as a proper occasion for the assumption of special emergency legal powers by government and for the imposition of exceptional or mass-affecting duties, such as military-service or additional taxes on citizens.

During the first centuries of the nation-state system, economic-welfare was thought to be advanced by extension of national-territory in the interests of trade and investment. Thus, during this era of so-called mercantilism the requirements of military-security were closely allied to those of economic self-interest. During the latter decades of the 20th century this linkage was largely destroyed by the virtually universal belief that prosperity derived from free-trade in global-markets. Concern about ecological issues generated new concepts of danger to national-welfare such as the effects of dangerous nuclear-installations or the destruction of forests or water-supplies. Possibility that military steps might sometimes be required to prevent such dangers raised the prospect of a new union between military and non-military elements in security, to succeed the former one between military power and economic prosperity.

Securitization-concept adopted consistent defensive-meanings/mechanism bearing more transparency and public acceptance in economics and finance

Black's Law-Dictionary defines 'securitization' as the process of homogenizing and packaging financial instruments into a new fungible one. Acquisition, classification, collateralization, composition, pooling and distribution are functions within this process.

Mark Fisher and Zoe Shaw defined 'securitization' as the packaging of designated-pools of loans or receivables with an appropriate level of credit-enhancement and the redistribution of these packages to investors. Investors buy the repackaged assets in the form of securities or loans which are collateralized (secured) on the underlying pool and its associated income stream. Securitization thereby converts illiquid-assets into liquid-assets. Securitization has two prototypical transaction types: cash and synthetic.

In **cash securitization**, the corporation pools assets together for purchase by a bankruptcy-remote **special-purpose-vehicle** (a limited-company/partnership created to fulfill specific-objectives to isolate financial/ taxation/ regulatory risks and bankruptcy where 'risk' generally means all insecurities and uncertainties); purchase is effected by issuing multiple trenches of securities based on the cash flow generating capacity of the asset pool. (For more on the capital-structure of SPVs please consult the section on asset-backed securities.) In **synthetic securitization**, the corporation buys a **credit default swap** (or, less commonly, a **total return swap**) on certain asset exposures as a kind of default insurance for credits that remain on balance sheet; the swap can be an outright trade or it can be embedded in the balance sheet of an SPE against which liabilities are issued. Financial-Institutions and businesses of all kinds use cash-securitization to immediately realize the cash-value of their illiquid-contracts or remove assets from their Balance-Sheets. However, Balance-Sheet restructuring so as to incorporate the accruing implications of and via securitization would be much harder to give effect under IFRS (International-Financial-Reporting-System) and US-GAAP (US Generally Accepted Accounting Principles).

To simplify, in 'economics and finance' the term is used to denote two meanings: something given by a borrower to a lender to secure a loan, that is, something that the lender will be able to sell and recover monies owed if the borrower defaults on repaying the loan; or a share in the equity (the assets minus the liabilities) of a business. Securities were originally the documents that proved ownership on property or rights to income that could be used as collateral (security) for a loan. Today, the term securities is generally taken to refer to interest-bearing shares or bonds traded on the capital (long term finance) or money (short term finance) markets. The past two decades have seen substantial growth in securitization, as companies have increasingly opted to raise finance through the securities market rather than through a loan from a bank or other financial intermediary. As a result the securities market has become remarkably diverse and sophisticated. Banks may have lost some of their traditional loan business, but they welcome the fact that the risk of lending is now spread among a wider range of suppliers of funds, and they now make money from arranging the issue of securities. The term 'securitization' is being used extensively also in "insurance-sector".

Corporations, through the technique of securitization, allows separation of their credit-origination and funding-activities. The technique comes under the umbrella of structured-financing as it applies to assets that typically are illiquid-contracts. It has evolved from tentative beginnings in the late 1970s to a vital funding source with an estimated total aggregate outstanding of $8.06 trillion (as of the end of 2005, by the Bond Market Association) and new issuance of $3.07 trillion in 2005 in the U.S. markets alone.

With the growth of securitization (the raising of corporate-finance through issue of securities rather than by bank loans), the market for 'derivatives' has also developed. 'Derivatives' are effectively assets derived from other assets; for example, an option (derived-asset) to buy a share (original-asset) at a certain-price at any time upto a specific period. In this instance, two markets operate: one for the original asset and one for the derived asset. Those who trade in options are in effect betting on the price of the share of which they have purchased an option to buy; if the share price goes up by more than the cost of the option, they can realize a profit or loss just from dealing in the option. Other derivatives include futures and swaps. In theory there could be derivatives of derivatives, such as an option to buy an option to buy a share. In practice, there are real worries that too much concentration on derivatives undermines the market for the original securities.

Germany's Bundesbank said that the growing use of derivatives "has reinforced the integration of financial markets and hence increased their vulnerability". The underlying problem is that many of those who trade in derivatives do not fully appreciate, let alone understand, the complexity of the market and its potential risks. These risks were graphically demonstrated early in 1995 when Barings, the oldest merchant bank in the City of London with capital of £541 million, was bankrupted by a single trader in its Singapore division who lost over £850 million through unsupervised derivatives trading in the Japanese markets. This prompted renewed calls for greater regulation of the derivatives trade, as well as admonitions to trading companies and exchanges to tighten their controls.

Technological advances in computers and telecommunications have fuelled growth in the trade of these sophisticated 'derivatives'. In 1994 the global derivatives market was estimated by one much-quoted source to be worth some US$16 trillion. According to the Bank of International Settlements, the total notional amount of outstanding over-the-counter derivatives at the end of June 2000 stood at just over US$94 trillion, a 30% increase since mid-1998.

Energy-Corporations not listed in stock-markets operate financial securitization procedures but in a very limited way. But, evaluating and measuring the implications on a country's future national-security of the securitized transactions of the related International Energy Corporations listed in one or more cross-country stock-markets and also dealing in 'derivatives', or 'sub-derivatives' committed to future transactions, remain under watch by the developed countries or expert agencies would call for a regular observation, analysis and administration. With India's expanding economic-liberalisation, it is expected that by the end of 11th Plan period (2012) many of Indian energy companies would have acquired assets/controlling-influence in foreign countries and similarly, foreign energy-corporations also would be acquiring assets/controlling-influence in India, all dealing in securities and derivatives/sub-derivatives. In this context it may be necessary that to counteract and balance the implications of any upheaval in the securities/derivatives market of those energy-corporations be addressed in advance.

Securitization in the context of International-Political-System

Securitization in international-political-system may exists in various forms: formal, informal, direct, indirect, bi-lateral, multi-lateral, regional, and universal as the United Nations (UN), whereby states plan to combine to repel and punish any aggression committed by one of their own members or collectively react to another group of nations. The international system of sovereign-states that has prevailed in politics since the 17th century is technically one of anarchy, with no overriding authority to govern the behaviour of the individual states. In such a system, states have sought security from each other by their own defensive-capability and by entering into alliances with others. The resulting relationship, often called a balance of power, has been characterized by frequent tests of the balance in war.

Such a system is commonly called collective-security. The League of Nations, established after World War I, was the first full-scale attempt to institute such a system. Its failure led to the modified form embodied in the UN, founded in 1945. During World War I the former United States President Theodore Roosevelt advocated a League to enforce peace that would constitute what he called the "posse of nations". Ideally, the known determination of all nations to band together against an aggressor should prove a powerful deterrent to aggression ever occurring, and collective security could be achieved with attractive cheapness. In practice, the system has serious flaws, some of which led to the collapse of the League. Universality of response requires great faith in the "indivisibility of peace". In reality, states are reluctant to become involved in distant disputes. In nearer disputes, nations often have interests of their own to pursue, which may entail being reluctant to offend, let alone fight, the aggressor. This was characteristic of efforts to enforce collective security against Italy when it attacked Abyssinia (Ethiopia) in 1935.

Where the aggressor is very powerful there may be doubt as to whether it would yield even to a powerful combination of states. It is to avoid this danger that the Big Five Permanent Members of the UN Security Council enjoy a veto that ensures collective-security cannot even be attempted against them. When the world was divided into camps in the Cold War, the vetoes and potential vetoes of the United States and the earlier Union-of-Soviet-Socialist-Republics (USSR) made the UN system incapable of implementing full-scale collective-security action. Indeed only two instances have come near realizing the formal conditions envisaged in the Charter: the Korean War, in 1950, when the Soviet Union had temporarily ceased attending the Security Council, and the Gulf War in 1991, when the period of harmony following the end of the Cold War permitted unanimity among the Council's permanent members. In the latter case, however, enforcement did not involve a UN command as in Korea, but a coalition licensed by the Council to act under US control. Various formulae have been used to justify intervention in the former Yugoslavia, but in the major campaign waged by the North-Atlantic-Treaty-Organization (NATO) against Serbia over Kosovo there was no clear UN mandate. NATO fell back on claiming that legitimacy for the action could be derived from the consensus of a large number of democratic nations. There are obvious severe difficulties with such a position, for the UN system depends precisely on universality.

In line with this stance some have begun to term NATO a regional organization within the terms of the UN Charter, something NATO always eschewed during the Cold War, precisely because under the Charter such organizations require Security Council authorization for the actual use of force. A similar difficulty would exist, as some have suggested, if the Organization for Cooperation and Security, which, like the Organization of American States and its African counterpart, the Organization of African Unity, is undoubtedly a regional security organization in terms of the Charter, tried to take enforcement action when the Security Council was deadlocked.

Securitization in the context of Economic-Policies

The 'Economic-Policy-measures' of a country intend to direct and regulate the behaviour of its domestic-economy and to influence the international-economy through its popular constituents: budget (a financial-tool that operates on whole economy), macro-economic policy-elements (operates on matters that are directly international, sectoral, inter/intra-sectoral affecting large group of organizations in economy), and micro-economic policy-elements (operates on matters that are international but small/indirect, inter-sectoral affecting limited organizations in economy). The two kinds of policy-elements encroach on one another, since measures affecting the whole economy necessarily affect the parts, and what affects any part or aspect of the economy registers in the performance of the whole.

The scope of 'macro-economic-policies' depends upon economic-system in operation, and the framework of laws and institutions governing it. The system may be capitalist or communist, free-market-economy or command-economy, pre-industrial or post-industrial. Macro-economic policies are designed to eliminate fluctuations in economic-activity, reduce unemployment, promote faster economic growth, create greater economic-quality, reduce the monopoly powers of large-corporations, and prevent deterioration of the environment. It has been accepted that fluctuations in economic-behaviour yielding both undesirable as well as desirable results increases with the increase in devising and implementing more number of macro-economic policies formulated to cope with the deficiencies of an economy.

The 'micro-economic-policies' are specific and multifarious, may be regulatory or recommendatory, relate to one industry or product, may have wider application/ implication. For example, they may involve nationalization/ privatization of the railway-system, prohibit import/export of specific commodities, regulate shops and establishments, prescribe new employment-conditions for labour, regulate production/ sale of certain products, and financial operations of various kinds. Some kinds of policy are regulatory; others seek to encourage particular activities. Micro-economic-policies very often have close links with social-policies. In general, micro-economic policy-elements structure the legal-framework within which socio-economic and particularly the market-forces operate and without which functioning and expansion of competition might no longer be fair or socially advantageous.

For **India**, pursuing very high economic growth-rate over world-average, in the context of securitization, its macro/ micro-economic policies and elements have to concentrate more on demand, investment, capacity and supply management and on all vital matters relating to all sources of **'energy'** through many measures that may include fiscal-policy, monetary-policy, and also an analysis of the favourable/ unfavourable influences, implications and obligations of the "invisible-hands" behind the market-forces. Policies may, however, do more harm than good if they are based on inadequate data and incorrect diagnosis of the economic-forces at work or if a country has not developed expert-agency dedicated to a specific focus for the sake of specialisation. The most-important task in macro/micro-economy of a country remains more of effective management of demand, investment, capacity and supply of energy in short-run than a visionary-formulation of policy and plans in medium/long-run.

Securitization in the context of International Relations

International Relations (IR) is a branch of political science, a study of **foreign-affairs** of and relations among states within the **international system**, including the roles of states, inter-governmental organizations (IGOs), non-governmental organizations (NGOs), and multinational corporations (MNCs). It is a public-policy field, can be either positive or normative, as it seeks to analyze and formulate **foreign-policy** affecting the population collectively. Apart from political science, IR draws upon such diverse fields as economics, history, law, philosophy, geography, sociology, anthropology, psychology, and cultural studies. It involves a diverse range of issues, from globalization and its impacts on societies and state sovereignty to ecological sustainability, nuclear proliferation, nationalism, economic development, terrorism, organized crime, human security and human rights.

The history of IR is traced back to the 'Peace-of-Westphalia' of 1648, where the modern state system was developed. Westphalia instituted the notion of **sovereignty**, which essentially meant that rulers, or sovereigns, would recognize no internal equals within a defined territory, and no external superiors. Classical Greek/Roman authority at times resembled the Westphalian system, but both lacked the notion of sovereignty. Westphalia encouraged the rise of the nation-state and the institutionalization of diplomacy and armies. This particular European system was exported to the Americas, Africa, and Asia via 'colonialism' and the 'standards of civilization'. The contemporary international system was finally established through 'decolonization' during the Cold War. However, this is somewhat over-simplified. While the nation-state system is considered "modern", many states have not incorporated the system and are termed "pre-modern". Further, a handful of states have moved beyond the nation-state system and can be considered "post-modern". The ability of contemporary IR discourse to explain the relations of these different types of states is disputed.

Securitization in international relations is a concept-of-thought connected with the 'Copenhagen-School-of-International-Relations', a **constructivistic** theory of international relations. It is a means to specify whether a given area of interest is merely ordinarily politicized or the area is considered essential for survival. The term was coined by Ole-Wæver in 1997, but seems to have become commonplace, at least within 'constructivistic' studies of international-relations. Besides **Constructivism,** other theories on international-relations are: Realism, Neo-Realism, Idealism, Liberalism, Neo-Liberalism, Marxism, Dependency-theory, Functionalism, Neo-Functionalism, and Critical-theory.

This field of 'constructivism' is closely associated with Alexander Wendt's idea of "social-constructionism" to the field of international-relations who laid (1992) the theoretical groundwork for challenging what he considered to be a flaw shared by both neo-realists and neo-liberal institutionalists, namely, a commitment to a crude form of materialism. By showing how even such a core realist concept as "power-politics" is socially constructed, that is, not given by nature and hence, capable of being transformed by human practice. Wendt opens the way for a generation of international-relations scholars who pursue work in a wide range of issues from a constructivist perspective.

Since the 1990s, 'constructivism' has become one of the major theories in the field of international-relations due to being propogated by many constructivist-scholars namely,

Ruggie, Martha Finnemore, Kathryn Sikkink, Peter Katzenstein, and Alexander Wendt whose work has been widely accepted within the mainstream IR community and has generated vibrant scholarly discussions among realists, liberals, institutionalists, and constructivists. Behind them, there are radical-constructivists who take discourse and linguistics more seriously. Constructivists optimistically analyze international-relations by looking at the goals, threats, fears, cultures, identities, and other elements of "social-reality" on the international stage as the 'social-constructs' of countries. India has the option to raise the issue of the need and extent of securitization of 'energy' by China as a commodity of extreme-crisis for international discussion to be proved as a "genuine and real social-reality" as it is believed that the International Court of Justice and International Judicial Bodies have developed ways of checking the powers of even the UN Security Council when it goes beyond the traditional modes of judicial review.

In this context, in one view, if a subject (here "energy") is successfully labelled as having security-implications or problem, the subject can be considered to be an illegitimate subject for political or academic debate. Barry Buzan, Ole Wæver and Jaap de Wilde ("*Security: A New Framework for Analysis*"), advocated that securitization can take place with integration of five political-sectors (Military, Political, Economic, Society, and Environment) in a country. However, a securitization could easily involve more than one of these sectors. In the case of the 2003 invasion of Iraq, one could say that the conflict was securitized militarily, weapons of mass destruction was one reason for the invasion. However, the war was also securitized as a societal-problem, human-rights (not 'energy') in Saddam's Iraq as was mentioned in the public rationale.

In another view, however, **India**, in the fast-changing world-scenario around energy, need to concentrate if the given subject, "energy", is to be 'securitized' and if so, to what extent. It does not necessarily mean that the subject is of super-objective-essence for the survival of a State, but only means that **China** has successfully constructed a series of circumstances around "energy" as an essential-dilemma which may implicate or even push India into a disadvantageous circumstance to the minimum. In principle, any country can succeed in constructing something as a security problem or securitize an object through speech and action. The ability to effectively securitize a given subject is, however, highly dependent on both the status of a country and on whether similar issues are generally or globally perceived to having security implications. However, if a subject is successfully securitized by a country of status, it is possible to legitimize extraordinary means to solve a perceived problem. This could even include ultimately declaring a state of emergency or martial law, mobilizing the military or attacking another country.

Energy-Consumers and Investors in energy-corporations can also take judicial-recourse compelling Govt. for securitization through legislative enactments

The future energy-companies and multi-national energy-corporations working in India will certainly operate through shares, securities, derivatives and stock-market and be more vulnerable to stock-market fluctuations with the investors and the energy consumers under the Companies Act and the Right to Information Act of India having a right to see not only the company's Memorandum of Association, Articles of Association, Prospectus, Forward-Looking Statements and Annual Reports but also the right to call for any specific-information about its functioning. If these corporations operate their derivatives and securitization financing at international markets, they may become more vulnerable to the 'hidden-forces', working from behind the market mechanism, who may exercise controlling influence or even dislocate the functioning of the companies if 'energy' becomes a fully securitized-commodity.

In the context of general public, the obtained information may include details with respect to: regulation and the status of retail generation, service-supply competition in states, company's financing-plans, demand for energy and the cost and availability of raw materials, provider-of-last-resort, power supply contracts, results of litigation, results of operations, internal controls and procedures, capital expenditures, status and condition of plants and equipment, accounting issues, company's statements showing estimates, expectations and projections and, as a result, are subject to risks and uncertainties. There can be no assurance that actual results will not materially differ from expectations.

In fact, company's actual results may vary materially and unpredictably from past expectations. Factors that could cause actual results to differ materially include, among others, the following: changes in the price of power and fuel for electric generation; general economic and business conditions; changes in access to capital markets; complications or other factors that may render it difficult or impossible to obtain necessary lender consents or regulatory authorizations on a timely basis; environmental regulations; the results of regulatory proceedings, including proceedings related to rates; changes in industry capacity, development and other activities by the competitors; changes in the weather and other natural phenomena; changes in the underlying inputs and assumptions, including market conditions used to estimate the fair values of commodity contracts; company's existing and future markets or its activities; the loss of any significant customers or suppliers; dependence on other electric transmission and gas transportation systems and their constraints or availability; changes in company's rules and tariffs; the effect of accounting policies issued periodically by accounting standard-setting bodies; and the continuing effects of global instability, terrorism and war.

There may exist many more risks and uncertainties that are not identified and discussed here and, therefore, the energy-companies may become more susceptible to disturbance, external obligation and litigation on this account.

Need to review the domestic and future financial-management-system-development requirements and reporting-regulations in the context of future multi-national energy-corporations to work in India

International Energy Corporations accustomed to a much-exposing financial-system-reporting, in particular, under IFRS and US-GAAP will enjoy by short/non-disclosure as IFRS/US-GAAP are not applicable in India and they will have to work in a new and limited/deficient environment of accessing finance and credit in India. In a developing country like India a systematic/comfortable access to large-scale financial-services is a major concern for the policy-makers. A systematic/comfortable access to bulk-credit-system, seen as a channel through which the financial-system foster innovation, entrepreneurship and economic growth is also a major concern. Mechanism, even economic-policies, to evaluate the levels of degree of access to finance and credit is yet to be developed in India which is often indiscriminately described as problem in many developing countries. With increasing trend in internationalization of financial market starting to operate from India, it appears essential that on international financial-management-system, still awaiting mass-scale intelligibility/ popularization, be reduced to a simplified yet all comprehensive learning package be developed for the investors and consumers of energy.

Presently India has low-level of financial-literacy and limited-scope policy/system-mechanism in the fields of international finance, security, credit, risk-evaluation and analysis, accounting and reporting management, and, if energy becomes a fully securitized commodity, then the profitability and sustainability of energy-companies will be a prime-concern because as compared to other companies the energy-companies will be more vulnerable to:

(i)   high macro-economic uncertainty (in inflation-rate, terms of trade, the real-interest-rate, and the real-exchange-rate);

(ii)   weaknesses in the contractual and informational environment (in poorly defined and difficult to enforce creditor rights, deficient accounting and disclosure practices, and lack of a well functioning credit bureau);

(iii) geographical limitations (in inter-regional-state communication and others);

(iv)   absence of systemic risk measurement and evaluation (if risk increases, undermines financial contracting and enlarges the set of borrowers/projects that find the cost of credit unaffordable and are thus priced out of the credit market);

(v)   companies may also get affected and constrained in areas of their internal and external costs and risks due to constraints from the "state variables" (i.e., variables that do not change in the short-run affecting all financial-sector activities across the board such as market-size, macroeconomic-fundamentals, available technology, average level and distribution of per capita income, and system-wise costs of doing related business, for instance, the quality of transport and communication infrastructure, the effectiveness of the contractual and informational frameworks, and the degree of general-insecurity associated with disruption, crime, violence, terrorism etc. whereas the real problem lies in the fact, in the countries of comparable economic development new energy-technologies are not available and that existing deficiencies in state-variables in India, when compared to countries of origin with higher levels of technology and economic development may bring many bottlenecks which may effectively disrupt the sustainability of the international-energy-corporations working in India);

(vi)   changes in the state-variables involve changes in fundamental institutions and, thus, take a long time to materialize, however, continuing with the existing deficiencies in the macro-economic environment and with the state-variables in India the scope for improvements in financial/credit policy and mechanism in the shorter-run may be allowed under compulsion to function below the optimum-level but should be done with a watch and safeguard-mechanism against all types of problems that may arise due to increased sub-optimizations with consequent improvements in cost and risk management also need to be developed parallel to it;

(vii) in India where its economy is not yet much diversified internationally, a slow and defensive premium-policy and mechanism also need to be developed on accessing the vast, yet vastly unexploited, risk pooling and diversification opportunities offered by international capital markets, which range potentially from catastrophic insurance to commodity price hedges, from weather and crop insurance to securitization of export receivables, and from currency swaps to GDP-indexed securities; and

(viii) development of government policies and mechanism to prevent the existing financial-system moving to unsustainable-equilibrium beyond the defined red-line parameters, but simultaneously developing policy and mechanism to help grow better and wider capital *market-harnessing* with improvised and competitive market-enabling policy/mechanism accompanied by a properly defined regulatory and supervisory safety-net to calibrate aggressive-risks; to further expand outreaching and door-accessing the bankable population in India; to develop new or specific financial products (for example, the asset holdings of households can be compared to collateral-requirements if legal-system reforms movable assets to be used as collateral) in place of the existing collateral-requirements of financial institutions which presently constrain the entrepreneurs from access to credit as they do not have assets that are acceptable as collateral.

Therefore, while securitization-measures of 'energy' in India is all the more necessary, as a short-run measure, in a moderate form and for a limited time-frame, due to the compelling and fast-changing energy-circumstances in the world, but it should constitute: (i) development of expert-agencies dedicated to their respective specific-specialized focuses (preferably issues and crises) which is otherwise essential in the vast area of overall energy-management; (ii) more effective-management of demand, investment, capacity and supply of all energy resources in short-run; (iii) development, modification and re-adjustment of short term fiscal-policy/monetary-policy elements, procedures and mechanism in a manner that will fully support and help implement the macro-economic policies developed on issues relating to all energy resources together; (iv) a continuous watch and analysis of the favourable / unfavourable influences, implications and obligations of the "invisible-hands" including the multi-national energy-corporations behind the energy market-forces acting both domestically as well as internationally; (v) immediate adoption/convergence of IFRS/US-GAAP (with necessary book-keeping/reporting-requirements as required to be modified on 'energy') with future Indian Accounting/Reporting Systems and (vi) watching and analyzing the Balance-Sheets of the International Energy Corporations to see whether or not their reporting-restructuring after securitization was effected under India-adopted IFRS (International-Financial-Reporting-System)/US-GAAP(US-Generally-Accepted-Accounting-Principles) as post-securitization Balance-Sheet reporting-restructuring if done in time-laggered pieces may be resented or objected to on technical grounds; and (vii) joining of Energy-Audit (Bureau of Energy Efficiency) with Cost-Audit (Institute of Cost and Works Accountants) to develop a better reporting-system to keep a watch both on engineering and economic aspects of technology-deployment, resource-consumption, productivity and pricing-mechanism of energy.

It may be a matter of discussion and controversy how far economic-policy should be governed by rule or discretion and to what extent securitization should be stretched, the above measures, when "energy" has already been securitized by China, becomes very necessary because the world economy has already turned more closely integrated and the global capital and investment become more mobile where one nation's economic-policy may have very little or limited impact internationally, where the problem of international-coordination particularly affects the international and the external-aspects of the economic-policy of a nation; where a very wide-range of international issues on trade and investment, exchange rate, balance of payments, tariffs, double-taxation, copyright-law etc. and also India's accordance to the terms of the international-agreements and so on. Changes in any of these have repercussions on India's domestic-economy is of the highest importance, so that the international and domestic-aspects of the policy is well coordinated and timely readjusted or modified.

Energy-Securitization Vs. Energy-Education

It is through a holistic-synthesis of learning-approaches applied to all the related branches of knowledge on any focused issue that makes a learner to see through a transaction, an organisation, a sector and an economy holistically in order to see through the complexly-networked impacts of globalization in order to be capable of acting global.

Thinkers and the analysts have been suggesting the need of 'energy-security' as a beta-blocker for India. But, in the transition to total 'energy-independence' the indispensable 'steroidal' milepost of 'energy-education' shall have to be synthesized symmetrically not only with each sector of Indian economy but also with her wide-stream population, in segments, in defined time-scale.

While 'Energy-Securitization' is objectively inbound, 'Energy-Education' is an outward-journey possibly to whole of the earth. Education should not be adopted as a means of securitization, rather securitization can be adopted as a means of education. 'Energy-Securitization', its need, extent and implications need to be studied separately in the light and requirements due to fast globalization of economy, complexity in the management of international financing and reporting requirements, to increase further with the future multi-national energy-corporations to work in India, 'Energy-Education' need to be formulated as a different Plan. In long-run 'Energy-Education' must supercede 'Energy-Securitization' as the later should be taken as a strategy in short-run, (immediate and effective) while the former is a development-programme in long-run (elongated, long-lasting, universally acceptable and all-welfare-oriented).

In other words, unlike China, India in the long-run must project and plan for 'Energy-Education' embedding the lessons learnt from 'Energy-Securitization'. The futuristic Energy-Educational-Plan should be *ab initio* industry-oriented, hence need to re-categorise the entire energy sector of India into High-Tech, Medium-Tech and Low-Tech with their varying levels of technology-deployment, R&D needs and prospects, investment-requirements and the required levels HR skills to help enable employment/man-power planning in future.

India's future 'Energy-Education-Plan' should be in the direction of developing the applied-consciousness and oriented-wisdom towards mastering the subject of 'Energy-Management' in totality, the currricula, at school-level, (from Class-V onward, Science-Labs of Schools also to give science-demontrations on 'energy') need to be revised in order to display, gradually and selectively, the theory, applied-science and technology, economics, National-Policy-Programmes on that energy-source, and industry information relating to all forms and sources of natural and man-made energy. The applied-science and technology (of homemade-battery, solar energy, wind energy and similar other) should be demonstrated in schools atleast through videos.

At college-level, integrated course on 'All-Energy-Management' can be planned to create a new-class of academia and profession in future similar to IT/BPO/KPO. At industry-level, corporate producers and consumers of energy can help sector-wise collection and integration of industrial-statistics (techno-economic) on all energy sources. This approach will ultimately enable integration of divergent branches of academic-knowledge and technology-management on a single platform in the line of Neo-Technology which itself inherently is an integration of diverse knowledge and without which energy sector may not be able to bring the expected breakthrough or revolution in India.

One of the Nextgen learning-approaches for the future India could be the holistic-synthesis of learning-approaches. It is only through a holistic-synthesis of learning-approaches (structurally, functionally, complementarily and objectively) applied to all the related branches of knowledge on any focused issue is complete at one stage, that the learner should be expected, in course of time-led wisdom and experience, to be able to develop the capacity of seeing through a transaction, an organisation, a sector and an economy holistically and then to start think universal in order to be able to see through the complexly-networked impacts of globalization in order, finally, to be able to act global.

Section – IX

Long-Run Implications of China's Energy Security Policies and Strategies on India

CHAPTER 21

Long-Run Implications of China's Energy Security Policies and Strategies on India

Energy security concern is an old issue for Asia

Energy security concerns are not new to Asia. These concerns have been around since at least the 1930s when anxieties over access to Southeast-Asian oil supplies became a key-reason for Japanese expansionism. Later, the first oil-crisis of 1973-74 battered the Japanese economy and provoked major new efforts by Japan to reduce its vulnerability to oil-supply-disruptions. However, the scale and scope of the concerns have broadened across the region since the early 1980s as the result of Asia's two decades of booming economic growth and energy-intensive economic development.

As economic growth is mostly linked to energy demand, the balance that China and India choose between cooperative and competitive strategies, and how these strategies intersect with each other, will determine whether energy becomes ultimately a stabilizing or destabilizing force in the region;

whether energy aggravates existing and looming rivalries or whether it reinforces impulses toward greater regional-cooperation and reliance on market-solutions. They will also determine Asia's inevitably growing role in the Middle East, Central-Asia, and Russia, and impact on U.S. interests in those regions.

Reasons behind China's Energy-Insecurity

Asia's limited oil-resource-base and slow energy-industry-reform have hobbled the region's ability to mobilize supplies needed to meet their booming demands resulting in rising dependence on energy imports, particularly for oil and gas to prevent energy from becoming a bottleneck undermining economic growth and social stability. As a result China's import-dependence may accelerate further high over the next two decades to sustain its highly accelerated economic growth-trend.

The result is a profound and deepening sense of energy-insecurity in Asia/China bringing important long term geo-political implications in the region for India, in particular, as the Asian powers, reaching out to secure future-supplies, are responding more with "energy-nationalism" than with 'energy-cooperation' due to risks of terrorist attacks on vital energy-infrastructure, fuel-supply-disruptions, and political-instability. The countries of other regions will also have major strategic-stakes in how Asian countries respond to their energy-insecurity and its impact on the region and global energy geo-politics. Nonetheless, there is a concern that actions by Chinese companies to acquire energy assets will "remove" energy resources from the competitive market, which, according to some, has the effect of constricting supply and thereby raising world prices.

However, because China can be expected to consume the vast majority of any resources it does acquire, the effects of these purchases should be economically neutral. Even if China's equity oil investments "remove" assets from the global market, in the sense that they are not subsequently available for resale, these actions merely displace what the Chinese would have otherwise bought on the open market.

Regardless of whether China secures its oil through equity investments or purchases on the global market, its increasing demand for these resources will continue to play a role in world oil markets (as will rising demand from other areas, such as the U.S. and India). [1]

China's energy security and strategy is not a simple situation of 'shortage' of energy

One view stresses that China's energy-deficit is not a simple situation of 'shortage' of energy as even today it continues to export energy, including certain kinds of crude and refined-oil. It is the ever growing demand for clean and efficient energy, especially oil that lie at the core of this energy security crisis in-the-making. The other view stresses that it is a problem of lack of vision, coordination and structural adjustment as China remains a typical example of a resource-rich (for example, even in clean-efficient energy-source like gas, China possesses abundant reserves of 53.3 trillion cubic feet) yet import-dependent country as its energy policy has not kept pace with the changing mode of country's energy-needs. While the debate on the reasons how energy-deficit becomes a security-threat in international relations remains inconclusive, the Chinese experts stress that it is the nature of international politics that made its energy dilemma 'securitized'.

Oil being the blood of industry, the life of economy, and a guard against aggression and therefore, the target of big-powers for use as an important weapon of diplomacy. As a result, security-implications for the Indian Ocean region, with sea-lanes ridden by turbulent-politics, are seen as resulting not only from China's energy-deficit but also from the fact that most of China's oil-imports flow through this region. The nature of threat-projections around an oil-crisis has more to do with events like the two Persian Gulf wars that made energy a 'flashpoint' in the Asia-Pacific region, the rising-demands for oil-imports only intensify the political-

1. China's Energy Supply and Demand EIA, 2003

skirmishes. In case of oil, most of the imports inevitably coming from politically turbulent and unstable-regions such as the Indian Ocean, Persian Gulf, and transported along potentially vulnerable sea-lanes and complex-pipeline-routes crossing several national-borders, the need to meet rising electricity-demand, in the face of oil and natural gas supply-constraints, will force heavy reliance on coal and nuclear power which, in turn, will aggravate future environmental and nuclear-proliferation-risks.

Besides, the extension of U.S. military power and influence in Central-Asia and the Persian Gulf has aggravated China's existing fears of U.S. hegemony and increased its sense of vulnerability from U.S. control over oil and gas flows to China. The high energy needs of China have been impelling it to become a major-player in the world's oil and gas exporting-regions and energy geo-politics. This is likely to make the complex web of diplomatic ties and alliances either more complicated or complement the inter-regional / international energy and security-interests. For example, Asia's rapidly growing involvement in helping Iran develop its energy sector is already adding to U.S. frustrations in its efforts to isolate Iran. The same is true in Sudan. Moreover, Asia's energy needs are inexorably drawing Russia back into Asia as a key strategic and commercial player.

Therefore, for China, energy is becoming a matter of "high-politics" involving national-security and no longer just the "low-politics" of domestic-energy policy. China is viewing that energy security is becoming too important to be left entirely to the markets, as its economic-prosperity is being increasingly exposed to global supply disruptions and instability in energy exporting regions. As a result China will respond to its growing sense of energy-insecurity with a broad range of strategies, in order to guarantee an uninterrupted greater supply, a price-stability and also a control in world market.

China's strategic efforts on energy will grow in scale, scope and complexity

Experts believe that China's strategic efforts will grow in scale, scope and complexity ranging from largely cooperative and market-oriented strategies to those that are deeply neo-mercantilist and competitive. China has already accelerated its efforts to gain more secure national-control of overseas-oil and gas-supplies by taking equity-stakes in overseas oil and gas-fields, promoting development of new oil and gas pipelines to Asia, developing broader trade and energy-ties, and following up with diplomatic-ties to cement relations with the major oil and gas exporting countries. Whether mercantilist or dominated by market motives, China's energy strategies will be critically important to future India's interests.

The energy demand boom has been spread across the range of primary-fuels, but the implications for China's energy security may vary significantly across the spectrum, depending on resource-availability, transport and infrastructure-costs, government-policies and its short/medium-term strategies. China's petroleum-dilemma is most acute. In broad-terms, oil/natural gas made up about 28/14% (Appendix-C) of China's energy-consumption, about the same share as the rest of the world. Looking ahead, China's import-dependence on oil and natural gas is likely to become even more acute in future.

It is important to note that much of increased demand is due to the high energy intensity of China's industry. Energy consumption per capita in China is still only a fraction of that of the U.S. or Japan. However, as in other countries that have experience rapid, sustained economic growth, there has been a significant rise in the middle-class, further increasing China's energy needs. Currently 40.5% of the population lives in urban areas and there are 25 cities with populations over 1 million. With average growth rates in urban areas of 1.4% per year, the percentage will increase between 55% and 60% by 2020. These urban populations consume approximately 35 times more energy than rural populations, significantly contributing to rising energy demand.[2] A rising middle class also means higher energy demand, as individuals demand higher living standards, more travel by air and more cars on the roads. Ownership of air conditioners in households has increased from 11.6% in 1990 to 61.8% in 2003.[3] The market for personal cars is growing at 50% to 60% annually and energy demand for all road transport is projected to grow by 4.6% per year from 2004 to 2030.[4]

According to research conducted at the Lawrence-Berkeley-National-Laboratory, transportation currently accounts for 38% of all oil demand. They further project that by 2020 transportation vill account for nearly 50% of all oil demand, with personal cars growing from 2% of demand to approximately 10% of demand.[5]

Impact of joint-declaration (21 Nov. 2006) mainly focused on trade and energy

Chinese President **Hu Jintao** visiting India released a **joint-declaration** (21 Nov. 2006) with Indian Prime Minister **Manmohan Singh** pledging to forge a socio-economic partnership between the two countries, signing 13 pacts covering an array of issues, from joint-scientific-initiatives, opening of new-consulates to promote increased bilateral trade/investment-flows pledged to more than double the rapidly-growing trade between the two countries to US$ 40 billion by 2010.[6] On energy both the governments promised

2. Kong, "An Anatomy of China's Energy Insecurity and Its Strategies," Pacific Northwest National Laboratory; November 2004, page 10

3. Crompton, Paul and Yanrui Wu, "Energy Consumption in China: Past Trends and Future Directions" Energy Economics: Volume 27, Issue 1, January 2005, Pages 195-208.

4. World Energy Outlook 2004, published by the International Energy Agency

5. Presentation by David Fridley of Lawrence Berkeley National Lab, "China's Energy Future to 2020 Initial Results" presented to Department of Energy, November 29, 2005.

6. http://meaindia.nic.in/declarestatement/2006/11/21jd01.htm)

to work-together to fulfill their soaring energy-needs by undertaking joint oil and gas exploration-projects in other countries, and also expand co-operation in civilian-nuclear-energy.

China, leaving India's worries on the impacts of highly expanding trade-flows flooded with cheap Chinese imports; China's increasing investments on its ports; dispute on the residence of the Dalai Lama in India advocating increased autonomy for Tibetans; and the long-pending territorial border-disputes after 1962 border war, however, successfully displayed its strong political-will and strategy by making the joint-declaration mainly focusing its interests on **trade** and **energy**, which China presently needs to sustain its dynamic economic development. Therefore, the possible impacts of joint-declaration (21 Nov. 2006), mainly focused on trade and energy needs to be examined at macro/micro/long term/short term levels in India.

Possibility of discontinuities in China's energy-future

Speculations are also trying to take on board that there could be categories of discontinuities that would significantly reduce region's energy consumption and demand and alter China's energy-future and reduce the scope of China's energy security challenges.

The sets of possible discontinuities, which may as well impact India's energy security and its strategies, may include: (i) China's own plan for much lower long term economic growth than being currently pursued; (ii) a serious impelling discontinuity could be the intervention of a major geo-political crisis having a decisive impact on China's long term growth; (iii) a major, trend-altering slowdown in energy demand through sharp technological innovation or policy shifts; (iv) a major environmental-disaster leading to a fundamental-shift in energy-policies across the region, with aggressive regulatory limits on energy-consumption like 'Three-Mile-Island' and 'Chernobyl' nuclear accidents; (v) development of new and aggressive energy demand management-policies in the region, similar to Japan's policies after the first two oil-shocks, which resulted in huge efficiency gains and sharply lowered per capita energy-consumption; and (vi) a highly energy supply-constrained world resulting in very high energy-prices, creating unexpected disincentives for Asia as well as globally.

In the panorama of world events it will not be a surprise if any of the above discontinuities comes to normal happening or factors in Asia's future energy-diplomacy. Although many energy-forecasts have over-estimated future demand-growth yet it is difficult to expect that China will alter its outlook for its booming energy demand without assuming a very major discontinuity in Asian economy or a calamitous geo-political event.

China's aggressively and globally-expanding energy security strategies

It can be accepted that 'Energy-Security' has firmly become the central-concern for China; its thrusts to secure future energy-supplies have become manifold and also taken on great urgency. Import-Energy dependence and vulnerability to global oil-supply-crises have acted as a catalyst to its leadership, which fears that energy-shortages and volatile world-energy-prices could prove serious impediments to economic growth. China has probably become the most aggressive of the Asian powers in securing its future energy-supplies. China's strategy has become increasingly wide-ranging over the past decade and is growing in sophistication. It is built on relatively tight coordination between state geo-political interests and energy interests. China, therefore, diplomatically, strategically and patiently pursued its energy security on a wide range of fronts:

First, it strengthened its supply relationships in key-areas, such as the Persian Gulf, while diversifying the geographic distribution of its crude-oil suppliers and transportation-routes, from Russia's East-Siberia and western Kazakhstan through long-distance pipeline-projects, which would have the added advantage of reducing vulnerability to disruptions in tanker-flows from the Persian Gulf and Africa.

Second, China's state oil companies have been aggressively buying equity-stakes in many existing or prospective oil-fields around the world in Kazakhstan, Sudan, Venezuela, Iraq, and Peru, Caspian-Sea area in Azerbaijan and Turkmenistan which include oil production, exploration, pipelines, refineries, and port-construction. Another element of China's energy-equity-strategy is to target countries subject to unilateral U.S. sanctions. These tactics improve the competitive-landscape of China offering greater opportunities.

Third, China's strategy involves extensive cross-investment and commercial ties with major exporting-countries in order to reinforce strong long term ties. China also invited the state-oil-companies in the exporting-countries (ARAMCO, a Saudi national oil company), to invest in downstream oil and petrochemical projects in China.

Fourth, China liberally encourages Foreign Direct Investments to acquire stakes in China's domestic and offshore energy fields and even in the disputed energy field. CNOOC has also been negotiating with Shell over the Bonan project in the Bohai-Sea. All this is aimed at building stakes of great-powers to ensure peace in China's immediate periphery.

Fifth, China's strategy involves an active oil-gas diplomacy, strengthening oil supply contracts, equity-stakes, and cross-investments with deeper and broader diplomatic and trade ties. For example, a "strategic-energy-partnership" (1999) between China and Saudi Arabia; broadening of energy, trade, and military ties with Moscow (2001); a stronger diplomatic and energy-ties with Iran; and China's extensive state involvement in contracts with Australia and Indonesia for its LNG needs. China's leadership pursued development of a broader diplomatic trade-ties and alliances as a key-element in securing its access to future oil and gas supplies which also included military sales and cooperation, sales of nuclear-equipment, and other potentially problematic trade-ties.

Sixth, China's strategy also involves continuing active-pursuit of its territorial claims in the surrounding maritime-region, to assert sovereignty and to claim control over potential oil and gas resources in these areas. China has repeatedly asserted its territorial interests in disputes over control of exploration and licensing blocks with Vietnam, Indonesia, and Japan over the past decade.

Seventh, China decided (2004) to follow the examples of the industrialized countries and its neighbours (Japan and South Korea) to construct a Strategic-Petroleum-Reserve. Beijing has been involved in discussions with Russia and South Korea on proposals to build a large regional natural gas pipeline from East-Siberia, southeast through China, and across the Yellow-Sea to South Korea to link Russian gas supplies to both markets.

Eighth, Chinese experts have expounded both defensive and offensive options for a new naval-strategy: by making quick-reactions, including military-reaction when a crisis occurs displaying its strength for safeguarding country's interests; and by showing the capability of reciprocal deterrence based on counter-threatening. Chinese scholars no longer shy away from stressing the link between China's military-ability and its energy security imperatives.

In sum, China's energy security-strategy is wide-ranging and increasingly becoming aggressive, sophisticated, competitive and strongly **diplomatic, statist** and **mercantilist,** built on a common vision of government-policymakers and state-oil-companies, increasingly linked to broader diplomatic relations and alliances, searching for energy security to become a major geo-political player in the Persian Gulf, Central-Asia, and Russia, with a growing capability to complement or complicate international interests in these regions.

Regional implications of China's energy security strategies

Analyzing the regional implications of China's energy security strategies, several basic trends can be seen across Asia that have important strategic, environmental, and energy implications for the region. Prospects appear extremely poor for large new oil-supplies within Asia. Existing exporters' oil prospects look poor who are shifting investment-priorities toward LNG exports. Consequently, barring a major political or economic discontinuity in the region, rising oil-demand in Asia will translate directly into deepening dependence on oil-imports from outside the region. By far the largest proportion of the imported-oil will come from the Persian Gulf, Russia, the Central-Asia/Caspian-Sea region, and Africa. These regions have the large-reserves to meet rising global oil demand over the next 25 years, likely to account for roughly 70% to 80% of the net global increase in oil production by 2030. The IEA's forecast (2004) indicates that Asia's natural gas imports is likely to become dependent on the same regions to the same extent as that it will depend on for oil-imports.

China, driven by its rising-demand for electricity, will continue to depend on coal as the only domestically plentiful power-generation-fuel. China's burgeoning coal-use will also be a serious and obvious area for concern in Asia. It is a strong possibility that China's expanding energy-deficit will cause at least some benign threats as it continues to produce large quantities of unclean and polluting energy resources. Continuance of a very high trend of coal-consumption in China will also create strong pressures for controlling environmental-degradation and for investments and research on clean technology, improving public health and safety and the environment-risks in the region. China's widespread use of Coal, for example, may also cause grave environmental implications for Asia in terms of air-quality, health, and global-warming and even acid-rains. If it be a disaster knowing no national-boundary, may, in turn, become a major hurdle in attracting FDI and the resultant economic-stagnation may create havoc, with a possible outpouring of Chinese populations to neighbouring countries.

China's nuclear-energy will also be boosted rapidly to help meet its rising electricity-needs with the consequence of a serious and growing concern as a potential source of nuclear-technology-proliferation, safety-problems, and nuclear-waste disposal challenges resulting in nuclear-proliferation and safety-issues generating strong pressures for improving the global regime to contain proliferation and for expending on research and remedial measures.

China's strategic foresight links bordering-geographies well

The rationale behind China's emphasis on building the Kodari Highway into Ńepal and the Karakoram Highway into Pakistan-Occupied Kashmir was simple enough, a strategic access to politically sensitive areas. China is now converting those strategic assets into economic opportunities. The two countries have just agreed to open four new road-links through the 'Khunjerab-Pass', bringing the total number of China-Pakistan roads links to eight. The two cargo-routes run from Kashi in southern-Xinjiang to Pakistan's ports of Karachi, Qasim and Gwadar. The passenger-lines run from Kashi and Taxkorgan, also in southern-Xinjiang, to Pakistan's Northern-Gilgit and Sost-Pass respectively. Developing better connectivity and promoting cross-border trade with neighbouring regions in the Subcontinent has now become China's major priority.

China is also planning to build many new highways into Nepal, to supplement the existing Kodari-Highway which eventually would open up access to the north-Indian-plains. Lhasa also announced that the new railroad between mainland China and Tibet would be extended from Lhasa to Shigatse, leaving small distance from Sino-Indian border. These include the constructions of small hydro-power projects, dry-port at Sust, water-diversion channels, bridges, and telecom facilities.[8]

---

8. Indian Express: 26 Mar. 2006: Diplomacy takes a high road.

China's "String-of-Pearls" strategy is ominously sensitive to India

China's "String-of-Pearls"[9] strategy though remained held back by the difficult terrain of the area/sea-distance, is again modernized with new investments in building railways, new transportation-lines, and roads to link its west to the oceans which will be the bearers of Chinese increased influence to Central, South-west and South-Asia. Pakistan identified Gwadar as a deep-sea port-site in 1964. It was only in 2001 that significant steps toward making the proposal a reality were taken, when China agreed to participate in its construction .

Gwadar provides China "a transit-terminal for crude-oil imports from Iran and Africa to China's Xinjiang region". The network of rail and road links connecting Pakistan with Afghanistan and Central-Asian republics that is envisaged as part of the Gwadar project and to which China will have access would provide China an opening into Central-Asian markets and energy sources, in the process stimulating the economic development of China's backward Xinjiang region.

But it is the strategic-significance of Gwadar port that is perhaps more important for Pakistan and China and a number of other countries as well. For China, Gwadar's strategic value stems from its proximity to the Strait-of-Hormuz. About 60% of China's energy supplies come from the Middle East, and China has been anxious that the US, which has a very high presence in the region, could choke off these supplies to China. A presence in Gwadar provides China with a "listening post" where it can "monitor US naval activity in the Persian Gulf, Indian activity in the Arabian-Sea and future US-Indian maritime cooperation in the Indian Ocean".

A recent report titled "Energy Futures in Asia" produced by Booz Allen Hamilton for the Pentagon notes that China has already set up electronic-posts at Gwadar, which are monitoring maritime-traffic through the Strait-of-Hormuz

9. Article "China's Pearl in Pakistan's Waters" by Sudha Ramchandran in 'Asia Times', 04 March 2005 (www.atimes.com)

and the Arabian-Sea. Drawing attention to China's "String-of-Pearls" strategy, the report pointed out that "China is building strategic relationships along the sea-lanes from the Middle East to the South-China Sea in ways that suggest defensive and offensive positioning to protect China's energy-interests, but also to serve its security-objectives". While Gwadar is part of the total "String-of-Pearls", the other "pearls" in the string include facilities in Bangladesh, Myanmar, Thailand, Cambodia and the South-China Sea that Beijing has acquired access to by assiduously building ties with governments in these countries.

Possibility of China's imminent leadership role in future energy market

China is seeking long term energy-ties but also is rapidly building diplomatic, trade, and military relationships to support those ties. All these trends suggest that energy will propel China into becoming Asia's major player in the Persian Gulf and broader Middle East, Russia, Kazakhstan, Central-Asia and Caspian-Sea region in the future.

China's growing energy-ties in all these regions will certainly have a significant impact on future international geo-political developments which by all means will affect India's energy security. The nexus of diplomatic, trade, and military ties with Asia also appeals to the Gulf producers, who are looking to broaden their economic and geo-political base beyond traditional dependence on the U.S. and European markets and diplomatic relationships. Russia also may like to diversify its growing energy export-base away from total dependence on European markets for both oil and gas desiring to use oil and gas as its strategic, diplomatic, and commercial levers to gain regional influence.

China is in the best geographical position to benefit and is pushing hard to make Kazakhstan a key oil supply source for the future through its equity investments in oil fields in western Kazakhstan. As part of this effort, China has been active in developing broader diplomatic alliances with Kazakhstan and the other countries of Central-Asia. The **Kazakhstan-China pipeline** (1,860 miles) will export (less than 5% of China's expected oil-demand) Caspian-oil to China's, progressing in spite of many difficulties viz., seismically active-area, lack of industry-infrastructure, climatic-problems, extreme-seasonal-temperature, high-level-

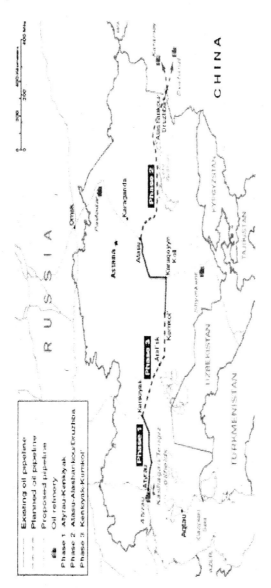

floods, and rain-waters. This new-route will ease China's excessive reliance on the Strait-of-Malacca, a traditional route for 80% of China's imported-oil.

It is apparent that Chinese government is largely choosing bilateral approaches that link energy, trade, strategy, and often military-cooperation rather than adopting multilateral, regional, co-operative and market approaches to linking energy and security interests. In course of time the key Asian powers may increasingly compete in the same producing areas and countries with examples of their state-owned, public or sponsored oil-companies going head-to-head to control the same large oil-fields and supplies. The analysis suggests that China's strategies for its deepening energy-insecurity will have important implications for India across a range of economic, geo-political, energy, and environmental issues.

Thus, China, as a major economic, stabilizing and balancing force in Asia, has a vital stake in how energy-insecurity impacts India's future geopolitical-architecture, either aggravating regional-tensions and rivalries or providing a platform for greater regional-cooperation. The foregoing analysis suggests that on balance Chinese strategies are showing a marked inclination toward a relatively narrow and a **mercantilist** approach to energy security that has the potential to be a major source of future tension/conflict in the region. "Mercantilism" means policies solely driven by economic-nationalism in which government pursues economic-goals as part of its effort to build and expand national, political and strategic power.

Chinese energy-nationalism and militarization of energy security strategy—a matter for concern

China is also believed to have evolved or accessed military-facilities in some of the states. In China's 'target' of military-engagement one could include countries like Nepal, Burma, Bangladesh, Sri Lanka, Pakistan, the Maldives, Iran, Sudan, South-Africa, Tanzania and Tonga. China's energy security strategies may also risk the aggravation of another long term regional-rivalry in Asia between China and India. China's strategists are increasingly concerned about India's naval-power and its capacity to interfere with oil-flows through the Indian Ocean to China, while India is concerned with China's growing ties with Burma and its efforts to extend its naval and other capabilities to the Indian Ocean. "Energy-nationalism" would also be likely to spill over into maritime-control of sea-lanes and transport-routes through the South-China Sea, Strait-of-Malacca, Indian Ocean, and East-China Sea.

In summary, the problems in these areas where China's growing presence is likely to introduce a more complex and challenging situation need to be recognised by India.

Security Atlas—Analytic Stories for the Security Community

To explore China's energy security issues, 40 international experts on China and energy gathered at the National Defense University in Washington, D.C. in recent past for a two-day conference on "China's Search for Energy Security and Implications for the U.S." co-sponsored by the Pacific Northwest Center for Global Security (CGS) and the National Bureau of Asian Research (NBR). Asian nations may have the greatest impact on world energy security over the next two decades and beyond. China's widening global quest for energy security is beginning to become a significant factor in United States-China relations, as demonstrated by China National Offshore Oil Corporation's (CNOOC) failed bid to acquire Unocal.

The Pacific-Northwest-Center for Global Security's work on Asia's security is a new endeavour on the part of Pacific-Northwest-National-Laboratory and are working closely with the National Bureau of Asian Research (NBR), on energy security issues in Asia, especially China. China's energy demand is changing the international energy balance and it is important for the U.S. to monitor and take stock on how this affects U.S. energy and other foreign policy options. Work has also started with NBR on a new concept called a "Security-Atlas."[10]

---

10. OKSANA ELKHAMRI Pacific Northwest Center for Global Security (Volume 2 / Issue 3) Spring 2006

In this context what is more of importance is the goal to create a "Security-Atlas" that will become a central-resource for the security community. The Atlas will provide visualizations of "analytic-stories" that will effectively communicate complex security issues to the decision makers. Illustrations can convey information gleaned from reading many articles or pages of text in a simple and intuitive-manner, enabling even non-experts to comprehend complex security situations quickly and more accurately. The collaboration is bringing together experts on particular security-issues, visual-representation, and presentation-tools to create the Atlas. The long term goal is to cover a broad array of global security-issues, starting first with energy security in Asia, for example, what are the key drivers leading Asian countries to seek energy resources offshore; what energy deals are Asian countries making or attempting to make around the globe; who are involved in these deals; how do these actions reflect or reveal national policies; what corollary agreements or exchanges are being made; and what are their implications for the dynamics of political and economic influence?

Possibility of regional-cooperation and market-mechanism also co-exist

Additionally, there also exists in the region a potential possibility for energy-insecurity to link with and encourage regional-cooperation and greater reliance on markets. In the war on terrorism there is a strong potential for India, China and other Asian-powers to work-together and also with the United States to prevent terrorist attacks on oil-fields, energy-infrastructure, vital-tanker-routes and transit-chock-points while the United States has already initiated discussions on this issue. Effectively pioneering and collaborative-efforts in this direction, more necessary to safeguard the proposed very large regional gas-pipeline linking Russia, China, South Korea, and Japan; integrated South-east Asian Natural Gas pipeline-system and other similar energy-infrastructures to come in future, are the important examples.

The International Energy Agency (IEA) needs to be approached to revamp its organization to include the major developing Asian-states, particularly China and India, directly into IEA emergency oil supply management process. Steps by India to build strategic-petroleum-stocks with China, though not a directly collaborative effort, may be a vital measure to help reduce the risks of a competitive regional scramble for oil-supplies in the event of global oil-supply disruptions. As the evidence suggests that "energy-cooperation" is falling behind competition, mercantilism and energy-nationalism in the search for energy security in the region, all these developments which are important and with potential possibilities should be recognized, encouraged and pursued. Recent efforts within APEC and ASEAN to promote regional energy-cooperation and energy security suggest the potential for developing regional energy security institutions similar to the IEA.

In addition, another area of important concern involves the potential for Asia to aggravate instability in global oil-markets and prices due to lack of adequate preparation for oil-supply-disruptions. Asia lacks the regional institutions to manage supply crises on a regional cooperative basis, and the key-buyers in the region are prone to panic-buying during oil-crises, fuelling-market instability. Both China and India were key-actors in panic buying during the Iraq war in 2003. Lack of effective policies also makes Asia a potential source of instability in global oil-markets. Asia's growing-consumption of coal and significant increases in transportation have grave environmental-implications for Asia in terms of air-quality, health, and global-warming. Concerns over long term global carbon-emissions, for which China has a very high share, simply cannot be effectively addressed without greater involvement of China and India. This needs to be addressed both on the demand side, by slowing the rise in electricity demand-growth particularly in China, as well as by showing the necessity and making improvements in clean coal-technology and government policies regarding the preparation, handling, and transportation of coal and disposal of wastes and emissions.

The Historical Links and the National Psyche

Many Chinese leaders including Premier Wen described the India-China relationship as being amicable over 2500 years except a 25 year hiccup. A testimony to the durability of the friendship is the statue in Kuche in China's Xinjiang region, built in honour of Kumarajiva, a fourth-century monk born of an Indian father and a Kuchinese princess, who more than any other individual inspired Chinese population to adopt Mahayana Buddhism.

As the principal guide and mentor to the Chinese emperor he pushed Buddhism to become the state religion in the fourth century after Christ. Kumarajiva's writings inspired Xuenjang two centuries later to undertake the monumental 18-year journey to India to bring back originals of Dharmasutras. The record of his journey became the primary source of Indian history as well as the planning document for the Tang Dynasty's expansion to the western regions.[11] The contribution of Buddhism to China was to underscore that there were sources of wisdom outside China which encouraged Chinese intellectuals to go abroad, particularly to India, in search of truth and enlightenment. Amartya Sen points out in his essay 'China and India': If China was enriching the material world of India two thousand years ago, India was busy, it appears, exporting Buddhism to China.[12]

Two thousand years of civilizational interaction and vibrations between India and China was characterized by **three elements** namely **pilgrimage, translation of Buddhist scriptures from Pali and Sanskrit into Chinese** and **trade and diplomacy**. It had given way to civilization dialogue in different times but without any clash of civilizations unlike in western hemisphere of world. Economic cooperation had also taken place between ancient India and China for material

---

11. Ref: Deccan Herald 03 May 2005

12. India in China's foreign policy–The China Thaw by CV Ranganathan

and economic benefit as well. India being the thoroughfare between the western and eastern hemisphere, has been receiving far greater external influence than China for many millennia.

As a result, the Indian civilization has projected a totality of heterodox past and pluralist present, to quote the Indian Nobel Laureate, Prof Amartya Sen. India is the 'unity in diversity' that projects more diversity than unity, China is the 'unity in diversity' that tends to replace diversity with unity.[13] These elements of basic building block which reflects the national psyche of China will have certain influence on the policies and thought process of China and proper understanding of this will help to build relations in spite of various constraints and uniqueness in their approach. Thus the historical influence helped to build Buddhism as the national faith of China.

Thus, in the area of "energy-cooperation" also India's wisdom inherits insight, scope and capacity to address, pursue and strengthen, after considering China's strong political will and perseverance toward more and more securitization of energy, country's efforts and interests on energy security and to generate controlling influence against the range of potentially significant implications and disagreements over how to ensure energy-stability and energy security at least in the region of Asia.

---

13. China Report Vol. 42 April-June 06 by Geng Yinzeng

Section – X

Conclusion And Recommendations

CHAPTER 22

Conclusion And Recommendations

Words are but Ghosts unless they speak of the heart.

– Sri Aurobindo

12.1 CONCLUSION

For both **China** and **India**, 'energy' and 'foreign-trade' are the two critical determinants for their accelerated, sustainable and peaceful economic development. In the 21st century, 'economic growth' is mostly linked to energy demand, especially in developing economies, but it is also strongly influenced by population-growth, urbanization, and industrialization. In the "Developing-Asia," excluding the mature, slower growing industrial countries of Asia (such as Japan, Australia, and New-Zealand), the dynamic economic growth patterns of **China** and **India** combined with all other factors, have driven a period of exceptionally strong energy demand growth particularly in the past two decades.

India's import-demands particularly for oil and natural gas is substantial, and will only increase as its economy grows and industrializes. Oil accounts for 33% of India's total energy-consumption and is expected to grow from 2.6 million barrels per day (mmbd) in 2005 to 3.7 mmbd in 2020

In the field of observation, opportunity favours only the prepared and the alert mind.

— Louis Pasteur (1822-1895)

and 4.5 mmbd in 2030. Based on conservative estimates, the imports will continue to grow as consumption needs will rapidly outpace growth in production capacity. Looking ahead, in 2020 India's production capacity will be 1.4 mmbd, leaving an estimated import demand of 2.3 mmbd.

Likewise, by 2030 import demand will continue to grow to 2.9 mmbd as production will only increase slightly between 2020 and 2030 (1.4 to 1.6 mmbd). Consumption of natural gas has risen faster than any other fossil fuel in recent years, from 0.63 trillion cubic feet per year (Tcf) in 1995 to 1.09 Tcf in 2004. Its use is projected to reach 1.5 Tcf by 2010 and 2.2 Tcf by 2020. China's import-demand projections particularly for oil and natural gas are much higher than those for India. The burgeoning consumption projection of oil in China is projected to shoot up from 10.8 mmbd in 2003 to 22.8 mmbd in 2020 to 30.7 mmbd in 2030; and that of natural gas to shoot up from 1.2 Tcf in 2003 to 4.9 Tcf in 2020 and to 7.1 Tcf in 2030 both may lead to higher import-dependence than before.

As compared to China, India's strategies on energy security has so far maintained a low, non-mercantilist, non-aggressive profile. On the contrary, to overcome its energy-deficit and insecurity, China pursued a two-directional, double-strategy petroleum-diplomacy focusing both on attracting foreign investments inward as well as penetrating investments outward by becoming nationalist, mercantilist and antagonistic in acquiring interests in foreign oil-fields/firms; and turning liberal, diplomatic and accommodative in inviting FDI for exploring, particularly, China's onshore and offshore gas and oil even in the disputed energy fields. This brought double advantages to China, one by developing its offshore-energy which was expensive, high-tech, and high-risk operation through foreign-enterprises; and the other by acquiring stakes/ controlling-interests in companies and oilfields overseas for import, profiting by export and a cautiously, a persistently developed captivating oil-diplomacy.

The U.S. anti-terrorism policies may inadvertently fuel the competitive, nationalist and mercantilist character of China's energy strategies if it aggravates Asian fears over the long term stability of key energy exporting regions. The deepening U.S. presence in the Persian Gulf and Central-Asia is also heightening China's insecurity over its future access to energy-supplies and is certain to make energy an increasingly important potential source of tension.

However, India's attempts in bringing about a positively strengthened U.S. efforts to help Asia solve its energy-problems could pay huge dividends along a broad range of larger geo-political and environmental issues. India need to participate in a bigger way in the trans-national piping system with Central Asian Republics, Russia and other neighbouring countries. High priority need to be given to resolve the border disputes with neighbouring countries to pave the way for secured trans-national piping system, keeping in view the future scenario of increased degree of inter-dependence among nations.

China's growing energy-insecurity and increasing diplomatic/ties with rising competition, mercantilism and energy-nationalism have broad ramifications for the region and for India, in particular, across a wide range of issues: geo-political, energy, defence, economy, health and environmental. It is vitally important that India's policymakers examine that energy is a central pivot influencing a series of otherwise apparently unrelated strategic, economic, and environmental interests. There is a high degree of inter-connectedness between energy and these other issues, suggesting that India needs to identify and examine all the favourable and unfavourable forces in the multiple multiplexes of possibilities.

It is, therefore, both pertinent and imminent for India's policymakers to understand the linkages between not only India's energy-insecurity and the much broader range of China's important geo-political, energy, and environmental-interests but also the linkages between Asia's energy-insecurity and the world geo-political and energy-interests so that India's energy security-dilemma against all possible unfavourable impacts could be analyzed comprehensively and determined on a long term basis by boosting sufficient and effective efforts, to help control the rapid regional-demand-growth by encouraging achievement of 'energy-security' more through regional 'energy-cooperation' and markets over the spread of energy-insecurity, mercantilism, energy competition and energy-nationalism.

India's plan and focus, therefore, should remain, with equal intensity, magnitude and priority from short-run to medium-run and long-run, on devising alternatives and more cooperative-strategies, on formulating opportunities out of risks and disfavours for managing the dilemma of 'energy-insecurity-competition' more aggressively and diplomatically, using the available energy resources more efficiently and judiciously with proper energy-mix on one side, and with advancing technologies in exploring alternative and renewable sources of energy on the other side, since in case of **India**, in particular, the nexus between the country's economy and prosperity with its security and peace has shifted closer to the dynamics of its energy-management in the continuing context of energy-dilemma of the Asian region, in particular, and the developing energy-trends of the world, in general.

Thus, it can be concluded that the dynamics of future energy-management of India should focus on aggressive exploitation of international-opportunities; extension of more flexible cooperative-approaches of mutual-benefits and participation in the building of energy-infrastructures in the surrounding regions; increase the level of energy inter-dependence with the bordering States; strategise management of energy, trade, transport and communication linking with and help resort the border-disputes; immediate attention to develop strategies to reduce overall losses relating to technology-deficiencies and distribution-systems in view of estimated tremendous increase in energy-consumption by the residential-sector; giving the highest priority to renewable energy sources even with technology-transfer and improvised energy-mix; capacity-building and technology-upgradation to be in line with the social-fabric and customs of India's divergent societies representing 20% of world population; integration of all energy resources, assets and power-grid systems; construction and consolidation of knowledge-base on all energy resources; and a nation-wide-programme steered to create mass education on energy efficiency, losses, mix, cost and prices.

12.2 Recommendations

(1) **Integrated-National-All-Energy-Plan**—The first and the foremost of all recommendations is that the "Energy" being the essential fuel and the enabling-cum-driving-force of India's ambitiously accelerated economy and having become a seriously competitive and a high-priority concern in international agenda, India, to marshal and support its Five-Year Plans, must develop, in correspondence and harmony with the main plan, a complementary 'National-Energy-Plan', as an accompanying or a follow-up document, to help attain and sustain the plan-objectives. The 'National-Energy-Plan' need to be 'techno-economic' and so comprehensive as to consider all sources of 'energy', their availability; renewability; cleanliness and efficiency; accessibility; production and productivity; technology; R&D; balancing and optimization; substitutability; demand and supply; infrastructure; transportation and distribution; ecology; sustainability; import and export; consumption; deficiencies and losses; costs and prices; subsidy; policy;

geo-politics; defence and security; priorities, strategies and contingencies embracing all the regional and national factors but aspected internationally.

The National-Energy-Plan should be developed after integration of different Ministries under the Government of India as presently the energy sector in India, at the apex level, is administered by five different ministries. Coordination and integration is achieved within the Government of India through the Cabinet, Planning Commission, and all Ministries, however a standing **Energy-Technology-Commission** representing all the concerned Ministries should be formed to be made responsible for the National-Energy-Plan.

There are four, to the minimum, major elements of an integrated approach to strategy-making: (i) Energy-Pricing - the pricing of different forms of energy has to be carried out on a relative-pricing basis and within an integrated framework and prices have to be determined by the markets; (ii) Energy-Substitution - there are possibilities of substitution between different forms of energy where the inter-fuel substitution is to be determined by relative pricing and a desirable mix of energy sources should guide pricing decisions; (iii) Energy Policies – to form effective policies it is important to have an integrated policy system for all sectors of energy, for example, regulatory-reforms in coal-industry accompanied by similar reforms in the power-industry will lead to effective-outcomes and promote efficiency; and (iv) Energy-Technology – innovation and R&D on technology is an important determinant of good energy-future, and hence policy-making across all fuels and forms of energy must be technology-based. The Government should fund on R&D in this area. Such funding should relate to both demand as well as supply sides of the energy-chain. This would also help alter the mix of energy demand substantially.

(2) Dual-Approach Energy Strategies—As faster economic growth and its sustainability are totally dependant on energy supply, India need to further strategise its energy security internationally and choose both cooperative and competitive strategies. While both the approaches and efforts should have the guiding criteria of diplomacy and international relations, the **'cooperative-strategies'** need to focus more on long term implications and interests rather than financial criteria alone, on the possibility and capability of bringing stabilisation, on immediate neighbouring countries, on development of regional-cooperation, on enhancement of inter-country trade and dependence, the **'competitive-strategies'** on the other hand should be guided more by extra-financial and commercial criteria, by energy-nationalism, by mercantilism, by short/medium-term implications and interests, by the largeness and distance of the supply-nodes and by the possibility and capability to destabilise the unfavourable implications. For example, on these lines, India, while in pursuance of its 'cooperative-strategy' should increase bilateral-trade and energy-dependence with Nepal, Bangladesh and Sri Lanka. Similarly, India, by going beyond the traditional business-principles/ criteria of corporate-level should frame and enhance its 'competitive-strategy' at national level with countries having large and long-distance supply-points.

(3) **Tapping of Renewable Energy Potentials In India—** The use of 'Renewable-Energy' accounted for only 6000 MW in 2004 in India. There is a huge potential that needs to be tapped. It will enhance the energy security and efficiency and is also environmental friendly. Government should fund on R&D and explore feasibility and investment-opportunities as India has immense potential in case of 'Renewable-Energy'. High-Efficiency Solar Power Plants using **nano-technology** with CNT based solar-photovoltaic-cells can provide an efficiency of 45%. The most significant aspect, however, would be that the power generated through renewable energy technologies may target 20 to 25% against the present 5%. In order to promote more effective use of renewable energy sources, which has tremendous potential in a vast country

like India, the existing infra-structures of the public sector oil-distributing companies such as Indian Oil Corp. Ltd., and Hindustan Petroleum Corp. Ltd., which already have very huge distribution-networks all over India including in the remotest villages, should be utilized for the distribution of different renewable energy items such as solar-lanterns, solar-panels etc. The existing retail pump-outlets and kerosene/lubricant-depots can be used as sales and service-centres for such items. Basic engineering skill pertaining to the servicing of solar-panels and small windmills can be taught to local students through workshops and training. Public-sector oil-companies with their massive, nation-wide infrastructure could organize a nation-wide educational-programme on regular basis in different locations. The training and promotional expenses would be less compared to the amount of subsidy the companies pay each year to sell kerosene and LPG in India.

(4) More Production of Bio-fuel - "Jatropha"—It is the bio-fuel which has 'oil- content' upto 30% and can be planted on wastelands. Government has made available 33 million hectares of waste land for its production. The Indian Railways have planted 75 lakh 'Jatropha saplings' and are running two passenger locomotives with a blend of 5% bio-fuel.

'Jatropha' can be grown on wastelands with little input. A yield upto 5 T/Hectare of oilseeds is possible under optimum-conditions. 'Jatropha' produces 2 tonnes of bio-diesel that could be used in automobiles, other agro-industrially useful by-products. If potentials fully realized, India's current annual diesel requirement (40 million tonnes this year) could be fully met. Use of bio-diesel is completely CO_2 emission free, the CO_2 fixed by the plantation could be used in emissions trading, thus leading to increased Energy-Security and Energy-Efficiency. The Chief Minster of Chattishgarh, has given great thrust towards the Jatropha cultivation and he is running his official cars using 100% bio-diesel. Similarly certain states such as Andhra Pradesh, Madhya Pradesh, Uttrakhand and Tamilnadu have already started the energy plantations in India.

(5) In India each industrial sector (Chemicals, Steel, Cement, Aluminium, Refractory etc.) has different sets of norms of production, consumption, operational-efficiency and operational-practices on 'energy'. Even within each sector, each industrial unit maintains different norms of energy-efficiency and different sets of best-practices for operational-efficiency. The desirability, the scope, and the extent of energy-savings in real-terms should be researched after introducing uniformity and/or similarity in norms of energy-consumption and the best-practices for operational-efficiency. The potential of energy-savings in Steel sector in India is reported to be significant when compared to world trend. According to Government of India estimates (1997) the potentials of energy-savings in Aluminium, Steel and Cement sectors are shown below –

Energy Savings Potential in Selected Industries/Sectors

Industry-Sector	India (Gcal/Tonne)	World (Gcal/Tonne)
Aluminium	14.55	12.35
Steel	8.00 – 9.55	4.00
Cement	1.00	0.80

(6) **Fuel-management for the Automotive/Transportation Sector**—To cope with massively increased future fuel-requirement of the 21st century India, strong innovative steps and formally funded R&D programmes are needed to develop and build energy-infrastructure, long term reserves and sustainability, technological innovations and alternative-energy sources on "Automotive-Fuel and Civilian-Transportation Systems" infrastructure together with the arrangement of the massive future investments required, is a continuing challenge to fuel-management for the automobile-sector. This problem has become increasingly complex due to fuel-technology evolution and requirement, development of alternative fuels, environmental-impact, cost-benefit analysis, need of subsidisation, and future energy security with their long-lasting implications.

For instance, introducing "Ethanol" in Brazil in the '80s required massive investment in fuel-processing, transmission, and distribution-infrastructure. Fuel-standards and suitable vehicle-technologies had to be co-developed by both energy and auto industry, while Government agencies assured the vehicles and fuels to meet safety and durability standards which combinedly determined the shape and success of Brazil's current "Ethanol" infrastructure. Use of compressed-air, Hydrogen Fuel-Cell and Hybrid-Vehicles in automobile sector need to be encouraged to the maximum.

The future fuel-scenario will need to consider decisions compounded on decisions analysing the critical issue of fuel-transitions for rapidly motorizing economies based on petroleum-based gasoline, natural gas, diesel, petrol, coal-based synthetic-fuels, electricity, battery and hydrogen (from coal, industrial, and renewable sources) with a need to understand the long term consequences (conventional vs. alternative transport-systems, fuel-octane ratings and fuel-purity standards, government regulatory environment, society and technology-absorption, fuel-infrastructural-development, transportation system evolution and innovation, supply, cost and price model, costs and benefits analysis, subsidisation, emissions and pollution-level, sustainable environment, public health, level of economic growth, uncertainty analysis, energy security issues etc.) of near-term policy decisions for complex fuel-technology and technology-transition systems. The above issues should be referred to a Standing Committee at the Centre for in-depth examination, research, analysis and recommendation.

(7) National Programme on Energy-Efficiency-Productivity Education—A National Programme committed to encourage and spread nation-wide general awareness on energy-efficiency and energy-productivity in the use of existing energy-technologies for reducing India's dependence on energy imports; to launch nation-wide programmes for developing more energy-efficient technologies/systems/practices; to identify and award energy-efficient products in

every sector; and deployment of advanced clean-efficient-energy technologies/systems/practices for buildings, homes, transportation, power-systems and in every sector of Indian industry. The programme activities should be conducted in partnership with the Central Government, private sector, state governments, local governments, national laboratories, universities and professional institutions.

Such educative, applied and innovative programmes and approaches to energy-management will create positive public-response and will impact the consumption, availability, efficiency, performance, operating-costs, optimization and management of all systems (Transport-System, Cooling-System, Heating-System, Ventilation-System, Hydraulic-System, Mechanical-System, Electrical-System, Electronic-System, Control-System, Lighting-System, Construction and Building-System, Power-System etc.) in all sectors (industrial, manufacturing, service, communication, health etc.) and at all technology-levels (low-tech/medium-tech/high-tech) in India.

The industrial units in India (the major ones) must develop and implement its own energy strategy including its alternative energy strategy to increase the performance of its systems and facilities while consuming less and less energy and operating fuel-resources through the mechanism of a Continuous Energy-System-Performance Measurement-System, Verification-System, Continuous Monitoring and Reporting System, Energy Information and Control System, Benchmarking and Consulting System; Predictive-cum-Proactive Testing System, Diagnostics System, Operations and Maintenance Services System; On-Site Management Expertise System, Continuous commissioning of energy consuming equipments, Energy Awareness Education and Training System and lastly the Quality-Assurance/Quality-Services/Quality-Control System.

At national level the above perspectives of Energy-Management-Strategies should be consolidated for analysis and policy-making considering the energy resources which are more of military importance and how their availability can be increased in a long term through alternating energy-management-strategies.

(8) High-Efficiency Solar Power Plants—When India's population touches 1.4 billion, demand from power-sector will increase from the existing 120,000 MW to about 400,000 MW. This assumes an energy growth-rate of 5% per annum. Electric power-generation in India now uses four basic energy sources: Fossil-Fuels such as oil, natural gas and coal; Hydroelectricity; Nuclear Power; and Renewable-Energy sources such as bio-fuels, solar, biomass, wind and ocean.

In India, 89% of energy used for power generation today is indigenous, from coal (56%), hydro-electricity (25%), nuclear power (3%) and Renewable (5%). Solar-energy segment contributes just 0.2% of our energy production. Thus it would be seen that only 11% of electric-power generation is dependent on oil and natural gas which is mostly imported at enormous cost. Only 1% of oil is (about 2-3 million tonnes of oil) being used every year for producing electricity. However, power-generation to the extent of 10% is dependent on high-cost gas supplies. The most significant aspect, however, would be that the power generated through renewable energy technologies may target 20 to 25% against the present 5%.

To meet this requirement, one of the innovative solutions can be the use of nano-technology using higher efficiency CNT based solar-photovoltaic-cells with an efficiency of 45%. This will enable setting up of modular 100 MW Solar-SPV plants in India in a reduced land with reduced cost when compared to present figure of Rs. 20 crore per MW-SPV plant with 14% efficiency photovoltaic-cells. Another solution can be development of novel hydrogen-storage-systems based on carbon nano-tube for energy storage.

(9) Similar to the recent efforts initiated within APEC and ASEAN to promote regional energy-cooperation and energy security, India, in a professional manner, should immediately construct first an 'Integrated-Energy-

Knowledgebase' and then also explore and suggest the potential for developing regional energy security institutions similar to the IEA, Department of Energy of U.S.A.

(10) India should pursue with the IEA (U.S.A.) to agree to revamp its organization to include India being one of the major democracy-based developing Asian-states directly into IEA's emergency oil supply management process. With its historical perspective, India should be recognized as stronger and more dependable a country to encourage and support "energy-cooperation" than China whose aggressive "energy security" strategies are known to have been totally based on competition, mercantilism and energy-nationalism.

(11) India may also examine the benefits and the implications in building strategic-petroleum-stocks with other countries in Asia region which may become a vital measure to help reduce the risks of a competitive regional crisis for oil-supplies in the event of global oil-supply disruptions. Like China, India should incorporate and expand its military-means as part of its efforts to ensure safety of its energy-infrastructures, both in terms of dedicated suppliers or sources as also supply lines, especially energy-flashpoints around India, SLOCs and similar others.

(12) Dependence on imported oil should be decreased through effective oil conservation programmes and inter-fuel substitution. Rural energy supply should be given overall improvement of rural-economy. Energy supply through integration of renewable energy sources in an effective manner should be worked out by the experts and implemented by local-bodies to ensure better participation of people. Both conventional and non-conventional sources are to be used for the time being, whenever conventional-sources are available and a judicious-mix of the two be planned and promoted.

(13) National Water-transport-network needs a review for energy-savings—A national plan to encourage and support water-transport should be developed and implemented because in India while the rail, road and aviation sectors are growing by consuming a large share of energy, the water-transport system, very cheap in comparison, is declining though 12 major rivers and hundreds of canals/small rivers crisscross India and prior to British rule waterways were the backbone of India's transport-system as India's rail-bridges with huge columns destroy the system as larger boats could not negotiate the columns under the rail-bridges unlike in Europe and other Western countries where more hanging-bridges were built across the rivers to facilitate movement of ships/steamers.

(14) National Rail/Road transport-network needs a review for energy-savings—In India the road-based transportation, costlier and bulk energy-consumer, continued to grow at the expense of rail though the National-Transport-Policy Committee (1980) noted the low-cost and high-energy-efficiency of the rail-mode and recommended measures to increase its share in total-traffic. As per GOI-Economic-Survey:2004-05 while Rail-Route increased (in '000 KM) from 59.8 (70-71) to only 63.1 (02-03), total length of Roads increased from 915 (70-71) to 2,483 (01-02. Highways/Super-highways/Express-highways being built across India as part of the globalization agenda entails very price that people are paying for in terms of financial, social and ecological costs outweigh the benefits encouraging the shift from sustainable methods of transport such as water and rail to non-sustainable movement of goods and people via roads thereby a resulting massive increase in energy-consumption.

The national modal split between rail and road (in %age terms) in 2000-01 was estimated at 26:74 for freight movement and 18:82 for passenger movement. India's Planning Commission observed (2005) that transporting goods by railways saves substantial amount of fuel and import of crude-oil. The share of railways in total tonne-kilometer of goods-traffic fell from 70% (70-71) to 39% (03-04). Had the Railways carried 70% of the goods traffic, it would have carried 300 btkm of additional traffic with a resultant saving in diesel-consumption by 5 MMT in 2003-04 only.

The future share of rail's future goods-traffic is projected to decline further. Since road-transport causes higher energy-consumption and high price in terms of financial, social and ecological costs outweighing the benefits encouraging the shift from sustainable methods of transport such as water and rail to non-sustainable movement of goods and people via roads thereby a resulting massive increase in energy-consumption, a strategic planning needs to be developed at national level.

(15) India historically subsidizes kerosene to help the poor. The 2001 census survey clearly revealed that only 1.62% of the households in rural areas use kerosene as the primary fuel for cooking but most of the kerosene consumed is for lighting purposes where the quality of light generated is extremely poor. From mid 1990s solar-photovoltaic has been receiving top priority by rural energy-planners globally. A study by 'Energy and Resources Institute' revealed that if solar-lanterns, in place of kerosene, is subsidized, the net-savings to government would increase substantially. The report demonstrated that a free solar-lantern to each of the households comprising the 57% population with no access to electricity, the annual subsidy-burden would reduce substantially. Moreover, by converting kerosene into higher value products the earnings of the refineries would be higher and also fetch higher tax-revenue to government from the converted higher value-added product. The proposal should be critically examined in the light of the current data at current costs for viability.

The next-gen, innovative, low-cost, long-life lighting-system, called LED-Lamps (Light-Emitting-Diodes) are four times more efficient than the conventional incandescent bulb. The white LEDS, can produce nearly 200 times more useful light than a kerosene-lamp and almost 50 times the amount of useful light of a conventional bulb. This technology is believed to have immense potentials to light the entire rural and remote India with much less energy than that used to light the conventional incandescent bulbs. LED-Lamps operate both on re-chargeable battery and solar-panel. LED lamps, more specifically LED lighting, like cell phones, is another example of a technology whose low cost could allow the rural and the remote India to leapfrog into the 21st century.

The two NGOs, 'Light-Up-the-World-Foundation' (Canada) and 'Grameen-Surya-Bijli-Foundation' (India) are working for the spread of the LED technology. This technology, which is not yet widely known in India, is awaiting encouragement, support and investments needed to set up LED and solar-panel manufacturing units in India, currently LEDs are being imported from China. The home-made units will be significantly low-cost in comparison to the unit-price with imported parts, both technologically capable and affordable too to revolutionize the lighting-system in rural and remote villages in India. This technology has the potentials to provide a high-efficient and low-cost solution to the energy problems of India.

(16) With the increasing awareness for the need to modernize country's energy-management and also improvise strategically, the need to establish better information management system on energy is also increasing in India where a lot of efforts are yet to be planned and monitored to harvest the fruits of programmes already implemented and investments already committed and those to come up in future. To achieve this, the key-element of an effectively and a fully functioning information-management system is the availability of timely and accurate data / information which necessitates much improvements on the existing technology, methodology, and techniques employed in India for collection of data / data-quality. Besides, Performance-Reviews and follow-ups, to be done effectively, will also need a parallely and professionally developed plan for Management-Information-System necessitating generation, preservation and reporting of both normative and actual data as defined and required in each such scheme and programme to enable correct and timely assessment and evaluation of the actual savings realized against the targets set by the Government.

(17) Integration of various electricity transmission and distribution assets of various electricity authorities need to be carried out to ensure full capacity-utilization of costly assets and also to ensure supply-demand matching. Any mismatch also leads to extra losses besides non-availability of electric supply to deficient areas. Capacity to generate power and the flexibility to distribute it to desired areas should be visualized as one entity (even with multiple authorities) as the end user is transparent to two different entities of generation and distribution. Assets of various electricity authorities who are directly participating in electricity business and other departments/agencies who have their own generation (Captive-Power-Generation) and distribution system need to be interlinked to ensure full capacity utilization of the overall system. The electric power-flow need to be transparent across various state-boundaries. Participation of Defence departments (spread across the country with electrical-assets more than some electricity board of states) in distribution network of states will help to ensure supply-demand matching, increased capacity utilization besides acting as conduit to supply power even in remotest areas of nation.

(18) It is estimated that each year over 300 million-gallons of used-oil is generated by the 'Do-it-Yourself' (DIY) oil-changers out of which only 7% is recycled. The used-oil generated annually by DIYs is estimated at 3 times more than Iraq dumped into the Persian Gulf and 30 times more than the Exxon-Valdez accident. Less than 10% of used-oil is properly recycled, the remainder ends up polluting the rivers, lakes, oceans and soils. The present disposal-methods of used-oil is a perennial threat to human-welfare as used-oil discharged by DIYs represents the nation's largest single source of petroleum-pollution as they contaminate the water and jeopardizes its eco-system. The 'Aaron-Oil-Company', joining with the 'International Used-Oil Research Institute' (IUORI), an organization devoted to the highest standards and best-management-practices for the Used-Oil Recycling-Industry in USA, has been working for over a decade with the Project 'ROSE' (Recycling Oil Saves Energy), by establishing used-oil collection-centres. If all industries in India use small-portions of the recycled-oil; the programme will prove, also in India, as a successful form of energy-recovery. The major problem with the programme at present is the lack of industrial-facilities' willingness to use recycled-oil for energy-needs.

India, in the lines of 'IUORI' can consider setting up a centre to conduct regular-surveys whereby the organization might gain insight into the industry's needs and most common perceived problems; to establish a nation-wide public-education programme for the use of recycled-oil; to continue with research in the fields of Microwave-Treatment, Line-Analyzers, Probe-Technology, etc.; to set up country-wide collection-centers in the service-centers of its oil-companies; and educate/encourage the industrial facilities / organizations in India to start and process opening-up of new-markets for used and recycled-oil.

(19) Development of a Long-Term "Energy-Education-Plan"—Unlike China, India, keeping 'Energy-Securitization' only as a short term strategy, should formulate an 'Energy-Education-Plan' (a development-programme, industry-oriented, universally acceptable and all welfare-oriented) as its long term measure, after re-categorising its entire energy sector into High-Tech, Medium-Tech and Low-Tech with their varying levels of technology-deployment, R&D need and prospects, investment-requirements and the required HR skills to help enable employment/man-power planning in future through integration of divergent branches of academic-knowledge and technology-management on a single platform in the line of Nano-Technology, to bring a real breakthrough or revolution in energy sector by creating a new class of academia/profession similar to IT/BPO/KPO.

(20) India's Electricity-Sector Reforms—A common knowledge-base cum soft-database must be developed to

enable inter-state/inter-corporate comparison along technical/operational/financial/economic parameters which will help strengthen policy formulation, regulation, governance, research and public awareness. The difficulties faced in the implementation of electricity-sector reforms and their possible implications need to be reviewed for lessons to be learnt with reference to similar reforms done in United States, Europe and China.

(21) A Task-Force at national level may be constituted to conduct cross-sectoral study and recommend against the technical and financial implications of perennial nature due to 'intermittency in energy sources'; on 'aggregate technical and commercial losses'; and on 'national-grid-system optimization' after considering all energy sources.

(22) Energy-Audit—A comprehensive implementation programme for effective conducting, reporting and follow-up of the recommendations after Energy-Audit in all the energy-sectors in India and joining of Energy-Audit (Bureau of Energy Efficiency) with Cost-Audit (Institute of Cost and Works Accountants) to develop an improvised joint-mechanism for techno-economic analysis and better reporting-system for a watch both on engineering/technology and economic aspects of the technology-deployment, resource-consumption, productivity and pricing-mechanism should be considered.

Appendices

Table - 6: World Per Capita Total Primary Energy Consumption (1980-2004)

(Region-wise and Country-wise)

(Million Btu)

Region/Country	1980	1985	1990	1995	2000	2004
World Total:						
(221 Countries)	63.7	63.6	65.8	64.2	65.7	70.1
I. North America: (6)	286.0	267.4	277.9	279.7	286.1	280.2
2. Canada	394.4	392.9	400.7	412.4	417.2	418.4
4. Mexico	54.6	58.6	59.4	58.4	63.3	63.0
6. United States	343.9	321.1	338.5	342.1	350.6	342.7
II. Central and South America:(45)	39.6	38.2	40.8	45.3	49.8	50.8
11. Bahamas,The	285.3	141.3	159.6	154.1	163.3	191.2
15. Brazil	32.8	33.7	38.3	43.1	48.9	49.3
17. Chile	38.5	33.1	42.9	54.0	66.9	74.6
36. Netherlands Antilles	1,021.5	628.7	780.4	766.1	738.6	703.1
41. Puerto Rico	133.2	91.9	84.6	99.0	115.4	141.2
45. Suriname	114.3	75.7	87.3	81.8	82.5	86.1
46. Trinidad and Tobago	159.7	235.0	188.7	280.7	376.0	546.8
49. Venezuela	107.6	102.5	107.9	114.5	117.5	115.3
III. Europe: (38)	135.7	135.1	137.3	134.8	140.8	146.5
53. Austria	145.0	144.3	150.6	159.2	170.3	178.1
54. Belgium	206.4	200.4	219.5	229.4	262.4	269.0
56. Bulgaria	149.4	159.8	132.6	110.2	111.1	112.6
59. Denmark	168.5	159.8	149.8	168.3	164.1	159.6
61. Finland	203.4	195.5	213.2	220.9	235.9	258.1
64. France	156.7	152.3	161.1	173.4	183.0	186.1
65. Germany	NA	NA	NA	175.2	173.5	178.3

68. Gibraltar	252.4	446.5	750.9	1,521.7	3,382.8	1,943.8
69. Greece	78.0	81.7	102.5	107.6	126.7	135.8
70. Hungary	112.7	117.7	112.9	100.8	101.3	106.1
71. Iceland	250.1	282.8	320.7	326.9	472.6	502.5
73. Italy	108.8	106.7	119.3	123.6	132.2	142.3
74. Luxembourg	389.6	340.6	378.7	339.7	350.6	432.5
77. Netherlands	226.0	207.8	221.5	231.3	238.5	251.4
78. Norway	328.2	373.2	403.9	409.6	435.2	424.2
79. Poland	142.4	131.9	103.6	96.3	93.9	95.1
81. Romania	124.4	128.3	123.0	88.8	70.6	73.5
86. Sweden	249.4	259.8	254.3	251.8	246.5	257.9
87. Switzerland	177.7	174.7	171.5	172.0	177.2	172.0
88. Turkey	21.9	26.1	35.2	40.7	48.1	51.3
89. United Kingdom	157.0	154.3	161.4	161.7	162.6	166.5
IV. Eurasia: (16)	175.7	200.4	211.2	145.7	140.4	157.2
93. Estonia	NA	NA	NA	121.3	142.7	165.8
96. Kazakhstan	NA	NA	NA	113.7	128.9	154.0
101. Russia	NA	NA	NA	188.2	187.1	208.8
103. Turkmenistan	NA	NA	NA	74.0	88.7	166.2
104. Ukraine	NA	NA	NA	141.0	117.4	137.1
105. Uzbekistan	NA	NA	NA	81.7	78.4	84.3
V. Middle East: (14)	62.3	75.2	83.8	91.8	102.7	116.0
106. Bahrain	395.7	483.4	512.0	495.1	575.0	611.5
107. Cyprus	68.8	72.2	102.0	125.9	135.6	147.3
108. Iran	40.0	49.5	54.3	62.0	76.2	95.5
109. Iraq	39.6	36.1	50.5	57.7	47.7	47.5
110. Israel	93.9	87.6	99.9	117.0	144.5	140.8
112. Kuwait	351.1	232.4	208.2	364.5	460.1	470.0
114. Oman	55.0	80.1	103.4	105.2	134.4	128.7
115. Qatar	929.2	704.8	711.1	917.8	865.7	840.4
116. Saudi Arabia	166.3	203.3	208.0	191.3	209.2	236.5
118. United Arab Emirates	267.2	507.6	629.4	737.3	757.9	925.4
VI. Africa: (56)	14.4	15.6	15.1	15.0	15.0	15.7
120. Algeria	42.6	47.6	48.5	46.4	40.7	38.6
134. Djibouti	79.0	36.5	63.4	58.9	57.1	55.8
152. Mauritius	14.2	14.1	25.8	31.4	41.6	45.0
163. Seychelles	47.6	61.8	85.5	94.5	101.9	147.7
166. South Africa	90.0	99.2	91.7	98.3	103.3	115.2
VII. Asia and Oceania: (46)	19.9	21.8	25.0	29.9	32.0	38.5
177. American Samoa	182.8	168.7	170.6	146.7	136.4	140.6
178. Australia	188.8	200.0	218.4	223.6	252.2	264.5
179. Bangladesh	1.5	1.7	2.3	3.2	3.9	4.7
180. Bhutan	0.1	0.5	8.2	9.4	8.5	9.0
181. Brunei	442.8	348.4	272.0	207.9	192.8	274.1
182. Burma	2.1	2.8	2.2	2.8	3.7	4.4

184. China	17.8	20.8	23.5	28.9	30.6	45.9
185. Cook Islands	23.2	47.5	36.6	34.4	39.1	40.8
186. East Timor	NA	NA	NA	NA	NA	NA
187. Fiji	30.7	20.2	26.8	21.6	20.6	31.6
188. French Polynesia	20.7	63.7	68.0	50.2	42.9	50.4
189. Guam	498.6	78.0	192.9	348.5	252.2	206.5
190. Hawaiian Trade Zone	NA	NA	NA	NA	NA	NA
191. Hong Kong	53.8	67.8	88.9	100.8	120.8	159.1
192. India	**6.1**	**7.7**	**9.5**	**12.5**	**13.5**	**14.5**
193. Indonesia	7.1	9.4	11.8	15.8	18.2	19.7
194. Japan	130.3	130.1	148.6	165.2	177.2	177.7
196. Korea, North	77.6	87.9	76.5	49.4	39.7	39.2
197. Korea, South	44.0	54.7	88.9	144.0	167.3	185.5
200. Malaysia	30.4	45.0	55.9	74.8	85.9	107.1
201. Maldives	1.4	5.0	6.3	18.7	21.9	44.7
202. Mongolia	51.9	54.6	49.1	39.8	31.5	33.7
203. Nauru	246.2	230.7	215.8	200.4	179.6	172.0
204. Nepal	0.6	0.6	0.9	1.4	2.3	2.3
205. New Caledonia	197.6	148.4	147.6	150.5	129.1	130.9
206. New Zealand	160.6	180.4	217.2	226.5	226.4	221.4
208. Pakistan	7.4	8.8	10.3	12.3	12.7	12.5
212. Singapore	183.0	181.1	262.7	333.7	376.0	444.6
215. Taiwan	62.6	75.9	100.6	134.4	170.1	193.3

APPENDIX - B (1)

Table - 7: Delivered Energy Consumption and Projections for CHINA by End-Use Sector/Fuel-Type: 2003-2030

(Quadrillion Btu) Sector/Fuel-Type	Actual		Projections				Average Annual % Change:
	2003	2010	2015	2020	2025	2030	2003-2030
1. Residential Total	**3.8**	**7.6**	**8.7**	**9.6**	**10.8**	**12.3**	**4.5%**
Oil	0.7	1.1	1.2	1.3	1.4	1.5	2.8%
Natural Gas	0.4	0.9	1.3	1.6	1.9	2.3	7.1%
Coal	1.6	3.1	3.0	2.7	2.6	2.4	1.5%
Electricity	0.8	2.0	2.7	3.5	4.4	5.6	7.4%
Heat	0.3	0.5	0.5	0.5	0.5	0.5	2.0%
Renewables	0	0	0	0	0	0	-
2. Commercial Total	**1.4**	**2.2**	**2.5**	**2.8**	**3.2**	**3.6**	**3.5%**
Oil	0.7	0.9	1.0	1.0	1.1	1.1	1.7%
Natural Gas	0	0.1	0.1	0.2	0.2	0.2	6.4%
Coal	0.2	0.3	0.3	0.3	0.3	0.3	1.6%
Electricity	0.4	0.9	1.1	1.3	1.5	1.8	5.5%
Heat	0	0	0	0	0	0	- 0.5%
Renewables	0	0	0	0	0	0	-
3. Industrial Total	**22.9**	**36.3**	**45.2**	**54.1**	**62.7**	**72.6**	**4.4%**
Oil	5.3	7.5	9.5	11.7	13.5	15.5	4.1%
Natural Gas	0.8	2.0	2.6	3.2	3.8	4.5	6.7%
Coal	11.2	18.6	23.1	27.3	31.4	36.5	4.5%
Electricity	4.4	6.6	8.1	9.6	11.2	12.8	4.0%
Heat	1.3	1.5	1.9	2.3	2.8	3.3	3.5%
Renewables	0	0	0	0	0	0	-
4. Transportation Total	**4.4**	**6.6**	**7.8**	**9.2**	**10.9**	**12.9**	**4.1%**
Oil	4.1	6.2	7.4	8.8	10.5	12.5	4.2%
Natural Gas	0	0	0	0	0	0	5.6%
Coal	0.2	0.3	0.3	0.2	0.2	0.1	1.6%
Electricity	0.1	0.1	0.1	0.1	0.1	0.1	3.1%
Renewables	0	0	0	0	0	0	-

All End-Use Sectors
- Total

Oil	10.8	15.7	19.1	22.8	26.5	30.7	3.9%
Natural Gas	1.2	3.1	4.0	4.9	6.0	7.1	6.8%
Coal	13.2	22.2	26.6	30.5	34.5	.9.3	4.1%
Electricity	5.7	9.5	12.0	14.5	17.3	20.4	4.8%
Heat	1.6	2.0	2.4	2.9	3.3	3.8	3.2%
Renewables	0	0	0.1	0.1	0.1	0.1	-
Total Delivered Energy	**32.5**	**52.6**	**64.1**	**75.7**	**87.6**	**101.4**	**4.3%**
Electricity-Related Losses	13.0	24.4	27.7	30.9	34.1	37.7	4.0%
TOTAL:	45.5	77.0	91.8	106.6	121.7	139.1	4.2%
%age of Electricity Related Losses	28.57%	31.69%	30.17%	28.99%	28.02%	27.10%	

Electric Power Total	**20.3**	**35.9**	**42.1**	**48.2**	**54.7**	**61.9**	**4.2%**
Oil	0.5	2.0	1.4	1.1	0.7	0.2	- 4.3%
Natural Gas	0.2	0.4	0.6	1.0	1.2	1.0	7.0%
Coal	16.3	26.6	32.0	37.4	43.3	50.1	4.2%
Nuclear	0.4	0.8	1.3	1.7	2.3	3.1	7.6%
Renewables	2.9	6.1	6.8	7.0	7.2	7.5	3.6%

Total Energy Consumption of CHINA (Average Annual Change in %age)

Oil	11.4	17.8	20.5	23.9	27.2	30.9	3.8%
Natural Gas	1.4	3.5	4.6	5.9	7.2	8.2	6.8%
Coal	29.5	48.8	58.6	67.9	77.8	89.4	4.2%
Nuclear	0.4	0.8	1.3	1.7	2.3	3.1	7.6%
Renewables	2.9	6.1	6.8	7.1	7.3	7.6	3.7%
Total	45.5	77.0	91.8	106.6	121.7	139.1	4.2%

Source: Energy Information Administration/International Energy Outlook-2006

APPENDIX - B (2)

Table-8: Delivered Energy Consumption and Projections for INDIA by End-Use Sector/Fuel-Type: 2003-2030

(Quadrillion Btu)

Sector/Fuel-Type	Actual		Projections				Average Annual % Change: 2003-2030
	2003	2010	2015	2020	2025	2030	
1. Residential Total	1.7	2.6	2.9	3.2	3.5	3.8	3.1%
Oil	1.0	1.3	1.4	1.4	1.4	1.4	1.2%
Natural Gas	0.0	0.0	0.1	0.1	0.1	0.1	4.9%
Coal	0.2	0.4	0.4	0.4	0.5	0.5	2.9%
Electricity	0.4	0.8	1.0	1.3	1.5	1.8	5.9%
Heat	0.0	0.0	0.0	0.0	0.0	0.0	-
Renewables	0.0	0.0	0.0	0.0	0.0	0.0	-
2. Commercial Total	0.4	1.0	1.2	1.4	1.6	1.8	5.4%
Oil	0.0	0.0	0.0	0.0	0.0	0.0	-
Natural Gas	0.0	0.0	0.0	0.0	0.0	0.0	-
Coal	0.1	0.3	0.4	0.4	0.4	0.3	3.6%
Electricity	0.3	0.7	0.9	1.0	1.2	1.5	6.0%
Heat	0.0	0.0	0.0	0.0	0.0	0.0	-
Renewables	0.0	0.0	0.0	0.0	0.0	0.0	-
3. Industrial Total	5.7	7.1	8.4	9.9	11.5	13.0	3.1%
Oil	2.2	2.8	3.3	3.7	4.2	4.6	2.7%
Natural Gas	0.6	0.7	0.9	1.2	1.6	2.0	4.8%
Coal	1.9	2.3	2.6	3.1	3.5	3.8	2.7%
Electricity	1.0	1.3	1.6	1.9	2.2	2.6	3.4%
Heat	0.0	0.0	0.0	0.0	0.0	0.0	-
Renewables	0.0	0.0	0.0	0.0	0.0	0.0	13.8%
4. Transportation	1.4	1.8	2.1	2.4	2.7	3.0	2.9%
Oil	1.4	1.8	2.0	2.3	2.6	2.9	2.8%
Natural Gas	0.0	0.0	0.0	0.0	0.0	0.0	-
Coal	0.0	0.0	0.0	0.0	0.0	0.0	-
Electricity	0.0	0.1	0.1	0.1	0.1	0.1	2.3%
Renewables	0.0	0.0	0.0	0.0	0.0	0.0	-

All End-Use Sectors

-Total	14.0	19.4	22.5	25.7	29.0	32.5	3.2%
Oil	4.6	5.9	6.7	7.3	8.1	8.9	2.5%
Natural Gas	0.6	0.8	1.0	1.3	1.7	2.1	4.9%
Coal	2.2	2.9	3.4	3.9	4.3	4.7	2.7%
Electricity	1.8	2.9	3.6	4.3	5.0	5.9	4.6%
Heat	0.0	0.0	0.0	0.0	0.0	0.0	-
Renewables	0.0	0.0	0.0	0.0	0.0	0.0	16.5%
Total Delivered Energy	9.2	12.5	14.6	16.8	19.2	21.6	3.2%
Electricity-Related Losses	4.8	6.9	7.9	8.9	9.8	10.9	3.1%
Total:	14.0	19.4	22.5	25.7	29.0	32.5	3.2%
% age of Electricity Related Losses	34.29%	35.57%	35.11%	34.63%	33.79%	33.54%	

Electric Power Total	6.6	9.8	11.5	13.2	14.8	16.8	3.5%
Oil	0.2	0.2	0.2	0.3	0.3	0.3	2.0%
Natural Gas	0.4	0.8	0.8	1.0	1.5	2.6	7.1%
Coal	5.0	6.9	8.2	9.2	9.9	10.3	2.7%
Nuclear	0.2	0.7	0.9	1.2	1.3	1.4	7.4%
Renewables	0.7	1.3	1.3	1.5	1.8	2.2	4.1%

Total Energy Consumption of INDIA (Average Annual Change in %age)

Oil	4.8	6.1	6.9	7.6	8.4	9.2	2.4%
Natural Gas	1.0	1.5	1.8	2.3	3.2	4.7	5.9%
Coal	7.3	9.9	11.6	13.1	14.2	15.0	2.7%
Nuclear	0.2	0.7	0.9	1.2	1.3	1.4	7.4%
Renewables	0.7	1.3	1.3	1.5	1.8	2.2	4.2%
Total	14.0	19.4	22.5	25.7	29.0	32.5	3.2%

Source: Energy Information Administration/International Energy Outlook-2006

APPENDIX - C (1)

World Trends In Energy-consumption By Energy-type and Region : Historical

Table - 1 :   World 'Petroleum' Consumption, 1980-2004
(Thousand Barrels per Day)

Region/Country	1980	1985	1990	1995	2000	2004
North America	20,203.8	18,732.8	20,494.6	21,369.3	23,772.2	25,003.4
Central/South America	3,613.4	3,225.7	3,760.6	4,458.2	5,229.9	5,384.0
Europe	16,034.0	13,765.6	14,642.4	15,262.2	15,814.5	16,307.8
Eurasia	8,995.0	8,950.0	8,392.0	4,604.4	3,721.3	4,105.8
Middle East	2,064.1	2,853.9	3,501.2	4,171.0	4,796.2	5,662.0
Africa	1,474.1	1,826.5	2,070.7	2,251.6	2,507.4	2,790.6
Asia and Oceania (+*)	10,729.1	10,730.6	13,684.4	17,795.7	20,846.2	23,341.0
World Total	63,113.6	60,085.1	66,545.9	69,912.3	76,687.8	82,594.7
*(China)	1,765.0	1,885.0	2,296.4	3,363.2	4,795.7	6,400.0
*(India)	643.0	894.9	1,168.3	1,574.7	2,127.4	2,450.0

Table - 2: World 'Dry Natural-Gas'
Consumption, 1980-2004 ((Billion Cubic Feet)

Region/Country	1980	1985	1990	1995	2000	2004
North America	22,559	20,436	22,470	26,122	27,723	27,597
Central and South America	1,241	1,755	2,024	2,581	3,304	4,077
Europe	11,193	12,286	13,360	15,252	17,394	19,897
Eurasia	13,328	20,302	24,961	20,553	20,532	23,388
Middle East	1,311	2,273	3,599	4,735	6,822	8,613
Africa	735	1,072	1,351	1,689	2,038	2,622
Asia and Oceania (+*)	2,523	4,120	5,605	7,790	10,462	13,472
World Total	52,890	62,244	73,370	78,723	88,275	99,665
*(China)	505	457	494	582	902	1,351
* (India)	51	135	399	628	795	1,089

Table - 3 : World Coal Consumption, 1980-2004
(Million Short Tons)

Country	1980	1985	1990	1995	2000	2004
North America	749.33	880.12	972.17	1,032.86	1,168.91	1,182.53
Central and South America	19.40	28.36	26.54	32.94	37.10	38.21
Europe	1,411.23	1,580.47	1,477.74	1,116.90	1,043.27	1,036.30
Eurasia	751.33	778.87	848.47	475.71	400.80	429.40
Middle East	1.08	4.81	5.68	9.28	14.02	16.27
Africa	112.50	150.72	151.70	174.77	187.22	205.83
Asia and Oceania (+*)	1,092.84	1,464.67	1,786.93	2,273.08	2,248.46	3,190.25
World Total	4,137.70	4,888.02	5,269.24	5,115.54	5,099.78	6,098.78
* (China)	689.74	911.21	1,124.13	1,494.76	1,282.30	2,062.39
* (India)	129.83	193.47	255.79	331.92	406.07	478.16

Table - 4 : World Net Hydro-Electric Power
Consumption, 1980-2004 (Billion Kilowatthours)

Region / Country	1980	1985	1990	1995	2000	2004
North America	546.91	611.08	609.97	670.65	663.30	627.61
Central/South-America	201.49	287.46	365.13	460.55	546.58	577.08
Europe	458.02	476.74	474.47	539.22	585.53	543.56
Eurasia	184.03	205.05	230.67	237.38	227.69	233.09
Middle-East	9.62	10.76	9.65	11.00	7.93	14.11
Africa	60.11	46.57	54.91	59.12	74.26	87.43
Asia and Oceania (+*)	262.70	317.26	404.14	479.36	542.21	664.00
World Total	1,722.88	1,954.91	2,148.92	2,457.29	2,647.51	2,746.88
* (China)	57.62	91.48	125.14	184.90	240.70	327.68
* (India)	46.54	50.51	70.94	71.87	73.72	83.76

Table - 5 :   World Net Nuclear Electric Power Consumption: 1980-2004 (Billion Kilowatthours)

Region/Country	1980	1985	1990	1995	2000	2004
North America	287.00	440.79	648.89	774.38	830.86	883.13
Central and South America	2.22	8.36	8.97	9.46	10.93	18.91
Europe	229.56	602.87	761.26	849.22	914.94	967.52
Eurasia	72.88	169.96	201.31	172.05	203.35	236.71
Middle East	0	0	0	0	0	0
Africa						
Asia and Oceania (+*)	92.73	198.25	279.93	393.64	476.80	498.62
World Total	684.38	1,425.54	1,908.81	2,210.04	2,449.89	2,619.18
* (China)	0	0	0	12.38	15.90	47.95
* (India)	3.00	4.70	5.61	6.46	14.06	15.04

APPENDIX - C (2)

Map of Six Country-Groupings/Regional-definitions

The 6 basic Country-Groupings/Regional-Definitions used in this report are defined as follows:

(1) **OECD** (18% of 2006 world population) : **North America**-United States, Canada, and Mexico; OECD Europe-Austria, Belgium, Czech-Republic, Denmark, Finland, France, Germany, Greece, Hungary, Iceland, Ireland, Italy, Luxembourg, Norway, Poland, Portugal, Slovakia, Spain, Sweden, Switzerland, Turkey, and the U.K. OECD Asia-Japan, South Korea, Australia, and New-Zealand.

Non-OECD (82% of 2006 world population) : **Non-OECD Europe and Eurasia & Non-OECD Asia :**

(2) **Non-OECD Europe and Eurasia** (5% of 2006 world population)-Albania, Armenia, Azerbaijan, Belarus, Bosnia and Herzegovina, Bulgaria, Croatia, Estonia, Kazakhstan, Kyrgyzstan, Latvia, Lithuania, Macedonia, Malta, Moldova, Romania, Russia, Serbia and Montenegro, Slovenia, Tajikistan, Turkmenistan, Ukraine, and Uzbekistan.

(3) **Non-OECD Asia** (53% of 2006 world population)-Afghanistan, Bangladesh, Bhutan, Brunei, Cambodia (Kampuchea), CHINA, Fiji, French Polynesia, Guam, Hong Kong, INDIA, Indonesia, Kiribati, Laos, Malaysia, Macau, Maldives, Mongolia, Myanmar (Burma), Nauru, Nepal, New-Caledonia, Niue, North Korea, Pakistan, Papua, New-Guinea, Philippines, Samoa, Singapore, Solomon-Islands, Sri Lanka, Taiwan, Thailand, Tonga, Vanuatu, and Vietnam.

(4) **Middle East** (3% of 2006 world population)- Bahrain, Cyprus, Iran, Iraq, Israel, Jordan, Kuwait, Lebanon, Oman, Qatar, Saudi Arabia, Syria, the United Arab Emirates, and Yemen.

(5) **Africa** (14% of 2006 world population).

(6) **Central and South-America** (7% of 2006 world population).

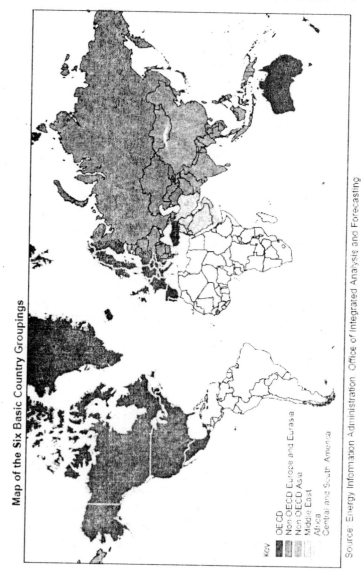

Map of the **Six** Basic Country Groupings

Key
OECD
Non OECD Europe and Eurasia
Non OECD Asia
Middle East
Africa
Central and South America

Source: Energy Information Administration, Office of Integrated Analysis and Forecasting

Energy Information Administration, International Energy Outlook 2006

APPENDIX - C (2)

Map showing Import-Export of 'Oil' and the growing oil-import dependence of 'Non-OECD-Asia' (including China and India)

Asia's Growing Oil-import Dependence:

Oil Imports/Exports for Selected Countries/Regions: Year **2000** to Year **2030.**

Imports or exports in millions of barrels/day during year:

Middle-East **China** Japan Pakistan South-East-Asia Africa **India** Korea Indonesia   Russia   Central-Asia

----

Exports - Imports (2000 -   2030) :

19-46   **2-10**   6-7   0-2   0-6   5-8   **1-5**   2-3   0-1   4-5   1-4

Sources: BP, 2004; International Energy Administration, World Energy Outlook, 2002

(Please see Map on page 368)

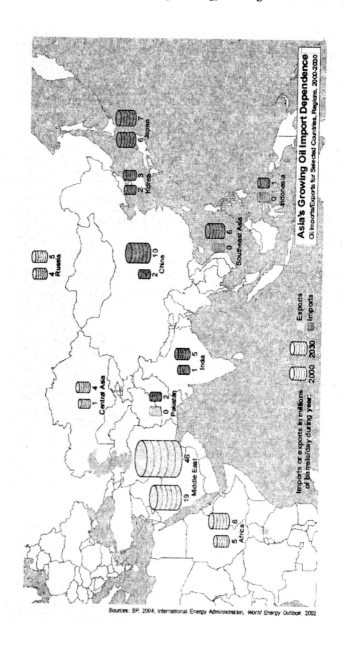

Asia's Growing Oil Import Dependence
Oil Imports/Exports for Selected Countries, Regions, 2000-2030

Sources: BP, 2004, International Energy Administration, World Energy Outlook 2002

APPENDIX-D

List of Abbreviations, Acronyms & Conversion-factors
Energy Related Abbreviations & Acronyms

AFVs - Alternative fuel vehicles

ADB- Asian Development Bank

CDM- Clean Development Mechanism

CERC- Central Electricity Regulatory Comm.

CMIE- Centre for Monetary Indian Economy

CNG- Compressed Natural Gas

CO- Carbon monoxide

CPCB- Central Pollution Control Board

DSM- Demand Side Management

GDP- Gross Domestic Product

GHG- Green House Gases

GOI- Government of India

IGCC- Integrated Gasification Combined Cycle

IMF- International Monetary Fund

IREDA- Indian Renewable Energy Dev. Agency

MNES- Ministry of Non-Conven. Energy Sources

MoEF- Ministry of Environment & Forests

NABARD- National Bank for Agriculture and Rural Development

NIPM- National Integrated Pest Management

NoX- Oxides of Nitrogen

PLF- Plant Load Factor

SoX- Sulphur Oxides

SPM- Suspended Particle Matter

SPR – Strategic Petroleum-Reserve

T & D- Transmission and Distribution

TERI- Tata Energy Research Institute

TNC- Trans National Corporation

AC/DC – alternate/direct current

FBR - fast breeder reactor

GHG - greenhouse gas

IEA - International Energy Agency

IAEA - International Atomic Energy Agency

OECD - Organisation for Economic Co-operation and Development

IIASA - International Institute for Applied Systems Analysis

OPEC - Organisation of the Petroleum Exporting Countries

IPP - independent power producer

OTEC - ocean thermal energy conversion

OWC - oscillating water column

PBMR - pebble bed modular reactor

PHWR - pressurised heavy-water-moderated and cooled reactor

API - American Petroleum Institute

PV - photovoltaic

PWR - pressurised light-water-moderated and cooled reactor

LNG - liquefied natural gas

SER - Survey of Energy Resources

LPG - liquefied petroleum gas

LWGR - light-water-cooled, graphite-moderated reactor

BWR - boiling light-water-cooled and moderated reactor

LWR - light water reactor

CHP - combined heat and power

CNG - compressed natural gas

DOWA - deep ocean water applications

ECE - Economic Commission for Europe

EIA - US Energy Information Administration

UNDP - United Nations Development Programme

contd.

CIS - Commonwealth of Independent States	HWR - heavy water reactor
IBRD - International Bank for Reconstruction and Development	NEA - Nuclear Energy Agency
OAPEC - Organisation of Arab Petroleum Exporting Countries	NGL's - natural gas liquids
	NPP - nuclear power plant
WEC - World Energy Council	UNFCCC – United Nations Framework Convention on Climate Change

APPENDIX-D *Contd.*

Energy Related Abbrevations & Acronyms

10^3 = kilo (k)	tC – tones of carbon
10^6 = mega (M)	Tce – tonne of coal equivalent
10^9 = giga (G)	Tcf – trillion cubic feet
10^{12} = tera (T)	m/s – metres per second
10^{15} = peta (P)	toe – tonne of oil equivalent
10^{18} = exa (E)	m^2 - square metre
Kgoe or Koe - Kg. of Oil Equivalent	tpa – tones per annum
MMT- Million Metric Tone	m^3 - cubic metre
INR- Indian Rupees	ttoe – thousand tones of oil equivalent
MT - Metric Tone	MJ – megajoule
MTOE- Million Tone of Oil Equivalent	tU – tones of uranium
	Ml – megalitre
MW- Mega-Watt	TWh – terawatt hour
Rs.- Indian Currency	Mpa – megapascal
J – joule	mPas – millipascal second
Kcal – kilocalorie	MT – million tones
Gcal – Gigacalorie	MMT – million metric tones
Ppm – parts per million	W – watt
b/d – barrels/day	Mtoe – million tones of oil equivalent
Bbl – barrel	MW – megawatt
Mmbd - million barrels per day	W_p - watts peak
	MW_e – megawatt electricity
kWh – kilowatt hour	Wt - weight
Bcm – billion cubic metres	GW_e – gigawatt electricity
kW_p - kilowatt peak	MWh – megawatt hour
kW_e - kilowatt electricity	GWh – gigawatt hour
Million - 10^6	MW_p - megawatt peak
Billion – 10^9	MW_t – megawatt thermal
Trillion – 10^{12}	Hz – hertz
kW_t - kilowatt thermal	Nm^3 - normal cubic metre
Lb – pound (weight)	..... $kWh/M^2/Day$ - Average Daily solar-radiation
Rpm – revolutions per minute	..... $kWh/M^2/Year$ - Average Annual solar-radiation
Bscf – billion standard cubic feet	W-hr/kg - watt-hours per kilogram
Btu – British thermal unit	(to express Energy-Density at atmospheric-pressure)

APPENDIX-D (*Contd.*)

Energy Related Conversion - Factors

Basic Energy Units

1 joule (J) = 0.2388 cal ; 1 calorie (cal) = 4.1868 J ; 1 British thermal unit [Btu] = 1.055 kJ = 0.252 kcal.

WEC Standard Energy Units

1 tonne of oil equivalent (toe) = 42 GJ (net calorific value) = 10 034 Mcal

1 tonne of coal equivalent (tce) = 29.3 GJ (net calorific value) = 7 000 Mcal

International Energy Agency Unit

1 tonne of oil equivalent (toe) = 107 kilocalories (equivalent to 41.868 GJ)

Volumetric Equivalents

1 barrel   = 42 US gallons   = 159 litres approx.

1 cubic metre = 35.315 cubic feet = 6.2898 barrels

Electricity

1 KWh of electricity output = 3.6 MJ = 860 KCal approx.

Representative Average Conversion Factors

1 tonne of crude oil = 7.3 barrels approx.

1 tonne of natural gas liquids = 45 GJ (net calorific value)

1000 standard cubic metres of natural gas = 36 GJ (net calorific value)

1 tonne of uranium (light-water reactors, open cycle) = 100 000 - 16 000 toe

1 tonne of peat = 0.2275 toe

1 tonne of fuel-wood = 0.3215 toe

1 kWh (primary energy equivalent) = 9.36 MJ = 2 236 Mcal approx.

Power

1 Horsepower = 0.7457 KW

1 Boiler HP = 9.803 KW

1 BTU/Hr = 0.293071 W

1 Ton Refrigeration = 3.51685 KW

1 KCal/Hr = 1.163 W

Material : Heat Content (BTU)

1 gallon of gasoline = 126,000 BTU (Heat Content)

1 cubic foot of natural gas = 1,030 BTU (Heat Content)

1 pound of bituminous coal 13,100 BTU (Heat Content)

One 42-gallon barrel of Oil (Distillate) = 58,00,000 BTU (Heat Content)

One 42-gallon barrel of Oil (Residual) = 63,00,000 BTU (Heat Content)

One 42-gallon barrel of NGL (Natural-Gas Liquids) = 37,77,000 BTU (Heat Content)

Generators and Engines

1 Horsepower (hp)   = amount of power required to lift 33,000 pounds 1 foot in 1 minute, or   550 foot-pounds per second

1 Horsepower (hp)   = 746 Watts (electrical equivalent)

1 Horsepower (hp)   = 2545 British-thermal-units per hour (heat equivalent)

1 Horsepower (hp)   = 4500 kilogram-meters per minute (in metric-system)

Battery-related measuring units

C   : nominal capacity, in Ah (or submultiplier mAh) for a given voltage.

W   : watt, unit of power. One watt equals one joule per second.

W/kg	: watts per kilogram, unit of mass power-density.
W/l	: watt per liter, unit of volume power-density.
W-h	: watt-hour, unit of energy, or work. 1 watt expended continuously for 1 hour equals 1 watt-hour. 1 watt-hour is equivalent to 3,600 J (joules) and 1 kWh is equivalent to 3.6 MJ.
W-h/kg	: watt-hours per kilogram, unit of mass energy-density.
W-h/l	: watts-hour per litre, unit of volume energy-density.
W-h/lb	: watt-hours per pound, unit of energy-per-mass.

Mass per
volume index : 1/kg of battery.

Energy-Efficiency/Energy-Intensity

"Energy-Efficiency" can indicate the efficiency of a process in terms of output per unit of energy-consumed. "Energy-Intensity" of a process (energy-consumed per unit of output) is the inverse of the "Energy-Efficiency" of the process (output per unit of energy-consumed).

The 'Aggregate-Energy-Intensity' or the 'Economy-wide Energy-Intensity' (Ratio of total energy consumed to GDP) can be expressed in 'Megajoules (mJ) per $' or in terajoules (TJ, 1012J) per $, petajoules (PJ, 1015J) per $, or exajoules (EJ, 1018J) per $.

Similarly, 'Energy-Intensity' can be measured and expressed for each 'Sub-sector' separately in terms of Megajoules (mJ) per tonne of goods produced; or Megajoules (mJ) per thousand/lakh of goods produced; or Megajoules (mJ) per passenger/vehicle-kilometers; etc.

APPENDIX-D (*Contd.*)

Thermal Conversion Factors

Thermal Conversion Factors used in the 'Annual-Energy-Review' published in the United States:

The Thermal-Conversion-Factors presented in the following tables can be used to estimate the heat content in British thermal units (Btu) of a given amount of energy measured in physical-units, such as barrels or cubic-feet. For example, 10 barrels of asphalt has a heat content of approximately 66.36 million Btu (10 barrels x 6.636 million Btu per barrel = 66.36 million Btu).

The heat-content rates (i.e., thermal-conversion-factors) provided in this section represent the gross (or higher or upper) energy-content of the fuels. Gross heat-content rates are applied in all 'Btu' calculations for the 'Annual-Energy-Review' published in the United States; net (or lower) heat-content rates are typically used in European energy calculations. The difference between the two rates is the amount of energy that is consumed to vaporize water that is created during the combustion process. Generally, the difference ranges from 2% to 10%, depending on the specific fuel and its hydrogen content. Some fuels, such as unseasoned wood, can be more than 40% different in their gross and net heat-content rates. Thermal conversion factors for hydrocarbon-mixes are the weighted-averages of the thermal conversion factors for each hydrocarbon included in the mix. For example, in calculating the thermal conversion factor for a 60-40 butane-propane mixture, the thermal conversion factor for butane is weighted 1.5 times the thermal conversion factor for propane.

The source of each thermal conversion factor is described in the section entitled "Thermal Conversion-Factor Source Documentation," available at : (http://www.eia.doe.gov/emeu/aer/append_a.html).

Thermal Conversion Factors

(1) Approximate Heat-Content of Petroleum Products (Million Btu per Barrel)

Petroleum Products	Heat Content (M Btu/Barrel)	Petroleum Products	Heat Content (M Btu/Barrel)
Asphalt	6.636	Natural Gasoline	4.620
Aviation Gasoline	5.048	Pentanes Plus	4.620
Butane	4.326	Petrochemical Feedstocks :	
Butane-Propane Mixture (60% -40%)	4.130	Naphtha less than 401° F	5.248
Distillate Fuel Oil	5.825	Other Oils equal to or greater than 401° F	5.825
Ethane	3.082	Still Gas	6.000
Ethane-Propane Mixture (70%-30%)	3.308	Petroleum Coke	6.024
Isobutane	3.974	Plant Condensate	5.418
Jet Fuel, Kerosene Type	5.670	Propane	3.836
Jet Fuel, Naphtha Type	5.355	Residual Fuel Oil	6.287
Kerosene	5.670	Road Oil	6.636
Lubricants	6.065	Special Naphthas	5.248
Motor Gasoline :		Still Gas	6.000
- Conventional	5.253	Unfinished Oils	5.825
- Oxygenated	5.150	Unfractionated Stream	5.418
- Reformulated	5.150	Waxes	5.537
- Fuel Ethanol	3.539	Miscellaneous	5.796

(2) Approximate Heat-Content of Bio-Fuels (Million Btu per Barrel)

Biodiesel	4.996		
Biodiesel Feedstock to Biodiesel (soyabean oil input) - (5.208 MBtu soyabean oil per barrel biodiesel)	5.208	Ethanol Feedstock to Fuel Ethanol (corn input) - (million Btu corn per denatured barrel ethanol)	3.539

(3) Approximate Heat-Content of Natural Gas (Btu per Cubic Foot)

Natural Gas Consumption, Electric-Power Sector Calculated annually by EIA by dividing the heat-content of natural-gas consumed by the electric power sector by the quantity consumed.

contd.

Natural-Gas Consumption, End-Use Sectors. Calculated annually by EIA by dividing the heat-content of natural gas consumed by the end-use sectors (residential/commercial/industrial/transportation) by the quantity consumed.
Total Natural-Gas Consumption - Calculated annually by EIA by dividing the total heat content of natural gas consumed by the total quantity consumed.
Natural-Gas Exports - Calculated annually by EIA by dividing the heat content of natural gas exported by the quantity exported.
Natural-Gas Imports- Calculated annually by EIA by dividing the heat content of natural gas imported by the quantity imported.
Total Natural-Gas Production (Dry) - Assumed by EIA to be equal to the thermal conversion factor for dry natural gas consumed.
Natural-Gas Production (Marketed) - Calculated annually by EIA by dividing the heat content of dry natural gas produced and liquids produced by the Natural-Gas Plant by the total quantity of marketed natural gas produced.

(4) Approximate Heat-Content of Coal and Coal Coke

Coal Coke Imports and Exports -	24.800 million Btu per short ton.
Coal-Consumption of Electric Power-Sector - Calculated annually by EIA by dividing the heat content of coal consumed by the electric power sector by the quantity consumed.	
Coal-Consumption, Industrial Sector, Coke Plants - Calculated annually by EIA by dividing the heat content of coal consumed by coke plants by the quantity consumed.	
Coal Consumption, Industrial Sector, Other - Calculated annually by EIA by dividing the heat content of coal consumed by manufacturing plants by the quantity consumed.	
Coal Consumption, Residential and Commercial Sectors - Calculated annually by EIA by dividing the heat content of coal consumed by the residential and commercial sectors by the quantity consumed.	
Total Coal Consumption - Calculated annually by EIA by dividing the total heat content of coal consumed by all sectors by the total quantity consumed.	
Coal Exports - Calculated annually by EIA by dividing the heat content of steam coal and metallurgical coal exported by the quantity exported.	
Coal Imports. • 1949-1963: Calculated annually by EIA by dividing the heat content of coal imported by the quantity imported. • 1963 forward: Assumed by EIA to be 25.000 million Btu per short ton.	
Coal Production. Calculated annually by EIA to balance the heat content of coal supply (production and imports) and the heat content of coal disposition (exports, stock change, and consumption).	

contd.

Appendices

(5) Approximate Heat-Rates for Electricity

Electricity Net-Generation (Fossil-Fueled Plants) - There is no generally accepted practice for measuring the thermal conversion rates for power-plants that generate electricity from hydro, wind, photovoltaic, or solar thermal energy-sources. Therefore, EIA calculates a rate factor that is equal to the annual average heat rate factor for fossil-fueled power-plants in US, using that factor makes possible to evaluate fossil-fuel requirements for replacing those sources during periods of interruption, such as droughts. The heat content of a kilowatthour of electricity produced, regardless of the generation process, is 3,412 Btu.

Electricity Net-Generation (Geothermal-Energy Plants) - • 1960-1981: Calculated annually by EIA by weighing the annual average heat rates of operating geothermal units by the installed nameplate capacities. • 1982 forward: Estimated annually by EIA on the basis of an informal survey of relevant plants.

Electricity Net-Generation (Nuclear-Plants) - • 1957-1984: Calculated annually by dividing the total heat content consumed in nuclear generating units by the total (net) electricity generated by nuclear generating units. • 1985 forward: Calculated annually by EIA by using the heat rate reported on Form EIA-860, "Annual Electric Generator Report" (and predecessor forms); and the generation reported on Form EIA-906, "Power Plant Report."

For details see: Energy Information Administration / Annual Energy Review 2006
(http://www.eia.doe.gov/emeu/aer/append_a.html)

APPENDIX - E

Frequently-asked-questions (FAQ) On Energy

Here is an illustrative list of Frequently-Asked-Questions on "ENERGY-BASICS", only some important ones, that many of us very often ask each-other, rather out of some necessity and not merely for the sake of curiosity or information:

Energy, General Awareness

What Priority-Rating should be given to spread Energy-Awareness in India?

How should we estimate the total impact of broad-spread 'Energy-Awareness' in India firstly in the area of 'saving/conservation of energy'?

Who is an 'Energy-Kid' and who is an 'Energy-Person'?

Can we plan to make Energy-Kids in India without a formal energy-education?

Can India make of us Energy-Persons without a formal Programme?

What is Energy-Intelligence? What is Energy-Compass?

What is energy efficiency? Do we measure energy-spent and energy-gained for each type of energy-generation?

How can we compare heating-fuels in terms of their efficiency and economics?

How can we compare lighting-devices in terms of their illumination and unit-cost?

What is alternative energy management?

What is 'Alternative-Fuel-Vehicle' (AFV)?

What is 'Fuel-Cell' and what is 'Solar-Power-Satellite'?

What is Energy-Conversion-Table and how it should be used?

How much total energy does a person need in a year to live comfortably?

How much energy does a person actually use in a year?

Which sources of energy are primary and which are secondary?

Which parameters and factors should be considered to determine inter-comparability and inter-substitutability of energy?

What will be the amount of annual saving if 10 incandescent-bulbs each of 100W and 10 fluorescent tube-lights of 40W of a house are replaced with 20 CFL or T-5/T-8 or LED lightings each of 25W?

Which Batteries will be most economic to purchase for a given purpose?

Energy, Nature and Environment

Which energy-resources the Nature has given to India in abundance and in scarcity?

Which energy-sources are natural and which ones are man-made?

Which sources of energy are non-renewable and which are renewable?

Which primary energy-sources are infinitely renewable?

By what percentage renewable-energy is being used out of the total?

How long the coal-reserve of earth will last at current rate of consumption?

How long the oil and gas reserves of earth will last at current rate of consumption?

Which sources of energy are 'clean-energy' and which ones are 'polluting-energy'?

Which source of energy pollutes air the maximum and brings acid-rains?

Which country has the highest level of gaseous emissions per capita?

What is India's rank in per capita gaseous emissions in the world?

How much fossil-fuel reserves (coal, petroleum, natural-gas, and oil-shale) India has and how long they will last at current rate of consumption?

Energy, Planning, Regulation and Governance

What has been India's research-scale and developments/ prospects on this source?

Are there national norm on energy consumption?

Which institutions in India preserve energy related statistics and which institutions undertake research projects?

Does India have the required soft-database on all energy-resources needed to do planning and research in a comprehensive manner?

Is energy audit compulsory and sufficient in India?

Does India have enactments to regulate all sources and types of energy?

Whether Indian enactments are presently sufficient to regulate and govern all aspects relating to all sources and types of energy?

Is India now facing the need to securitize its energy-policy? Is 'energy-management' being best done under existing corporate-governance?

Whether the best practices and canons under existing corporate-governance will be sufficiently able to administer all issues related to energy management in the country?

Whether 'energy-management' need to be a subject of strategic-governance at the national level?

Does India need a Central-Coordinating-Agency or a Unified-Regulatory-Authority or a single Ministry and a separate Budget to regulate, plan for and govern all sources of energy?

Energy and National Economy

What is the role of 'Energy' in a country's economy and in the development of human-civilisation?

What is scale of human-deployment in energy-sector or on each energy-source?

What are the potentials of future employment opportunities in energy sector?

How the criteria for investment-decisions at national level best-optimized, cross-optimized and sub-optimized among all energy-resources?

Which class of 'industry' and 'economy' in India is more dependants on which type of 'energy'?

Which class of 'industry' consume the highest share of energy?

Which class of 'industry' has the highest need for energy saving?

Which section of 'population' consume the highest share of energy?

Which age-group of 'population' consume the highest share of energy?

What are the per capita energy-consumption for each type of energy in each State?

Energy and the World

Which countries have very high/very low levels of per capita energy-consumption?

Which countries in the world have done spectacularly excellent work in 'energy-management'?

How energy-dynamics shape and direct international relations and politics?

What is securitization of energy?

Should India go for the securitization of energy?

What should be the necessary level of energy-cooperation and energy-dependence in the neighbourhood of India?

Can we estimate the extent and strength of the dynamics of future cross-country energy corporations?

Is India's reporting-regulations sufficient to understand and control the extent and strength of the dynamics of future cross-country energy corporations?

Which are the major international energy agreements signed by India?

Which are the major international agreements on environment in which India is a member?

Energy, Cost, Prices and Subsidy

Which is the cheapest option in the comparative energy-economics of power-generation out of many alternatives?
Is it high time to introduce Life-Cycle-Costing methodology on energy-resources?
How the prices of each form of energy is determined?
How much per capita subsidy we enjoy every year on petroleum products?
What are the costs, and the subsidies given on each energy-form in India?

What is the annual total amount of subsidy on energy allowed by India?
What is the total amount of energy-subsidy consumed annually by different consumer-groups in India?
How do we find or calculate diesel fuel surcharge?

Why are diesel fuel prices higher than gasoline prices?
What are the products and uses of petroleum?
What are the differences between various types of coal or crude-oil prices?

How the international prices of gasoline are determined?
Can we tell which country the gasoline at our local station comes from?
How the petroleum-products distribution-network functions in India?

How many retail gasoline stations are there in the country?
What are the major factors that affect the prices of oil and natural-gas?

Energy, Production and Consumption

Which is the most basic and most abundantly available fossil-fuel energy-source that is used in many industries, including, steel, power, cement, paper and others ?
With what efficiency-ratios coal is used in different industries?
What are the by-products of coal and petroleum and their market/end-uses?

What is the impact of coal and coal using industries on environment?

What is the national annual consumption-requirement, total-reserves, total annual production-capacity, coal prices in India?

Do we have enough oil worldwide to meet world's future needs of oil?

How much oil and natural-gas is produced and consumed in India (total and by end use)?

How to convert fuels from one unit of measure to another (from gallon to barrel, for example)?

How many gallons of gasoline does one barrel of oil make?

How do you convert short-tons to metric-tons?

How many coal-fired and other type(s) power-plants are there in India?

Why India need to import coal in spite of huge reserves?

What is the share of production of renewable-energy in India?

How much dependent India is on imported coal, oil and natural-gas?

Which countries have made 'Strategic-Petroleum-Reserves'?

What is the average per capita production and consumption of electricity in India?

What is %age of 'Aggregate Technical & Commercial' (AT&C) losses of electricity in each State of India?

How do we compare the efficiency and cost of electricity produced in a typical nuclear power-plant with that in coal-based, solar or tidal or hydro power-plants?

How many 'Alternative-Fuel-Vehicles' were made available for Indian roads in the 10th Five-Year Plan?

How many alternative fuel vehicles are being planned for use by the Central Government, State Governments, Central/State Public-Sector-Undertakings, National agencies, and fuel providers in the 11th Five-Year Plan?

Whether electricity is a primary or secondary source of energy?

Whether the energy-sources that are used to make electricity

can be renewable or non-renewable?
By what percentage nation's renewable and non-renewable energy-sources are used for generation of electricity?

Whether electricity itself is a renewable or non-renewable energy?
What is the national annual consumption requirement, total installed capacity, total annual actual production, total losses, prices and subsidization in petroleum industry?

Which alternative transportation fuels are renewable and which are non-renewable?
By which %age renewable alternative-transportation-fuels are being used in India?
What are the comparative cost and prices of renewable and non-renewable energies?
What are the comparative cost and prices of alternative-transportation-fuels?

How much nuclear-power accounts for in the total electricity-generation in India/World? Which are the raw-materials and what their current prices used in a nuclear-power plant installed to generate electricity?
Why is the analysis through a Life-Cycle-Assessment of a nuclear-power plant is necessary?

What is the comparative Life-Cycle Costing and environmental impact analysis of a nuclear-power plant over a conventional fossil-fuel plant installed to generate electricity?

APPENDIX – F

World-Bank : 55 Development Parameters – CHINA

CHINA: Parameters	2001	2002	2003	2004	2005	2006
Agricultural land (% of land area)	59.52515	59.43916	59.49245	..	..	..
Agriculture, value added (% of GDP)	14.14983	13.49505	12.56635	13.10749	12.54704	11.90916
Births attended by skilled health staff (% of total)	..	97	96	97.3	..	..
Cash surplus/deficit (% of GDP)	..	-2.57353	-2.35424	-2.11595	..	..
CO_2 emissions (metric tons per capita)	2.363746	2.720112	3.216	..	..	..
Electric power consumption (kWh per capita)	1069.308	1184.223	1378.527	1585.122	..	..
Energy imports, net (% of energy use)	-0.12576	0.867065	2.071314	4.509031	..	..
Energy use (kg of oil equivalent per capita)	880.9372	947.2251	1072.103	1241.63	..	..
Exports of goods and services (% of GDP)	22.60025	25.13327	29.55604	33.95057	37.29692	36.77002
Fertility rate, total (births per woman)	..	1.88	1.88	1.85	1.813333	..
Fixed line and mobile phone subscribers (per 1,000 people)	255.6811	328.1998	413.4586	498.8437	570.2269	..

Foreign direct investment, net inflows (BoP, current US$)	4.42E+10	4.93E+10	4.71E+10	5.49E+10	7.91E+10	..
Forest area (sq. km)	..	..	..	..	1972900	..
GDP (current US$)	1.32E+12	1.45E+12	1.64E+12	1.93E+12	2.24E+12	2.67E+12
GDP growth (annual %)	8.3	9.1	10	10.1	10.2	10.7
GNI per capita, Atlas method (current US$)	1000	1100	1270	1500	1740	2010
GNI, Atlas method (current US$)	1.27E+12	1.41E+12	1.63E+12	1.94E+12	2.27E+12	2.64E+12
Gross capital formation (% of GDP)	36.26775	37.86576	41.20289	43.26324	43.27007	40.69522
High-technology exports (% of manufactured exports)	20.56835	23.30854	27.09555	29.80557	30.60326	..
Immunization, measles (% of children ages 12-23 months)	85	85	85	86	86	..
Imports of goods and services (% of GDP)	20.48037	22.56195	27.35739	31.39927	31.73516	32.90485
Improved sanitation facilities, urban (% of urban population with access)	..	..	..	69	..	..
Improved water source (% of population with access)	..	..	..	77	..	..

contd.

Indicator						
Industry, value added (% of GDP)	45.15252	44.78988	45.96865	46.22525	47.34212	47.00047
Inflation, GDP deflator (annual %)	2.052264	0.584614	2.611465	6.912397	4.360426	2.881533
Internet users (per 1,000 people)	26.49684	46.15745	61.70444	72.52205	85.09007	..
Life expectancy at birth, total (years)	..	70.65854	..	71.44171	71.83415	..
Literacy rate, adult total (% of people ages 15 and above)	..	..	..	..	..	..
Long-term debt (DOD, current US$)	1.29E+11	1.2E+11	1.2E+11	1.32E+11	1.33E+11	..
Malnutrition prevalence, weight for age (% of children under 5)	..	7.8	..	..	..	..
Market capitalization of listed companies (% of GDP)	39.54933	31.85239	41.51247	33.11907	34.79563	90.93932
Merchandise trade (% of GDP)	38.46989	42.69863	51.8591	59.76854	63.36896	65.991
Military expenditure (% of GDP)	1.969814	2.102499	2.083594	2.026545	1.974242	..
Mortality rate, infant (per 1,000 live births)	..	..	..	..	23	..
Mortality rate, under-5 (per 1,000)	..	..	..	..	27	..

contd.

Net barter terms of trade (2000 = 100)	102.5022	102.7052	98.6925	93.10394	86.82748	..
Official development assistance and official aid (current US$)	1.47E+09	1.47E+09	1.33E+09	1.69E+09	1.76E+09	..
Population growth (annual %)	0.726381	0.67	0.622861	0.600296	0.641573	0.557865
Population, total	1.27E+09	1.28E+09	1.29E+09	1.3E+09	1.3E+09	1.31E+09
Poverty headcount ratio at national poverty line (% of population)	..	..	..	..	..	..
Present value of debt (current US$)	..	..	..	2.42E+11	2.76E+11	..
Prevalence of HIV, total (% of population ages 15-49)	..	..	0.068	..	0.081	..
Primary completion rate, total (% of relevant age group)	..	..	..	97.69748	..	..
Ratio of girls to boys in primary and secondary education (%)	98.95143	..	98.45143	99.70194	99.44751	..
Revenue, excluding grants (% of GDP)	7.86193	8.671139	8.759562	9.468469	..	..
Roads, paved (% of total roads)	..	78.34	79.49	81.03	82.5	..

contd.

Appendices

School enrollment, primary (% gross)	117.7282	116.0057	115.0183	117.6239	112.7774	..
School enrollment, secondary (% gross)	65.09779	67.19827	70.26487	72.53048	74.34348	..
School enrollment, tertiary (% gross)	9.816322	12.60529	15.41669	19.09544	20.30731	..
Services, etc., value added (% of GDP)	40.69764	41.71507	41.465	40.66726	40.11084	41.09037
Surface area (sq. km)	9598060	9598060	9598060	9598060	9598060	9598060
Time required to start a business (days)	..	..	48	48	48	35
Total debt service (% of exports of goods, services and income)	7.922806	8.280203	7.332966	3.415015	3.104496	..
Workers' remittances and compensation of employees, received (US$)	8.39E+09	1.3E+10	1.78E+10	1.9E+10	2.25E+10	2.25E+10

Source: World-Bank Online Data-Query accessed on 15.01.2008
(http://ddp-ext.worldbank.org/ext/DDPQQ/)

APPENDIX – G

World-Bank : 55 Development Parameters – INDIA

INDIA: Parameters	2001	2002	2003	2004	2005	2006
Agricultural land (% of land area)	60.65539	60.64866	60.54104	60.61503	60.60158 ..	
Agriculture, value added (% of GDP)	23.19141	20.86607	20.93192	18.78997	18.30423	17.54967
Births attended by skilled health staff (% of total)	..	..	..	..	..	..
Cash surplus/deficit (% of GDP)	-4.41322	-4.72714	-3.67168	-3.56858	..	..
CO_2 emissions (metric tons per capita)	1.128304	1.172499	1.196145	..	..	..
Electric power consumption (kWh per capita)	403.0312	416.5955	434.8098	457.3245	..	..
Energy imports, net (% of energy use)	17.9901	18.22428	17.87898	18.5001	..	..
Energy use (kg of oil equivalent per capita)	503.4377	508.9551	515.4657	530.5546	..	..
Exports of goods and services (% of GDP)	12.74658	14.46476	14.74613	18.20034	20.32767	..
Fertility rate, total (births per woman)	..	2.92	2.92	2.88	2.839333	..
Fixed line and mobile phone subscribers (per 1,000 people)	43.55338	51.59788	64.0309	84.52182	127.6742	..

contd.

Foreign direct investment, net inflows (BoP, current US$)	5.47E+09	5.63E+09	4.58E+09	5.47E+09	6.6E+09	..
Forest area (sq. km)	..	..	..	..	677010	..
GDP (current US$)	4.78E+11	5.08E+11	6.02E+11	6.96E+11	8.06E+11	9.06E+11
GDP growth (annual %)	5.208022	3.726654	8.391931	8.325039	9.23218	9.19511
GNI per capita, Atlas method (current US$)	460	470	530	630	730	820
GNI, Atlas method (current US$)	4.79E+11	4.93E+11	5.69E+11	6.8E+11	8.04E+11	9.07E+11
Gross capital formation (% of GDP)	24.45137	25.57427	27.45111	30.98203	33.35161	..
High-technology exports (% of manufactured exports)	5.393494	4.759841	4.753784	4.884294	..	..
Immunization, measles (% of children ages 12-23 months)	58	58	58	58	58	..
Imports of goods and services (% of GDP)	13.63622	15.45842	16.03325	20.02002	23.28671	..
Improved sanitation facilities, urban (% of urban population with access)	..	..	..	59	∵	..
Improved water source (% of population with access)	..	..	..	86	..	..

contd.

Industry, value added (% of GDP)	25.30879	26.41915	26.19551	27.46584	27.32813	27.71214
Inflation, GDP deflator (annual %)	3.128165	3.889109	3.795513	4.368794	4.448521	5.274544
Internet users (per 1,000 people)	6.779836	15.81094	17.36289	32.41578	54.8154	..
Life expectancy at birth, total (years)	..	63.38049	..	..	63.50049	..
Literacy rate, adult total (% of people ages 15 and above)	61.01456	..	..	..	..	..
Long-term debt (DOD, current US$)	9.57E+10	1.01E+11	1.08E+11	1.17E+11	1.14E+11	..
Malnutrition prevalence, weight for age (% of children under 5)	..	..	..	..	..	..
Market capitalization of listed companies (% of GDP)	23.08131	25.79372	46.37427	55.73708	68.64243	90.35723
Merchandise trade (% of GDP)	19.60169	20.82364	21.85356	25.22406	29.64273	32.50078
Military expenditure (% of GDP)	3.020318	2.916849	2.751378	2.935603	2.872983	..
Mortality rate, infant (per 1,000 live births)	66	64	..	61.6	56	..
Mortality rate, under-5 (per 1,000)	..	..	..	..	74	..
Net barter terms of trade (2000 = 100)	97.82919	88.62537	96.22765	83.40168	87.45467	..

contd.

Official development assistance and official aid (current US$)	1.7E+09	1.44E+09	9E+08	6.94E+08	1.72E+09	..
Population growth (annual %)	1.615975	1.553746	1.491518	1.42929	1.367061	1.381639
Population, total	1.03E+09	1.05E+09	1.06E+09	1.08E+09	1.09E+09	1.11E+09
Poverty headcount ratio at national poverty line (% of population)	..	..	..	..	..	..
Present value of debt (current US$)	..	..	..	1.1E+11	1.11E+11	..
Prevalence of HIV, total (% of population ages 15-49)	..	..	0.887	..	0.915	..
Primary completion rate, total (% of relevant age group)	75.83665	79.14167	83.62301	88.52859	89.84878	..
Ratio of girls to boys in primary and secondary education (%)	77.97435	79.71802	87.68122	88.10804	88.65115	..
Revenue, excluding grants (% of GDP)	11.2055	11.757	11.91474	12.49106	..	..
Roads, paved (% of total roads)	47.74	47.4	..	..	..	..
School enrollment, primary (% gross)	98.3035	98.94653	107.429	116.1999	119.2455	..

contd.

School enrollment, secondary (% gross)	48.01569	49.79887	52.28518	53.51369	56.55942	..
School enrollment, tertiary (% gross)	10.49468	11.03815	11.49818	11.76135	11.40989	..
Services, etc., value added (% of GDP)	51.49979	52.71478	52.87258	53.74419	54.36764	54.73819
Surface area (sq. km)	3287260	3287260	3287260	3287260	3287260	3287260
Time required to start a business (days)	..	..	89	89	71	35
Total debt service (% of exports of goods, services and income)	14.68581	17.32037	19.10136	..	..	..
Workers' remittances and compensation of employees, received (US$)	1.43E+10	1.57E+10	2.1E+10	1.88E+10	2.13E+10	2.57E+10

Source: World-Bank Online Data-Query accessed on 15.01.2008
(http://ddp-ext.worldbank.org/ext/DDPQQ/)

APPENDIX - H

List of Useful Web-resources Relating to 'Energy'

The detailed list given below will be useful for further studies and reaearch by energy professionals, entrepreneurs, teachers, students and scholars:

Note: The list of web-based energy-education resources shown below contain online treasure of information that can be downloaded for free or at a low cost. The information on intermediate and advanced energy-education and environment are useful both for entrepreneurs, researchers and learners/students. Most sites are equipped with search-engines and have hyperlinks to other web-pages related to energy and energy-education. Some of the web-sites are often updated and redesigned, and over the course of time, a few of the addresses listed below could change in which case backing up to the home-page for that site or using a search-engine (www.google.com or www.yahoo.com) on the home-page will help guide to the page needed.

(1) Overall/Primary Energy Related Institutes:Web-sites

1. Energy Institute (http://www.energyinst.org.uk/)

2. World Forum on Energy Regulation (http://www.worldforum2006.org/)

3. Strategic Energy Institute (http://www.energy.gatech.edu/)

4. Energy Information Administration (http://www.eia.doe.gov/)

5. Wikipedia (http://en.wikipedia.org/wiki/Energy_Information_Administration)

6. World Energy Council (http://www.worldenergy.org/)

7. Deptt. Of Energy (USA) (http://www.doe.gov/energysources/)

8. First Gov for Science (http://www.science.gov/)

9. UK Energy Research Centre (http://www.ukerc.ac.uk/)

10. Encyclopedia Britannica (http://www.britannica.com/)

11. Canadian Energy Research Institute (http://www.ceri.ca/)

12. Alberta Energy Reseach Institute (http://www.aeri.ab.ca/)

13. Indian Institute of Science, Bangalore (http://wgbis.ces.iisc.ernet.in/energy/)

14. The Institute for Energy Research (http://www.energyrealism.org/)

15. Research Institute for Sustainable Energy-RISE (http://www.eco-web.com/)

16. MSN Encarta (http://encarta.msn.com/)

17. Oxford Institute for Energy Studies (http://www.oxfordenergy.org/research.shtml)

18. World Energy Efficiency Association (http://www.weea.org/Directories/Directory-othergovs.htm)

19. California Energy Commission:ForKids (http://www.energyquest.ca.gov/story/)

20. Energy Facts:For Kids (http://www.eia.doe.gov/kids/energyfacts

21. http://www.thermaldepolymerization.org/

22. http://www.renewableenergyaccess.com/

23. http://fatknowledge.blogspot.com

24. International Energy Outlook (http://www.eia.doe.gov/oiaf/ieo/index.html)

(2) Energy-securitization: Web-sites

1. Securitization.Net (http://www.securitization.net/)

2. Securitization:Peace and Conflict Issues (http://shss.nova.edu/pcs/journalsPDF/V7N2.pdf)

3. Securitization in Emerging Markets (http://www.securitization.net/pdf/sp/EmergingMrkts_10Oct06.pdf)

4. Wikipedia (http://en.wikipedia.org/wiki/Securitization)

5. Allegheny Energy (http://www.alleghenyenergy.com/)

(3) China's Industrial and Economic Development: Web-sites

1. World Bank Online (http://publications.worldbank.org/online)

2. World Bank's World-Development-Report (http://0-web.worldbank.org. library.vu.edu.au/WBSITE/EXTERNAL/)

3. World Bank's Annual Reports (http://0-web.worldbank.org. library.vu.edu.au/WBSITE/EXTERNAL/)

4. China Through a Lens (http://www.china.org.cn/)

5. Peoples' Daily Online (http://english.people.com.cn/)

6. Association for Asian Research (http://www.asianresearch.org/articles/2756.html)

7. China Economic Review (http://www.chinaeconomicreview.com/)

8. World Socialist Web-Site (http://www.wsws.org/articles/2006/mar2006/chin-m23.shtml)

9. Answers.com (http://www.answers.com/topic/five-year-plan)

10. The Hindu BusinessLine (http://www.thehindubusinessline.com/)

(4) India's Industrial and Economic Development: Websites

1. Answers.com (http://www.answers.com/India%27s%20Economy)

2. Indian Economy (http://indianeconomy.org/)

3. Economy Watch (http://www.economywatch.com/)

4. The Economic Times (http://economictimes.indiatimes.com/)

5. India Brand Equity Foundation (http://www.ibef.org/economy/)

6. Indira Gandhi Institute of Development Research (http://www.igidr.ac.in/lib/ineco.htm)

7. United Nations Development Program (http://www.undp.org.in/)

8. Planning Commission (http://planningcommission.nic.in/plans/planrel/11thf.htm)

9. Planning Commission (http://planningcommission.nic.in/reports/publications/pubbody.htm)

10. Union Budgets/Economic Surveys of India (http://indiabudget.nic.in/welcome.html)

(5) Coal Energy Institutes:

1. China Coal Research Institute (http://www.ccri.com.cn/)

2. World Energy Efficiency Association (http://www.weea.org/)

3. IEA Clean Coal Centre (http://www.iea-coal.org.uk/)

4. National Research Center for Coal and Energy (http://www.nrcce.wvu.edu/)

5. Western Research Institute (http://www.westernresearch.org/)

6. Central Fuel Research Institute (http://cfriindia.nic.in/)

7. National Institute of Industrial Research (http://www.niir.org/)

8. Ministry of Coal, Govt of India (http://www.coal.nic.in/)

9. World Coal Institute (http://www.worldcoal.org/)

(6) Oil Energy Institutes:

1. Oil.com (http://www.oil.com/)

2. Oil India Ltd. (http://oilindia.nic.in/)

3. Indian Oil Corporation (http://www.iocl.com/)

4. Wikipedia (http://en.wikipedia.org/wiki/Oil)

5. Oil Online (http://www.oilonline.com/)

6. Research Institute of Petroleum Industry (http://www.ripi.ir/en/)

7. Strategic Research Institute (http://www.srinstitute.com/)

8. International Used Oil Research Institute (http://www.aaronoil.com/)

(7) Gas Energy Institutes:

1. Naturalgas.Org (http://www.naturalgas.org/)

2. Wikipedia (http://en.wikipedia.org/wiki/Natural_gas)

3. ONGC (http://www.ongcindia.com/)

4. Energy Information Administration (http://www.eia.doe.gov/oil_gas/natural_gas/info_glance/natural_gas.html)

5. Wiley   InterScience   (http://www3.interscience.wiley.com/)

6. Gas Authority of India Ltd. (GAIL) (http://www.gailonline.com/)

(8) Electricity Energy Institutes:

1. Electric Power Research Institute (http://www.epri.com/default.asp)

2. Static Electricity Research Institute (http://www.nenu.edu.cn/webE/academic/research/)

3. Central Electricity Authority (http://cea.nic.in/)

4. EnergylineIndia.com (http://energylineindia.com/)

5. Wikipedia   (http://en.wikipedia.org/wiki/Power_station)

6. PowerPlants (http://www.powerplant.com/)

(9) Nuclear Energy Institutes:

1. Nuclear Energy Institute (http://www.nei.org/)

2. World Nuclear Association (http://www.world-nuclear.org/)

3. Wikipedia   (http://en.wikipedia.org/wiki/Nuclear_power)

4. Energy Information Administration (http://www.eia.doe.gov/fuelnuclear.html)

5. US Deptt.of Energy (http://www.ne.doe.gov/)

6. NEI Science Club (http://www.nei.org/scienceclub/index.html)

7. International Atomic Energy Agency (http://www.iaea.org/)

8. World Nuclear Association (http://www.world-nuclear.org/)

(10) Renewable-energy - Related Institutes:

1. Global Energy Network Institute (http://www.geni.org/)

2. Shell Global Solutions (http://www.shell.com/)

3. Renewable Energy (http://edugreen.teri.res.in/EXPLORE/renew/renew.htm)

4. Renewable Energy (http://www.energ.co.uk/)

5. Wikipedia (http://en.wikipedia.org/wiki/Renewable_energy)

6. Indian Renewable Energy Development Agency (http://www.iredaltd.com/)

7. RenewableEnergyaccess (http://www.renewableenergyaccess.com/rea/tech/geothermal)

8. West Wales Eco-Centre (http://www.ecocentre.org.uk/renewable-energy.html)

9. EnergyTech (http://www.energetech.com.au/)

(11) Wind-energy - Related Institutes:

1. Indian Wind Energy Association (http://www.inwea.org/)

2. Wikipedia (http://en.wikipedia.org/wiki/Wind_power)

3. European Wind Energy Association (http://www.ewea.org/)

4. Ministry of New and Renewable Energy(India)-(http://mnes.nic.in/windp.html)

5. American Wind Energy Association (http://www.awea.org/)

6. New Wind Energy (http://www.newwindenergy.com/)

7. Lovearth Network (http://www.windenergy.net/)

(12) Solar energy Related Institutes:

1. Wikipedia (http://en.wikipedia.org/wiki/Solar_power)

2. Solar Energy (http://www.history.rochester.edu/class/solar/solar.htm)

3. TERI (http://edugreen.teri.res.in/explore/renew/solar.htm)

4. Ministry of Non-Conven. Energy Sources(India)-(http://mnes.nic.in/solarenergy)

5. Solar Energy International (http://www.solarenergy.org/resources/)

6. Gujarat Energy Development Agency (http://www.geda.org.in/solar/)

7. Solar/Wind Energy (http://ces.iisc.ernet.in/hpg/cesmg/tvrsolwind.html)

8. Global Solar (http://www.globalsolar.com/)

(13) Geo-thermal Energy Related Institutes:

1. TERI (http://edugreen.teri.res.in/explore/renew/geo.htm)

2. US Energy Efficiency and Renewable Energy (http://www1.eere.energy.gov/geothermal/)

3. International Geo-Thermal Association (http://iga.igg.cnr.it/index.php)

4. Idaho National Laboratory (http://geothermal.id.doe.gov/)

5. Geo-Thermal Energy Association (http://www.geo-energy.org/)

6. Earth Energy (http://www.earthenergy.co.uk/)

7. California Energy Commission (http://www.energy.ca.gov/geothermal/)

(14) Tidal Energy Related Institutes:

1. Wikipedia (http://en.wikipedia.org/wiki/ Tidal_power)

2. Tidal Energy (http://www.renewingindia.org/ tid.html)

3. World Energy Council (http://www. worldenergy.org/wec-geis/publications/reports/)

4. Blue Energy (http://www.bluenergy.com/)

5. California Energy Commission (http:// www.energy.ca.gov/development/oceanenergy/)

6. UN Atlas of Oceans (http://www.oceansatlas.org/)

7. Alternative-Energy(http://www.alternative-energy-news.info/tidal-energy-industry-boom/)

(15) Wave Energy Related Institutes:

1. Wave-Power (http://home.clara.net/darvill/ altenerg/wave.htm)

2. World Energy Council (http://www. worldenergy.org/wec-geis/publications/reports/ser/ wave/wave.asp)

3. Wavegen (http://www.wavegen.co.uk/)

4. Ocean Wave Energy Company (http:// www.owec.com/research.html)

5. Coordinated Action on Ocean Energy (http:// www.ca-oe.net/home.htm)

6. WaveDragon (http://www.wavedragon.net/)

7. Pure Energy Systems (http://peswiki.com/energy/ Directory:Ocean_Wave_Energy)

8. University of LimeRick (http://www.ul.ie/wert/ wave_energy_tech.htm)

(16) Ocean-thermal Energy Related Institutes:

1. National Renewable Energy Laboratory (http://www.nrel.gov/otec/)

2. Wikipedia (http://en.wikipedia.org/wiki/Ocean_thermal_energy_conversion)

3. World Energy Council (http://www.worldenergy.org/wec-geis/publications/reports/ser/ocean/ocean.asp)

4. Cogeneration Technologies (http://www.cogeneration.net/ocean_thermal_energy_conversion.htm)

5. NOAA Coastal Services Center (http://www.csc.noaa.gov/opis/html/summary/otec.htm)

6. Pure Energy Systems (http://peswiki.com/index.php/Directory:Ocean_Thermal_Energy_Conversion)

7. University of Missouri (http://www.ece.umr.edu/power/ocean.htm)

8. US Energy Efficiency and Renewable Energy (http://www.eere.energy.gov/consumer/renewable_energy/ocean/index.cfm/mytopic=50010)

(17) World Pollution And Enviroment:

1. World Resources Institute (http://www.wri.org/)

2. Global Environment Facility (http://www.gefweb.org/)

3. Environmentalist for Nuclear Energy (http://www.ecolo.org/)

4. Wikipedia (http://en.wikipedia.org/wiki/Pollution)

5. Pollution (http://www.pollution.com/)

6. Pure Energy Systems (http://peswiki.com/index.php/Directory:Environment/)

(18) World Energy Security:

1. Defense Energy Support Center (http://www.desc.dla.mil/default.asp)

2. Sohbet-Karbuz (http://karbuz.blogspot.com/)

3. Allegheny Energy (http://www.alleghenyenergy.com.)

4. Institute for Analysis of Global-Security (http://www.ensec.org/)

5. Energy Information Administration (http://www.eia.doe.gov/emeu/security/)

6. US Deptt.of Energy (http://www.energy.gov/nationalsecurity/)

7. Energy Security Council (http://www.energysecuritycouncil.org/)

8. Foreign-Policies Archive and related articles: (www.foreignpolicy.com.)

(19) Govt. of India–list of Ministries and Departments:

Planning Commission (http://planningcommission.gov.in/)

Ministry of Agro and Rural Industries (http://ari.gov.in/)

Ministry of Coal (http://coal.nic.in/)

Ministry of Commerce and Industry

Ministry of Defence (http://mod.nic.in/)

Ministry of Development of North Eastern Region (http://mdoner.gov.in/)

Ministry of Earth Sciences (http://moes.gov.in/)

Ministry of Environment and Forests (http://envfor.nic.in/)

Ministry of Finance (http://finmin.nic.in/)

Ministry of Mines (http://mines.nic.in/)

Ministry of New and Renewable Energy (http://mnes.nic.in/)

Ministry of Petroleum and Natural Gas (http://petroleum.nic.in/)

Ministry of Power (http://powermin.nic.in/)

Ministry of Railways (http://www.indianrailways.gov.in/)

Ministry of Rural Development (http://rural.nic.in/)

Ministry of Statistics and Programme Implementation (http://mospi.gov.in/)

Ministry of Steel (http://steel.nic.in/)

Department of Atomic Energy (http://www.dae.gov.in/)

Bureau of Energy Efficiency (http://www.bee-india.nic.in)

ANNOTATED-GUIDE TO WEB-RESOURCES

This is an 'Annotated-Guide' (© 2006 Pacific Gas and Electric Company, San Francisco, CA) to World-Wide-Web Resources which serves as an educational resource on energy.

1. Alliance to Save Energy

www.ase.org/educators/download.htm - This page provides elementary, middle, and high school hands-on, multidisciplinary lesson plans and activities on energy.

www.ase.org/greenschools - The Green Schools Project of the Alliance to Save Energy is designed for K-12 schools, to create energy awareness and encourage experiential learning and money savings on energy costs. The Web site provides an in-depth description of the programme, newsletters on recent developments, a bibliography of resources, online forums for teachers and students, and lesson plans (also found at www.ase.org/educators/download.htm).

2. Bonneville Power Administration Audit

www.bpa.gov/Corporate/KR/ed/energyaudit/homepage.shtml - High school students study the science of energy while working as members of a student team conducting an energy audit of their high school. This programme integrates learning about all the major building systems with lessons on the environmental costs of energy use, the physics of energy, and historical and biological perspectives on energy. The audit component ensures hands-on learning as students perform a real service for their school, potentially saving at least 10% of the previous year's energy bill. The complete curriculum was prepared by the Bonneville Power Administration and Oregon State University Extension Services.

3. California Department of Education - Office of Environmental Education

www.cde.ca.gov/cilbranch/oee - This Web site offers information on environmental educational projects and programmes that utilize community partnerships. The site includes applications for the Environmental Education Grant Programme (EEGP), and links to the Environmental Education Compendia of K-12 Curriculum References and a Child's Place in the Environment (ACPE) site (a K-6 environmental curriculum integrating science content standards with English language arts).

4. California Energy Commission - Energy Quest

www.energyquest.ca.gov - The redesigned Energy Quest site opens on an animated drawing of a student's room, over which the mouse is moved to access interactive energy games and puzzles, resources, newsletter, projects, homework help (Ask Professor Quester) and more (requires Flash player). Click on red apple for teacher's resources, including background material, recommended books and extensive links to K-12 energy education lesson plans on other sites.

5. California Environmental Education - Interagency Network (CEEIN)

www.calepa.ca.gov/education/CEEIN/Resources - CEEIN is a collaboration of twenty State of California agencies that provide environmental materials. The Web site provides links to compendiums on environmental education, resource guides, K-12 curriculum, teacher guides, student workbooks, brochures, posters, and information on classroom speakers.

6. California Integrated Waste Management Board (CIWMB)

http://ciwmb.ca.gov/Schools - At the CIWMB site is a listing of environmental educational publications (elementary and secondary) and schedules for teacher training workshops related to the waste prevention materials. These include Closing the 0Loop, Earth Resources, a Case Study: Oil, The

Worm Guide and modules developed by Project Learning Tree. There is no charge for the training or for the curriculum distributed at the workshops. Teachers will also find information at this site on developing school waste prevention and recycling programmes, a searchable online publications catalogue and a listing of funding sources for environmental, recycling or science literacy projects.

7. California Regional Environmental Education Community (CREEC Network)

www.creec.org - A Web site of the California Department of Education for environmental education in the state. Visitors to the site can click on regions in California to access information specific to that area. Information is also available on how to correlate programmes to state content standards. There are links to a library of Internet environmental education curricula resources, a statewide searchable resource directory, and other tools to help teachers make students environmentally aware. Workshops and grants are also listed.

8. California State and Consumer Services Agency (SCSA)

www.scsa.ca.gov/energy_education.htm - The site offers free energy education programmes and information on SCSA grants for teachers. The Kids' Flex Your Power Energy Challenge introduces 4th-6th grade students to energy conservation and provides teachers with lessons and online resources. The Recycle Rex School Assembly Programme, a game show format, also includes materials on energy conservation. California K-12 teachers can apply for grants to support innovative projects to teach energy conservation and efficiency from the SCSA Energy Education Grants Programme.

9. California State Parks: Folsom Powerhouse SHP, Electricity Unit

www.parks.ca.gov/default.asp?page_id=501 - Folsom Powerhouse State Historic Park provides a downloadable teacher's guide with 14 detailed lessons on electricity for 4th graders. The lessons, all keyed to California Science Standards, explore the history of electricity via the old Folsom Powerhouse. It offers investigations, instructions for making models and student handouts.

10. Charles Edison Fund

www.charlesedisonfund.org - The Fund's site offers 82 science-teaching experiments, including those focused on energy, for grades 4-8. The experiments are designed to stimulate an interest in science and technology through easy-to-perform experiments using basic scientific concepts. Information about the Edison Awards Programme for student participation in scientific projects is also available at the site. Click on Science Teaching Experiments.

11. Consortium for Energy Efficiency (CEE)

www.cee1.org - The CEE is a national, non-profit public benefits corporation promoting the manufacture and purchase of energy-efficient products and services. The U.S. Department of Energy and U.S. Environmental Protection Agency both provide the CEE major support through participation and funding. The CEE publishes a comprehensive Directory of Energy-Efficient Schools, Programmes and Resources, listing over 35 national, regional, state and local programmes. The directory is found in the Commercial Programmes section of the Web site.

12. Current Energy Supply of and Demand for Electricity in California

http://currentenergy.lbl.gov/ca - For a graphic representation of electricity used in California in real-time over the course of a day, direct students to this Web site. There are definitions for all the terms used in the charts with the two key ones being "Online Capacity," which is the amount of electricity currently available, and "Current Load," which is the electricity currently being used. The graph can be used as the basis for educational activities. It shows that households and businesses use more electricity in some parts of the day than others. Electricity production must accommodate the highest, or peak, usage. If peak usage can be reduced, then total electric generating capacity can be lowered. Ask students how they can reduce peak usage (conservation, shift usage off-peak). Ask students what happens when "Current Load" is greater than "Online Capacity." Answer: a blackout occurs. See the "Graph Archive" section of the Web site for a graphic display of a blackout.

13. Earth 911, Making Every Day Earth Day

www.earth911.org - This site is the result of a public and private partnership with the U.S. Environmental Protection Agency, all 50 states and several organizations and companies. It features geographically specific information about recycling programmes. Click Kids/Education for games, activities and information for students, elementary through high school.

14. Education for a Sustainable Future

http://csf.concord.org/esf - The Resource database on this site includes books, articles, Web sites and student activities for educators interested in sustainable development. The Teacher Center offers professional development (online tutorials). Click on Curriculum for online, printable lessons for grades K-12.

15. Eisenhower National Clearinghouse

www.enc.org - This site provides information for teaching K-12 science and math classes, including energy-related topics. The site features a searchable database and comprehensive descriptive catalogue of resources from hundreds of organizations and publishers. Links may be found to workshop materials, online teacher courses, teacher talk sites and education periodicals.

16. EnergyNet

www.energynet.net - EnergyNet is a classroom project that integrates technology, standards-based learning, and workplace skills for students for grades 6-12. Students develop skills in math, science, technology, and language arts while working as "energy consultants" on this project. A network for teachers and students to work online with their peers is also at the site. The programme is managed by the consulting firm Educational Dividends.

17. Flex Your Power

www.flexyourpower.ca.gov - This is the Governor's energy Web site for California. The site provides energy-saving ideas, information about energy-efficient products, and answers to questions about energy issues in the state.

18. Florida Solar Energy Center

www.fsec.ucf.edu/Ed/Teachers - Teacher Resources on this site include information on environmental issues, curricula on alternative energy sources for grades 4-8 and energy activities for students. Curriculum units are printable html files. The Center is situated at the University of Central Florida.

19. Franklin Institute Science Museum - Community Science Action Guides

www.fi.edu/guide/hughes/energy_us.html - Energy resource guides on energy efficiency, oil supply and global warming for upper elementary and high school. Each guide is an online collection of information and resources for teachers. Some include lesson plans that support National Science Standards.

20. GE Lighting Auditor

www.gelighting.com/gelauditor/school - The Lighting Auditor from General Electric is a Web-based programme for auditing and calculating the energy use of a school's lighting system. It consists of an online form for entering information about the lighting system's characteristics, such as type of lighting, hours of operation, and number of lamps. Illustrations and short descriptions of the various lighting systems make it easy for students to identify the different types of lighting. As a result, students can use the Lighting Auditor without extensive training.

21. How Stuff Works

www.howstuffworks.com - Students, teachers and parents can find what they want to know (and more) about science and technology on this site. Information is included on power plants, solar cells, and other energy topics. Some of these html pages have printer-friendly versions; others include advertisements. There are also links to more resources on each topic.

22. The Learning Team

www.learningteam.org - This Web site offers educational materials on CDs, tapes and books, among these The Sun's Joules, an educational CD-ROM for grades 8-12 about renewable energy and the environment with nearly 1,000 screens of text, graphics, videos, and interactive exercises, as well as a detailed index, charts of U.S. energy consumption by state, and an energy glossary. A teacher's guide that provides background information on renewable energy and six activities for classroom use is also available. It was produced for the U.S. Department of Energy - National Renewable Energy Laboratory.

23. National Energy Education Development (NEED) Project

www.need.org - The goal of the NEED project is to promote an energy-conscious society by creating networks of students, educators, business, government, and community leaders. NEED designs and delivers K-12 energy education programmes. The Web site provides information on teacher/ student training opportunities and curriculum guides and activities, downloadable in pdf format from the site.

24. National Energy Foundation (NEF)

www.nef1.org - The National Energy Foundation is a nonprofit educational organization. Its Web site offers an online catalogue of energy and environmental resource educational materials for grades K-12. The Foundation also provides professional development via the NEF academy (in-service training programmes on energy education materials that can be integrated into existing school curriculum) that earn teachers graduate credit. Some free instructional materials are offered to K-12 teachers on natural gas safety, energy awareness and alternative energy sources. These must be ordered online (except for Fueling the Future, available as downloadable pdf files).

25. The National Hydropower Association

www.hydro.org - The National Hydropower Association has a downloadable publication in pdf of a teacher's guide, Hydro for Kids: A Curriculum (Water Works: a Question of Balance). Designed for students in grades 3 through 8, this curriculum teaches about hydropower's role in providing electricity. Click on Publications.

26. North American Association for Environmental Education (NAAEE)

www.naaee.org - NAAEE is a network of professionals, students, and volunteers working in the field of environmental education throughout the world. The association offers a variety of programmes and activities, including an annual conference, publications and links to other environmental education resources on the Internet.

27. Northeast Sustainable Energy - Educational Materials

www.nesea.org/education/edmaterials - Curricular units and lesson plans for K-12 on energy conservation and non-polluting, renewable energy technologies. Contact information must be submitted before free materials can be downloaded.

28. The Northern California Solar Energy Association (NCSEA)

www.norcalsolar.org - NCSEA is a non-profit, member-supported association for ongoing education in the many aspects of solar energy. The Web site provides a calendar of events, announcements, bibliography, glossary of terms and links to related sites and K-12 curricula.

29. Northwest Foundation for Water and Energy Education

www.fwee.org/education.html - This page is a gateway to several resources on water power and energy efficiency. There is free downloadable curriculum on this site on the nature of water power (pdf files).

30. Pacific Gas and Electric Company (PG&E)

www.pge.com/energenius - On PG&E's home page teachers will find a link to the Energenius® Educational programme, which focuses on energy efficiency and gas and electric safety education for grades K-8. Curriculum materials are provided at no cost to schools within the PG&E Service Territory. The Energenius Educational Series comes complete with teacher curriculum guides and sets of student activities. The core of the series consists of multi-lesson classroom programmes designed to engage students in active, age-appropriate learning. Programmes include materials on energy efficiency that students complete with family members.

31. PG&E Home Energy Analyzer

www.pge.com/energysurvey - Audit home energy use with this interactive Webbased survey that produces a report with tailored recommendations for saving energy and reducing utility bills. From your answers to simple multiple-choice questions about your home and household appliances, the Home Energy Analyzer generates a list of Ways to Save energy and compares your home energy use to that of other similar homes. Illustrations and hyperlinks to definitions enliven the survey and make the Home Energy Analyzer an entertaining activity that can involve the entire family.

32. Peninsula School District - Gig Harbor, Washington

www.peninsula.wednet.edu/conservation/energy/e_info.htm - The How to Save Energy page on this school district's Resource Conservation Homepage site lists 69 helpful hints on saving energy. Topics include lighting and heating; cooling appliances; water, windows and doors; and energy saving at work.

33. Project Learning Tree

www.plt.org - Project Learning Tree (PLT) is an award-winning, interdisciplinary environmental education programme for K-12 grades, administered by the American Forest Foundation with the Council for Environmental Education. PLT focuses on students gaining awareness and knowledge of the environment and their place within it, as well as their responsibility for it. The site offers curriculum modules including energy materials, correlations to national and state standards and sample activities; an online newsletter and an educator exchange section. The free or low-cost modules are obtained at training workshops. Click on I Want PLT Materials for information.

34. Rebuild Hawaii: Energy $mart Schools Project

www.hawaii.gov/dbedt/ert/rebuild/projects/k12s.html - Managed by Hawaiian Electric Company, Inc. (HECO) in partnership with Rebuild Hawaii, the Energy $mart Schools Project trains high school students to perform energy audits in school buildings and neighboring small businesses. The Energy $mart Schools Project is a multidisciplinary programme that incorporates hands-on math, science, computer, marketing, advertising, and public speaking instruction. Students learn how electricity is produced and distributed, how to perform energy audits using state-of-the-art devices and computer spreadsheets prepared by HECO, how to apply critical thinking, problem solving and decision making skills, and how to present the benefits of lighting retrofits.

35. Rocky Mountain Institute (RMI)

www.rmi.org - This nonprofit organization works to foster the efficient and restorative use of resources to create a more sustainable world. Web pages are designed to give students and teachers information about energy and how it is used. Resources include a library of Rocky Mountain Institute publications available on line and the RMI for Kids pages with energy information for grades 4-6 students, as well as extensive links to other sites.

36. Science NetLinks

www.sciencenetlinks.com - The American Association for the Advancement of Science site for K-12 science educators includes online lesson plans. All site content is organized around Benchmarks for Science Literacy, by grades. Energy-related lessons include home energy conservation, energy sources and use, renewable energy, urban ecosystems (ecology) and more. There are links to other web resources.

37. Southern California Edison - Electrical Safety World

www.sce.com/site - Electrical Safety World features lively animated pages describing the principles and practices of electrical safety, interactive games and activities, a teacher's guide and links to related sites. The site is designed for a range of interests and reading levels and can be used by students in elementary and middle school.

38. Sprint's Kid's Page

www.sprint.com/epatrol - This Web site presents an interactive game on energy-saving measures that children can play. Users click on parts of a house to uncover energy tips. The site also offers students an Epatrol they can join by printing a certificate and signing a pledge.

39. Union of Concerned Scientists (UCS)

www.ucsusa.org - Click on Publications for USC environmental reports, such as Confronting Climate Change in California: Ecological Impacts on the Golden State. An eight lesson curriculum guide (with the same name) for grades 9-12, designed to be used with the report, is described at: www.ucsusa.org/climatechange/ccteachers.html. The pdf file may be printed or downloaded, and teachers may sign up for future updates to the curriculum on this page.

40. United Kingdom Department of Trade and Industry

www.dti.gov.uk/energy/renewables/ed_pack - Planet Energy is a United Kingdom site that guides visitors around its "Energy Trail" to learn about renewable energy technologies. It is divided into three sections: the teacher information zone, the information zone for ages 7-11, and a zone for ages 12-16.

41. University of Northern Iowa - Energy Education Curriculum Project

www.earth.uni.edu/EECP - Middle school modules for teaching about energy sources and efficiency, available on line (printable html files), from a local as well as global perspective.

42. U.S. Department of Energy - Energy Information Administration

www.eia.doe.gov/bookshelf/eer/kiddietoc.html - This Publications site, maintained by the Energy Information Administration, provides lists of energy education resources for grades K-12. Each entry includes the address, telephone number, a description of the organization and the energy-related materials available. Most entries also include Internet and e-mail addresses. Buttons on the home page link to the Department of Energy's Kid's Page and the Kidszone sites (see below).

43. U.S. Department of Energy - Energy Information Administration Kid's Page

www.eia.doe.gov/kids - This is the DOE Web site developed especially for kids and hosted by "Energy Ant." It offers an explanation of energy, a quiz, fun facts and a Kid's Corner with information on energy pioneers, news and virtual field trips.

44. U.S. Department of Energy - EnergySmart Schools

www.eren.doe.gov/energysmartschools/ - EnergySmart Schools is part of the U.S. Department of Energy's Campaign to Rebuild America. A Teaching page lists extensive teacher resources, including lesson plans (at www.eren.doe.gov/energysmartschools/lesson_plans.html). Scroll down this page with its links to Web sites that offer lessons plans for teaching about energy, energy efficiency and the environment, to find the downloadable EnergySmart Teacher Guide for grades 4-6. This guide provides in-class activities to illustrate the benefits of energy-efficient appliances and practices as well as how energy can affect the environment. A Home Energy Quiz may be found at www.eren.doe.gov/energysmartschools/quiz/quiz.html.

45. U.S. Department of Energy - Kidszone

www.energy.gov/engine/content.do?BT_CODE=KIDS - The DOE's Kidszone pages feature a Museum of Solid Waste, an Energy Ant game and other energy activities, a page with links to energy dictionaries and a Teaching Tools page with links to lesson plans and activities for grades K-12 on other sites.

46. U.S. Department of Energy - National Renewable Energy Laboratory

www.nrel.gov/education - This site offers information on research internships and fellowships, mentoring, tutoring, seminars, competitions, awards, special events, and after school programmes. In addition to instructional development opportunities, teachers are provided with renewable energy and energy efficiency curricula for grades K-12, aligned with national educational standards for science, mathematics, and technology (pdf or html files on this site or other linked sites).

47. U.S Department of Energy - Office of Energy Efficiency and Renewable Energy

www.eere.energy.gov/education/lesson plans.html - The Energy Lesson Plans, Curriculum, and Educational Materials page features links to educational and training resources on energy, particularly energy efficiency and renewable energy.

This page is a portal to a range of curricula and activities. A search engine and site index accesses the entire Department of Energy site. For "Dr. E's Energy Lab," games and activities for young students that explore alternative fuels: www.eere.doe.gov/kids .

48. U.S. Department of Energy - Roofus' Solar and Efficient Neighbourhood

www.eren.doe.gov/roofus - An animated cartoon site describing how people can save energy by using solar power and conservation techniques. Activities and experiments for children demonstrate the scientific evidence. There are also resources for teachers.

49. U.S. Environmental Protection Agency - Global Warming Visitor Center

http://yosemite.epa.gov/oar/globalwarming.nsf/content/VisitorCenterEducators.html - This page is a directory to educational materials available on the site for classroom activities, including climate change, potential global warming impacts, and mitigation options.

50. U.S. Environmental Protection Agency - Office of Environmental Education

www.epa.gov/enviroed - This site offers links to free online, EPA educational resources compiled by environmental topic, and an alphabetically indexed and searchable catalogue of K-12, EPA environmental education materials and resources. It provides ordering information and brief descriptions of educational tools of all types, including curriculum guides, fact sheets, pamphlets, and resource guides.

51. U.S. Environmental Protection Agency - Pollution Prevention Toolbox

www.epa.gov/RCRIS-Region-5/wptdiv/p2pages/toolbox.htm - The "toolbox" contains a series of four-page lesson plans with hands-on activities on pollution prevention and energy conservation concepts. Also included are sample content standards and frameworks with correlations to the lesson plans. Other pollution prevention education resources are included on the site. All are pdf files.

52. U.S. Environmental Protection Agency - Student Center

www.epa.gov/students - A Web site dedicated to students, with links to environmental club projects, careers, internships, and scholarships, environmental youth awards, and basic information about human health, waste and recycling, and air and water conservation.

53. U.S. Environmental Protection Agency - Teaching Center

www.epa.gov/teachers - A Web site for teachers who want background information for teaching about the environment. The site offers a collection of fact sheets, brochures, links to downloadable curricula from the EPA and other sites and to EPA sites for students and kids: the Student Center site provides background and activities on environmental issues for grade K-12 students (www.epa.gov/students); and the Kid's site, or Environmental Explorer's Club, a collection of interactive activities for younger children (www.epa.gov/kids).

54. Watt Watchers of Texas

http://wattwatchers.utep.edu/pages/Projects.htm - Hands-on, online energy-related activities for students K-12, developed by the Energy Center at the University of Texas at El Paso. Under High School Activities, click on Monitor Power Management for a comprehensive guide to forming and implementing energy patrols (downloadable pdf).

55. Wisconsin K-12 Energy Education Program (KEEP)

www.uwsp.edu/cnr/wcee/keep - KEEP initiates and facilitates the development, dissemination, implementation, and evaluation of energy education programmes. The site provides teacher-developed, hands-on, interdisciplinary lessons on energy and links to other resources. Click on More Energy Education, then Teaching Ideas.

Index

Index